Ethics in a Changing Society

Mapping the Terrain

James P. Wind,

J. Russell Burck,

Paul F. Camenisch,

and Dennis P. McCann,

editors

The Park Ridge Center
for the Study of Health,
Faith, and Ethics
Chicago, Illinois

Westminster/John Knox Press
Louisville, Kentucky

© 1991 The Park Ridge Center for the Study of Health, Faith, and Ethics

All rights reserved—no part of this book may be reproduced in any form without permission in writing from the publisher, except by a reviewer who wishes to quote brief passages in connection with a review in magazine or newspaper.

Scripture quotations marked NRSV are from the New Revised Standard Version of the Bible and are copyrighted © 1989 by the Division of Christian Education of the National Council of Churches of Christ in the U.S.A. and are used by permission.

Book design by Gene Harris

First edition

Published by Westminster/John Knox Press
Louisville, Kentucky

PRINTED IN THE UNITED STATES OF AMERICA

9   8   7   6   5   4   3   2   1

Library of Congress Cataloging-in-Publication Data
Clergy ethics in a changing society : mapping the terrain / James P.
Wind . . . [et al.], editors. — 1st ed.
       p.   cm.
   Includes bibliographical references.
   ISBN 0-664-25161-7
   1. Clergy—Professional ethics.   I. Wind, James, 1948–
BV4011.5.C44 1991
241′.641—dc20   91-3325

Contents

89763

Acknowledgments

Portions of the chapters by Martin Marty and Langdon Gilkey were printed in the *Bulletin of the Park Ridge Center,* May/June 1988, and an earlier draft of the article by William F. May, "Images that Shape the Public Obligations of the Minister," was printed in the *Bulletin of the Park Ridge Center,* January 1989.

An earlier draft of the chapter by Paul Camenish, "Clergy Ethics and the Professional Ethics Model," appeared under the title "Integrity in Ministry: Can Professional Models Help?" in *Sharing the Practice,* 12, no. 4 (Fall 1989), published by the Academy of Parish Clergy.

Portions of the chapter by M. L. Brownsberger, "Ethos, Incarnation, and Responsibility," appeared in *The Christian Century,* August 27–September 3, 1986, under the title "From the Other Side"; in *The Chicago Theological Seminary Register,* 79, no. 4 (Fall 1989), under the title, "Christian Faith and Business: A Story"; and in a paper titled, "Doing Business: A Theocentric Approach to Business Ethics," by M. L. Brownsberger and Dennis McCann, presented at the January 1988 meeting of the Society for Christian Ethics.

Chapter 13, "An Ethics for the Interpretation of the Contemporary Jewish Experience," originally appeared in *Tikkun* magazine, a bimonthly Jewish critique of politics, culture, and society published in Oakland, California, under the title "The Rabbi and the Abyss of AIDS," and is reprinted with permission of *Tikkun.*

Contributors

Don S. Browning, Alexander Campbell Professor, The Divinity School, University of Chicago

M. L. Brownsberger, Pastor, Immanuel Congregational Church (United Church of Christ), Dubuque, Iowa. Former Vice-President, ORGANICS/LaGrange, Inc., Chicago

J. Russell Burck, Director, Section on Ethics, and Associate Professor, Department of Religion, Health, and Human Values, Rush-Presbyterian-St. Luke's Medical Center, Chicago

Paul F. Camenisch, Professor and Chair, Department of Religious Studies, DePaul University

Rebecca S. Chopp, Associate Professor of Theology, The Candler School of Theology, Emory University

Joseph A. Edelheit, Rabbi, Emanuel Congregation, Chicago

Robert Michael Franklin, Associate Professor of Ethics and Society and Director of Black Church Studies, The Candler School of Theology, Emory University

Langdon Gilkey, Shailer Mathews Professor, Emeritus, The Divinity School, University of Chicago

Ann O'Hara Graff, Assistant Professor of Pastoral Studies, Institute of Pastoral Studies, Loyola University

Dennis P. McCann, Professor, Department of Religious Studies, DePaul University

Martin E. Marty, Fairfax M. Cone Distinguished Service Professor of the History of Modern Christianity, The Divinity School, University of Chicago

William F. May, Cary M. Maguire University Professor of Ethics, Southern Methodist University

Eleanor Scott Meyers, Academic Dean and Professor of Church and Society, St. Paul School of Theology and President-elect of the Pacific School of Religion

James P. Wind, Program Director, Religion Division, Lilly Endowment, Inc.

Introduction

This volume is the product of the joint efforts of the authors of the individual essays and the members of the Chicago Area Clergy Ethics Study Group listed at the end of this Introduction. The formation and work of the Study Group were guided by the founding members' understanding of the current situation of the clergy and of the current status of professional ethics.

The Study Group sensed that a widespread concern about ethics in the workplace—whether in business, politics, or the established or the fledgling professions—was emerging in the society at large. That concern was likely to have some staying power; it was not simply a passing fad. In academic circles there was a rapidly proliferating parallel development of applied ethics. Any specific work or professional group ignored these developments at its own peril, because the citizenry increasingly demanded a high level of conduct from it and even expected public declaration of the standards to which it could be held. Those expectations were increasingly being brought to the law courts for enforcement in the form of malpractice suits and other forms of litigation from which the clergy were not immune.

A preliminary look at the situation revealed that the clergy had made rather minimal response to these developments. There were older resources on the ethics of the clergy, but they reflected the times in which they had been written and spoke with neither clarity nor authority to the contemporary situation. A few more recent works were available, but for the most part they either combined clergy ethics with a treatment of other professions, with which there were only limited parallels, or they developed a single area or theme from clergy ethics and left the larger territory unexplored.

A fresh approach was needed. The status and role of organized religion in society are changing. The profile of its professional leadership is shifting. In some religious communities, a serious decline in recruits is forcing a reassignment of clerical tasks. In others, the increasing number of female and minority leaders are challenging the former "ethical" standards that seem to many too rooted in gender and class, and to others to be more a matter of style and etiquette than of ethics as such. The changing meanings of work and of profession in the larger society, of which religious communities and their leaders are always a part, are generating an ethos different from that which previously informed and guided most economic activity.

These realizations convinced us that a first step had to be taken toward an adequate ethic for the contemporary clergy, one that took advantage of all the resources now available for the study of religious experience, religious communities, and religious leadership.

Once we were determined to take up the task, several convictions guided us as we structured the project. In some sense they all involved inclusiveness, diversity, and plurality.

Perhaps most important was our conviction that we had to be as inclusive as possible with regard to racial, gender, ethnic, and religious diversity. On one level this had to do with the makeup of the group; on another level it had to do with the diversity of perspectives and experience we would let shape our work. Our efforts to achieve these very demanding objectives were blessed by the caliber of authors we were able to attract from around the country and by the rich talent pool of metropolitan Chicago, which provided us with a gifted and dedicated panel of clergy and academics who constituted the ongoing Study Group. Largely because of these factors, we believe this volume represents the most wide-ranging and the most inclusive study of clergy ethics currently available.

At the same time, several factors prevented our realizing our hopes to the fullest. We found it impossible to represent the astonishing diversity of contemporary urban America in a relatively small Study Group and in a relatively small number of topics to be addressed. The diverse ways of understanding the role of clergy or of religious leaders often led to very different assessments of the importance of particular issues.

And in spite of our best efforts, minority clergy and minority experience, even from the biblical traditions, much less from beyond them, were underrepresented.

It should be stressed that we sought to be inclusive in the above regards, not in order to discover the lowest common denominator and to declare that to be the ground for contemporary clergy ethics. Rather, we believed that knowledge of others' traditions and of their insights on these matters would give all a fresh perspective on their own traditions and would increase their respect for each other's. Our hope was that together we would learn from the particularities and celebrate the commonalities of the various traditions.

Although the project began in part with an eye to the flowering of professional ethics, we wanted to be more inclusive also in the approaches we took to the issues. This concern arose from the evident limitations of the professional ethics model: its emphatic rejection by some religious communities as inadequate or simply wrong as a model for their leadership; the power, status, and sometimes elitism associated with the professions that generate tensions with other elements of religious communities' faith and practice; current professional ethics' largely secular bases; its inability to capture or organize a "profession" as diverse—some would say as fragmented—as the contemporary clergy. As the following essays testify, we worked to include a variety of approaches: historical, theological, scriptural, cultural, feminist, literary, sociological, liberationist, political, experiential, and tradition specific.

It was our hope in this inclusiveness to draw not only on the resources of various academic disciplines and approaches, but on the experience and wisdom of seasoned clergy-practitioners as well.

Finally, we wanted to be inclusive with regard to the ethical problems facing the contemporary clergy. We soon discovered, however, that the specific issues met by modern clergy are simply too numerous and too varied to be covered by any one such project. Therefore, we surrendered the idea of treating, or even enumerating, all such problems faced by the clergy and settled for a terrain-mapping model. Our hope was to explore the major approaches to such problems and the major dynamics at work in them. If we were successful, the reader would then be equipped to explore various problem areas—such as confidentiality, personal ambition, appropriate use of one's position, professional competence, exploitation of the vulnerable, and the like—and the specific issues or cases falling within them.

The Formation of the Study Group

These hopes and goals, however, developed gradually over a period of time as the original nucleus of the Study Group felt its way toward an appropriate organization and format for a serious examination of clergy ethics. The work of the group grew out of early discussions of the subject of clergy ethics initiated by a meeting of the Professional Development Committee of the Chicago Presbytery with the staff of the Center for the Study of Ethics in the Professions at Illinois Institute of Technology. That meeting inspired Mark S. Frankel, the director of the Center at that time, to pursue the issues of clergy ethics in other contexts. He took up these issues again in September 1983 with seminary educators and officials of various religious bodies, including the Chicago Board of Rabbis.

In November of that year, the Center assembled a group of persons to form the Clergy Ethics Working Group. In correspondence with prospective members of the group, Frankel expressed the hope that the group could produce a concept paper outlining a project that would have some tangible and useful outcomes. These included (a) a *survey* of clergy and faculty to determine their perceptions of and experiences with ethical issues; (b) a *symposium* on clergy ethics in order to give the issues higher visibility and to produce a compilation of papers to serve as an intellectual basis for further serious discussion and analysis; (c) a *commissioning of papers* without a symposium; and (d) the preparation of *teaching materials* in clergy ethics.

The Clergy Ethics Working Group met for the first time in December 1983. It consisted of the Reverend J. Russell Burck of the Department of Religion and Health, Rush-Presbyterian-St. Luke's Medical Center, Paul F. Camenisch of the Department of Religious Studies at DePaul University, Frederick Elliston of the Center for the Study of Ethics in the Professions, Father Tim O'Connell of the Institute of Pastoral Studies at Loyola University, Rabbi E. H. Prombaum of the Chicago Board of Rabbis, the Reverend David T. Stein of Project Ten of Lutheran General Hospital (later the Park Ridge Center), and Mark Frankel.

Members of the Working Group recommended the formation of a somewhat larger Study Group consisting of representatives from the Jewish and Christian traditions. From the beginning, the group sought to combine inclusiveness with optimal size. Deciding not to define ministry in terms of the work of clergy only, the group included Margaret A. Grant,

House Counsel of Lutheran General and a Catholic sister. Ellen Renée Dill, a Methodist minister, joined the group, and David Stein later introduced his new colleague, James P. Wind, to the group.

When Frankel left to join the American Association for the Advancement of Science in 1986, the Study Group's future hung momentarily in the balance. Initially, it considered seeking a home in the major institutions represented by group members: DePaul University's Center for the Study of Values, the Park Ridge Center, and Rush-Presbyterian-St. Luke's Medical Center. Eventually, it was the Park Ridge Center that provided the decisive leadership and financing that brought this collection of essays into being. The project took a decisive step toward its final shape when it was decided to invite a group of scholars to address issues in clergy ethics under the concept of "mapping the terrain." The major work of the group in its final stages consisted of presentations of these papers, which follow, to the Study Group, followed by extended discussion between the group and the author. Authors were then asked to revise their papers for publication, taking into account the points raised in those discussions. To degrees varying among the group members and among the different papers, the members of the group were significant collaborators in generating what follows.

The Results of the Study Group's Work

What shows up on any map depends upon which features of the terrain are selected for display. The overall shape of the territory remains the same, but the information conveyed varies significantly when different features are emphasized. There are several paths that could be pursued through the papers presented for the Clergy Ethics Study Group, but the following guideposts are meant to highlight the most consistently prominent features. In retrospect, the Study Group seems to have intended a new kind of theological discourse on the meaning of ministry. It took as a given the significance of the specific traditional teachings of the various biblical communities of faith. But it then examined those teachings and the resulting practices in the context of a more or less common experience within the emerging cultural landscape of a secular and pluralistic America. Only in this way could the group expect its insights and conclusions about clergy ethics to be valid and helpful. With little hesitation, therefore, the Study Group approached the task of interpreting clergy ethics as an integral part of the challenge of living faithfully in America, and sought to understand how that challenge affects the communities' expectations of the clergy who serve them.

Given such a broad cultural horizon, it is not surprising that the papers providing a general orientation to the terrain of clergy ethics focused on how religious traditions have been transformed in America. Though the perspectives offered by Martin E. Marty, Langdon Gilkey, William F. May, Rebecca S. Chopp, and James P. Wind all speak directly from the experience of mainline Protestantism, they highlight cultural trends that have also affected Roman Catholic and Jewish communities and their clergy. Thus Marty's opening paper, "Clergy Ethics in America: The Ministers On Their Own," profiles the long-term cultural consequences of the American constitutional principle of the separation of church and state. It argues that the ensuing change in the relationship between clergy and laity is so striking as to warrant the construction of a typically American pattern of practical ecclesiology, what Marty himself names the "contractual-entrepreneurial" model of ministry. Lest Marty's point be misunderstood, it is important to note that the American pattern imposes upon ministers, as it does upon practitioners in a variety of other professions, a significant degree of governmental regulation, at least with respect to the enforcement of minimum standards of professional conduct. Nevertheless, as the label "contractual-entrepreneurial" implies, this pattern tends to leave both clergy and laity free, as it were, to shop around for a religious community in which their own distinctive needs and aspirations can be fulfilled. The pattern also carries with it the long-term and pervasive expectation of the professionalization of ministry, as both clergy and laity seek to define standards of accountability appropriate to the American situation.

Just how far removed this situation is from the ecclesial traditions inherited from European Christianity is the point of Langdon Gilkey's paper "Forgotten Traditions in the Clergy's Self-Understanding." Gilkey reviews the European landmarks mapped out in Ernst Troeltsch's typology of "church," "sect," and "mysticism," their distinctive conceptions of Christian ministry, and the expectations for clergy ethics implicit in them. Nevertheless, he emphasizes that the continuing impact of these traditions in contemporary America amounts to little more than a "haunting," which should lead us to deeper theological reflection on what we really take to be sacred. Similarly, William F. May's paper, "Images that Shape the Public Obligations of the Minister," has recourse to the classically Protestant theology of ministry implicit in the Christological titles of Priest, Prophet, and King. Yet in order to confront the challenge of living faithfully in contemporary America, May moves on to new ground and considers a variety of images of the minister embodying the new ideals of leadership implicit in the communities' experience of democratic pluralism.

Whereas Gilkey's and May's reflections seem to illustrate the process of theological accommodation predicted by Marty, the papers by Rebecca S. Chopp and James P. Wind confront us with voices from the periphery that would resist the hegemony of the contractual-entrepreneurial model of ministry. Chopp's paper, "Liberating Ministry," sees clergy professionalization as an index of the triumph of liberal modernity. She denounces the ensuing bureaucratic captivity of Christianity and calls for radical renewal within the church in order to render it the kind of community in which the oppressed may find a home. No less radically, James P. Wind's essay, "Clergy Ethics in Modern Fiction," looks to the work of contemporary American writers to discern what is usually left inarticulate about clerical morality in studies dominated by the conventions of academic theology. The results of Wind's literary expedition echo Chopp's perspective in some respects, and Gilkey's in others. Struggling with the inherited theological tradition is very high on the agenda of Wind's novelists, but equally pronounced is a disenchantment with the normal experience of religious community that borders on anti-institutionalism. Viewed from the periphery, the bold new path laid out in the contractual-entrepreneurial model looks suspiciously like a dead end.

As we move beyond these general surveys of the terrain and into regional studies, the tension between inherited ideals of religious community and the exigencies of professionalization continues to shape decisively our map of clergy ethics in America. The first region explored includes those institutional sectors of American society where these exigencies have advanced the farthest, namely, business and the professions. The papers in this section, authored by Paul F. Camenisch, M. L. Brownsberger, and Dennis P. McCann, seek to define the common ground shared by clergy ethics with business and professional ethics, in order to clarify the distinctiveness of each. Camenisch's "Clergy Ethics and the Professional Ethics Model" discusses the characteristics traditionally ascribed to the professions, including their atypical moral commitment to the interests and well-being of the client, and possibly to those of the larger society, and the various institutional mechanisms by which that commitment is monitored and sanctioned. His analysis suggests specific ways in which clergy ethics can and ought to parallel these developments within the professions, even though he insists that there may be a higher ethic for clergy based on the transcendent source of their ultimate authority as religious leaders. M. L. Brownsberger's "Ethos, Incarnation, and Responsibility" makes a similar argument from the perspective of business and managerial ethics. Citing personal experience as both a clergyperson and a business executive, Brownsberger tries to overcome the mutual incomprehension that he considers typical of the interaction between these two groups by discerning an ethic of managerial responsibility at the core of normal American business practice, an ethic of institutional edification and human empowerment that he regards as exemplifying the moral logic of the Incarnation. Brownsberger's aim is to establish a point of convergence between the actual practice of ministry and that of business management in order to promote a new dialogue between practitioners involved in either of them. Without denying the convergences established by either Camenisch or Brownsberger, Dennis P. McCann's "Costing Discipleship: Clergy Ethics in a Commercial Civilization" tries to determine, within a similar set of assumptions, what ought to be distinctive of clergy ethics. His thesis is that, because learning and teaching the ways of sacrifice have defined the social practice that is distinctive of clergy in virtually all religious traditions, a capacity for self-sacrifice ought to be the hallmark of clergy ethics. Because McCann's argument is based on anthropological perspectives not directly derived from biblical sources, it suggests that what ought to limit the convergence between clergy ethics and business and professional ethics is itself a reflection of the social function of ministry rather than any religious dogma about it.

If business and professional ethics represents one important region of the terrain of clergy ethics in America, its relationship to the therapeutic social practices derived from clinical psychology is surely another. The essays of J. Russell Burck and Don S. Browning provide an initial survey of this region. Like the previous set informed by the disciplines of business and professional ethics, Burck's "Pastoral Care and Clergy Ethics" and Browning's "Family Ethics and the Ethics of Ministerial Leadership" reflect the concerns of those actively involved in preparing clergy for their responsibilities as pastoral counselors, especially in situations where there is the greatest overlap between ministry and psychotherapy. Burck's essay explores the special problems of ethical accountability relative to both the faith of communities and the individual clients involved in pastoral care, particularly in clinical pastoral education. Browning, on the other hand, is concerned to resist the so-called triumph of the therapeutic in the communities of faith by integrating this and other forms of clinical practice within a view of ministry that emphasizes the clergy's role as moral teacher. Implicit in both perspectives is the same kind of ambivalence about the impact of professionalization on traditional understandings of ministry that the Study Group experienced throughout its deliberations.

The final set of papers maps this general theme in the distinctive region of concern created by the struggles of women and minorities for full and equal participation in ministry. Two of them, those by Ann O'Hara Graff and Eleanor Scott Meyers, explicitly carry on the debate about professionalization within a shared Christian feminist perspective on ministry. Graff's paper, "Women in the Roman Catholic Ministry. New Vision, New Ethics," welcomes professionalization because it offers grounds on which to assess and, where needed, to challenge the authority of Roman Catholicism's clerical patriarchy. Meyers' effort, "A Sociology of Ministerial Preparation," on the other hand, sharply criticizes the same professionalization for helping to create and legitimate patriarchal hierarchy in her denomination, the Disciples of Christ, a denomination that had enjoyed a more egalitarian tradition of ministry. So it seems that a professionalized ministry may or may not be liberating, depending, among other things, on what groups are empowered by it within distinctive denominational traditions. What may be liberating for Roman Catholic women may be oppressive for their sisters in other communities.

Though the final contributions do not address the trend toward professionalization explicitly, they do argue impressively for the traditional understandings of ministry distinctive of religious communities within American Judaism and African American Christianity. Rabbi Joseph A. Edelheit's contribution, "An Ethics for the Interpretation of the Contemporary Jewish Experience," emphasizes the rabbi's traditional role as interpreter of religious texts, as a basis for understanding a distinctively rabbinical approach to congregational ministry as a whole. Robert Michael Franklin's essay, "Clergy and Politics: The Black Experience," similarly insists upon the distinctive ways in which political leadership quite regularly becomes an extension of the pulpit ministry in African American communities. Though neither Edelheit nor Franklin wishes to generalize for all religious communities on the basis of their own distinctive experiences, they do imply that mainstream, predominantly Protestant understandings of clergy ethics will be inadequate so long as they ignore the distinctive patterns of clerical leadership exercised within minority communities. The questions usually raised by the professionalization of ministry simply may not be relevant to religious communities whose relation to the larger society diverges significantly from that of mainstream groups.

This one path through these papers suggests that the prospect for developing a single set of professional norms for clergy ethics, analogous to similar efforts in the professions of medicine, law, and—increasingly—business management, is to be greeted with a prudent degree of ambivalence. On the one hand, society's expectations, stemming from America's positive experience of regulated professionalism as a means of ordering the potential chaos of a polity committed to democratic pluralism, as well as the religious communities' own emerging American tradition of interdenominational collaboration, make something like a professionalized model of clergy ethics seem very desirable. On the other hand, accountability to the distinctively religious claims cherished in each particular community's history of faithfulness demands that such a model must sanction something more than the lowest common denominator languages of ministerial effectiveness. At stake, no doubt, is the range of responses to the Sacred, which first called the communities into being and has continued to nurture their distinctive traditions of ministry. As should now be clear, the papers presented at the Clergy Ethics Study Group do not propose any single, definitive resolution of this tension between professionalization and inherited communal identities. It is our hope, however, that they do accomplish what the Study Group proposed to do, which was to offer a map of the terrain upon which such resolutions might be formulated and tested.

JAMES P. WIND
J. RUSSELL BURCK
PAUL F. CAMENISCH
DENNIS MCCANN

November, 1990

Clergy Ethics
Study Group Participants

Rev. Samuel Acosta, First Spanish United Church of Christ, Chicago

Rev. Phyllis Anderson, Director of Theological Education, Division for Ministry, Evangelical Lutheran Church in America, Chicago

Rev. Bliss Williams Browne, Vice-President and Division Head of Midwest Banking, First National Bank of Chicago

M. L. Brownsberger, Vice-President, ORGANICS/LaGrange, Inc., Chicago

Rev. Ellen Renée Dill, Clair-Christian United Methodist Church, Chicago

Rabbi Joseph A. Edelheit, Emanuel Congregation, Chicago

Rev. Ralph H. Elliott, North Shore Baptist Church, Chicago

Mr. John Fontana, Executive Director, Cross Roads Center for Faith and Work, Old St. Patrick's Church, Chicago

Rev. Paul Golden, Director of the Institute for Leadership of Religious Organizations, DePaul University, Chicago

Rev. Susan B. W. Johnson, Hyde Park Union Church, Chicago

Rev. Charles Jordan, St. Mark's United Methodist Church, Chicago

Rev. Deborah L. Kapp, Fourth Presbyterian Church, Chicago

Ms. Maria Leonard, Morton International Corporation, Chicago

Rev. Glenn Loafman, St. Paul's United Church of Christ, Chicago

Rev. F. Dean Lueking, Grace Evangelical Lutheran Church, River Forest, Ill.

Rabbi Robert Marx, Congregation Hakafa, Glencoe, Ill.
Rev. Fumitaka Matsuoka, Dean, Bethany Seminary, Oak Brook, Ill.
Rev. David T. Stein, Apostles Lutheran Church, Melrose Park, Ill.

Steering Committee

Rev. J. Russell Burck, Associate Professor of Religion and Health, Rush-Presbyterian-St. Luke's Medical Center, Chicago
Paul F. Camenisch, Chair, Department of Religious Studies, DePaul University, Chicago
Dennis P. McCann, Associate Professor, Department of Religious Studies, DePaul University, Chicago
Rev. James P. Wind, Senior Associate, The Park Ridge Center, Chicago (during the time of the seminar; currently Program Director, Religion Division, Lilly Endowment, Inc.)

1

Clergy Ethics in America: The Ministers On Their Own

Martin E. Marty

He must not be made by the office he holds; he must make the office respected and honoured.

Rabbi Isaac Meyer Wise, 1876

All ethics makes sense only in context. How clergy are to act depends in no small measure on their setting. One glance at the military chaplaincy illustrates this. Ministers who draw their salary from the United States government and take military oaths know that they must make their ethical decisions with different factors in mind than do civilian clerics. Pastoral ministers who want to sustain long-term relations to their members may well make moral choices about what to say when or about what to do in different ways than would the Visiting Prophet who comes to town for a brief crisis situation. All these clergy will be responsive to some norms that are independent of context. They draw these from ancient scriptures, theology, and the statutes and standards of their religious bodies. But the way one acts on these norms depends upon how one relates to a larger contemporary environment.

As a historian drawn into this discourse about clergy ethics, I will stress the change in context as a result of changes in culture and society. To come right to the point: I will defend the thesis that in recent decades the American context for clergy ethics has changed. Whereas formerly the main ele-

ment was the sanction one received from the authority of the
believing community—we can code-name that the *ecclesia*—
and from clear theological warrants, today the clergy use
approaches that imply a more privately contracted entrepreneurial understanding. To say this does not mean that *ecclesia*
and theology play no part. It is, however, to contend that the
sanctions derived from these all acquire a different color in
the situation of personal enterprise. Let it also be said that it
makes little difference whether the cleric is active in episcopal,
presbyterian, congregational, or other polities. In practice, he
or she reflexively reflects the contractual individualized approach. And the constituents, clienteles, and congregants they
serve, to say nothing of the general public, appraise them in
this context.

One way to condense the whole proposition is to borrow
from show business, as one minister informally did. He observed that whereas once upon a time being part of a church
establishment (which implied governmental support and sanction) or being part of a denomination gave one the context,
now "you are only as good as your last act."

When a historian is called to give some accounting of past
and present, of the "from what" to the "to what" an institution
or society is supposed to be moving, an early question he or she
has to ask of the present subject is, Compared to what? If
clergy ethics is conceived as confused, blurred, foundering,
not-yet-defined, under stress, or in crisis, one must ask what
was the situation of earlier presumed clarity, boundary, direction, definition, taken-for-grantedness, or absence of such crisis. There is a tendency when doing analysis of a contemporary
situation to heighten the drama of study by contrasting it with
vastly different earlier circumstances. In the present case, we
have to ask to what we should contrast the current scene and
what boundaries there should be spatially, temporally, and
conceptually around the subject under examination.

Here the boundary for clergy ethics has to be "Western,"
the Protestant-Catholic-Jewish triad that is so familiar in American studies. It does not include Islam, now represented by
more hundreds of thousands of followers than many Christian groups can count. Islam has no professional clergy. It was
under-represented in the longer American past. Nor do we
include Asian religions or "New Religions" because of their
late arrivals, exceptionality, or minority status. Older New
Religions that have clergy (Mormonism and Christian Science, for example, do not) tend to take on the color of their
environment and fit into our picture, but we allude to them

only incidentally. However, many of these alternative or exceptional movements in the American environment do fit well. Studies of the forms and ministries of the Buddhist "Church" in America tend to show that it takes on the structural character and color of traditional Christian institutions and expressions.

If we speak chiefly of the West, this means two Wests. First is the Europe from which so many of the colonists and people on the frontier came. Africa produced its millions for America, and there may be traces of African "shamanisms" in some African American ministries in America. Yet socially and culturally, the black church ministries have more in common with those derived from the European West than from patterns in non-Christian sub-Saharan Africa. In the larger society, black ministry today is judged by and finds many of its norms in the forms of ministry derived from Europe.

Second is the North American past, the colonial and earlier national period backgrounds for ministry and clerical ethics. For most Americans, beginning with 52 million Catholics and millions of Episcopalians, Presbyterians, Reformed, Lutheran, and other Protestants, this meant that the clergy were in church traditions that had been established by law. They had been state and tax-supported in Europe and were privileged in the cultures from which the migrants came. Or they had thus been established in earlier America (Congregationalism in New England is an example). They might have been derived from churches with establishmentarian outlooks, as Methodism came from Episcopalianism; or they may have been so successful in America, as was this Methodism, that they were all but legally established at some time or another.

There are great exceptions here, notably in the largest of the white and black denominations, the Baptists. It may be to them that we must eventually turn to see some specifically American emergences. Other never-established, dissenting, or minority colonial or national-period churches may have further contributed to trends in ministry associated with what I call the "Baptistification" of American religion. In short, their ministries may belong more to the "where we are heading" part of a historical essay than from the longer past of "whence we came."

Even as I write such paragraphs, I am tempted to ruin the plot of this paper by issuing all the qualifiers or adding all the color of thick and lively experience and exception, as historians are wont to do. How does one speak about the ministry in America where ministers run the gamut all the way from Judaism, where rabbis are not technically clergy, through Catholic cardinals; from high church Episcopalianism, where theological and ecclesiastical sanctions are supposed to dominate, to storefront churches where inventive enterprisers set up shop and set out to draw a crowd? From cathedral to tent, from New England village to Crystal Cathedral, we have a spectrum so vast and so complex that one hesitates to generalize as we may and must, but it is possible to see some contours and landmarks from which to measure emergent clergy ethics contexts.

One difficulty in discussing clergy ethics in contemporary contexts is the widespread belief that once upon a time, in the Good Old Days or Golden Age, ministers lived in a simple world and could more easily be good, or do good, or know what was good. In the American context, this would mean first the colonial days. The picture that moderns carry in their minds suggests that in such times, when a single church dominated in at least nine of the thirteen colonies, it was easy to reflect on ethics. One simply looked up the rules of the dominant and supportive church. The public had no choice but to go along with what the minister found in the rule books. There was little space for ambiguity.

It is true that when ministers were dependent upon a paycheck from a legally official body, when they presided over First Church in a town where there was no Second Church, they occupied a different situation than do those who compete for the loyalties and attention of citizens who can look up "Churches—Religious Organizations" in the Yellow Pages of the phone book and find a congenial place whose norms will match what they find ethically satisfactory.

Yet living in that establishment context did not mean that clergy always knew what to do or how to be ethical. One could recount the complex decisions clergy made in such times. Bartolomé de Las Casas, perhaps the first ordained cleric active in the hemisphere, knew that his bread was buttered by Roman Catholicism. He knew which bishop to obey, which rule book to use. But even as he was "ethical" in fighting against the enslaving of native Americans, he allowed for the introduction of African slavery into the Western Hemisphere. In New Amsterdam, the official clergy had to struggle with pluralism: should they allow Jews and then Catholics, Lutherans, and Mennonites into "their" colony? How should establishment clergy relate to dissenters?

The ministers of today are not likely to reach back to the sixteenth and seventeenth century for good or bad examples. They need only the reminder that the "world we have lost" to pluralism, individualism, and entrepreneurship in the clergy was not a world that made ethical decision easy; it was merely different. The business at hand is to show how clergy ethics from 1607, when the Episcopalians arrived in Virginia, or from 1787–1791, when the United States Constitution preset the terms for the voluntary church, has seen a constant development from the theologically-ecclesiastically sanctioned norm (in which most clergy believe) to the contractual-entrepreneurial one (with which most of them live or which they are perceived to foster). I will point to five elements that indicate this development and intensification of a centuries-long trend. From them and similar themes that others could and may offer, we can proceed to study contemporary clergy ethics. What gave encouragement to the tendency for change?

American clergy norms developed in a "secular" epoch. By secular I mean what British sociologist Bryan Wilson means: that no single symbol system dominates or gives shape to a whole society (Wilson 1986). In medieval Christendom, for example, no matter how many paganisms were smuggled in plain brown wrappers by the ordinary people, elites at least promoted a single Catholic symbol system. Of course there were varieties and schools of thought and local color, and moral lapses in the clergy were documentably frequent, if not constant. But all were responsive to a single hierarchy, informed by a sacramental system, given norms by a Natural Law-based ethic connected with biblical revelation, Catholic tradition, and magisterial teaching. (I do not want to romanticize the notion of coherence within that worldview and polity, but *something* happened with the Reformation, Renaissance, and Enlightenment to alter the picture.)

Many colonial religious migrations were intentional efforts to repeal the secular trend in Europe, to "regress" to Protestantized medieval patterns. The Puritan movements of New England can be seen as efforts of that sort. Still, in much of colonial America, the sanctions for ministry and its ethics now no longer applied to whole societies, particularly where polities allowed for pluralism, as they did in Rhode Island, Pennsylvania, New Jersey, New York—colonies to whom the future belonged. The "metaphysics" or "metaethics" that may have inspired a particular form of clergy conduct among, say, the Lutherans or "Mennonists" of New Amsterdam would carry no force among the Catholics or Reformed who were presumed to be there, or who were.

When the moderate Enlightenment came to America in the

decisive period of national formation, with founders and framers like Thomas Jefferson speaking of the evils of "priestcraft," the secular context developed. The metaethical background for sanctions for ministry was seen as complex or was outright dismissed. Where asserted most strongly, as in the theological and ecclesiastical sanctioning of the Catholic priesthood, it was most questioned or denounced by all the other Americans who were *not* of the Catholic confession and communion. Society, it was at least tacitly agreed, could function without prior commitment of its members to a single symbol or value system— the very kind of system that would provide norms for clergy and clergy ethics. Societally, in a secular age, the clergy is very much on its own.

From then until now we have seen an extension or expansion of this fundamentally secular view of the clergy (or of clergy outside one's own subsociety or subculture). There may be respect for the clergy, and there often has been in America. The public is offended by lapsing and offensive clergy. But the norms for measurement of performance do not derive from the "credentialers" or the credentials but from other standards imposed on the "credentialees," the individuals in the clergy. This is a situation quite different from the one that persists where the whole society at least officially and presumably lives by a single norm enforced by God and the legal arms of society.

The fact that clergy ethics in America developed in an officially secular society has many bearings on the way decisions are made and enforced. To take an extreme example: in the Middle Ages, if a king were out of favor with the pope, he might face an interdict. This meant that the priests, as agents of the pope but as monopoly clergy, withheld the sacraments from the people and thus threatened their eternal salvation. In a society that is legally secular, there is a clear assumption that decisions made by the clergy have no effect unless they can participate in getting the political arm to act, through passage of laws. No one is "spooked out"; no one need turn reverential just because some clergy in the competitive society argue, "Thus saith the Lord, . . ." There are too many "lords," too many interpretations of the Lord's will, too many ways to escape unconvincing interpretations.

Clergy ethics in a secular society is effective chiefly among those citizens, be they members of a particular cleric's *ecclesia* or not, who come to be convinced that this minister is exemplifying, embodying, and propagating a believable and admirable pattern of action. One can argue that the new situation that began to be worked out in eighteenth-century America is purifying; it certainly changed all the contexts of ministry and decision.

The American polity subordinates church and clergy to civil concerns of the republic. When we look at how clergy act and should act, we instinctively pay attention to the national contexts in which they work. In the United States, the constitutional arrangements affecting religion resituated the church and the clergy. When the nation's founders struggled with a constitution and a legal framework, they saw religion as a problem. There was almost universal respect for religion in general as a basis for morality, and thus for civic virtue and respect for the Constitution. Yet there was widespread suspicion of religious sanctions voiced by clergy of competing "denominations" in various colonies. Many of the political leaders saw the clergy as wanting a "piece of the action," if not the whole action, when it came to determining what was ethical.

The resolution was ingenious. It allowed for unimaginably broad measures of religious freedom and contributed to the vitality of the churches because they did not bear the stigma of being part of governmental and thus coercive life. But to work out this resolution, religion had to be put in a legally subordinate situation in civil life, where so many ethical decisions are made.

To make religion legally subordinate does not mean that the state can render the clergy morally subservient. "We ought to obey God rather than men," a biblical line, serves as a prophetic reservation against such moral imperialism by government. Yet legally it is manifest: The church exists as an institution with charters from the state, with tax-exemption privileges; it seeks a law of conscientious objection to military service and follows police and fire laws in municipalities. The state does not come to ask exemption from stewardship campaigns, nor do its agents fear excommunication or interdicts.

What does this have to do with clergy ethics? It means that ministers, through their preachments and examples, have the most direct effect on private and personal life. They have a measure of unimpeded influence on those who choose to affiliate with the religious body they serve. They also find themselves "boxed in," segregated as it were, in the private sphere. "Religion is a private affair" is an effective way of cutting off the influence of clergy ethics. Public ethics belongs to philosophers in universities, authors of secular books of advocacy, and the like. But to introduce a religious backdrop or argument appears to be an intrusion into the civil fabric.

When religion is subordinate to the state, the government in effect sets some legal boundaries within which clerical actions and clerical ethics will operate. So great is the experience of religious freedom in America that it is clear, in a climate of "benevolent neutrality," that the government will not set forth many norms and will be reluctant to act on the basis of them.

Still, this subordination by law yet opposition by clergy to subservience in morality or doctrine leaves the clergy in an anomalous circumstance. One never knows when clerical moral claims will finally bump into governmental legal norms. Now and then they collide, as when the Internal Revenue Service sees a transgression against the tax-exemption codes. But there is great reluctance to measure the clergy by formal legal norms, and it is just about impossible to provide guidelines, principles, patterns, or laws for the clerical profession of the sort one finds in, say, the legal and medical professions. So how can there be regulations policing judgment?

The new strains on clerical ethics—visible to anyone who studies, as I have, the bibliography of articles and instances having to do with recent clerical ethics—occur in part because of the growth of our litigiousness. People take clergy to court over their counseling practices; clergy take out malpractice insurance; clergy are sued as partners in alienation of affection cases; the state requires clergy who run parochial schools to apply certain minimal credentialing standards that they often choose to transgress and defy. The fact that state and not church courts are last resorts in such cases shows that the church and clergy are legally subordinate, but there will be confusion when norms clash.

The American clergy and, derivatively, clergy ethics, developed and develop in the context of modernity and modernization. Modernity and modernization are processes and not events, argued-over trends and not clearly defined moments. They mean many things to many people. Rather than have many people take responsibility for what I mean or without having me take responsibility for all that modernization can mean, let me simply and clearly point to two factors: differentiation and choice.

Let us consider differentiation first. (See Cuddihy 1976 for a description of the differentiation process.) Although in the longer history of the West there were beginnings of differentiation in matters clerical (as in the "encyclopedia" of the theological curriculum, the specializations of parish clergy versus monastics, roving preachers, evangelizers, and healers), modernity brings a great increase in differentiation of roles and functions. We can think of what some of these mean for ministry and clerical ethics.

Differentiation, for Catholics, between church and state; for Jews, between religion and ethnicity; for Protestants, increasingly, between religion and regional-base or tie; differentiation between sacred and secular; between week and weekend, worship place and workplace, spiritual time and ordinary time, sanctuary and marketplace; differentiation between clergy and laity; between types of clerical roles—pastor, chaplain, missionary, bureaucrat, professor, and the like. All this was implied in what I call the unsigned pact modernity made with religion, which it then chopped up into specialties and then put in certain boxes.

It is one thing to provide clerical ethics for ministers who are in one of these boxes, slots, categories, or cocoons, and another to define ethics for people in other boxes. Thus there can be regularization of some ethical norms for denominational parish ministers, but this may be different from these norms applicable in clinical pastoral education credentialing. Again, they will be different if the employer is the military or a university or an ecumenical agency or even a private secular or public institution that employs ministers.

In addition to this web of credentialing networks, differentiation also connotes the idea that the various spheres of life were not to be transgressed. But today there are strains because there are impingements from both sides. When advice columnists, bridal counselors, undertakers, champagne salespersons, or psychiatrists invade what once were clerical preserves for confession, marrying, carrying on funeral rites, baptizing, or counseling, clergy find their ethical norms compared to nonclerical invaders of their turf. And when clergy compensatorily move into social, economic, artistic, literary, or political public spheres, they find applied to them the same norms that apply to people with "merely" secular credentials. One can easily observe this when "reverends" enter politics or endorse politicians. The investigative reporters and cartoonists do not go easier on them than on nonclergy candidates; they may go harder on them. So we think of the clergy as an impinged-upon and impinging profession for whom implicit bargains struck with modernity no longer satisfy or serve.

Implied in this change is the stress put upon clerical ethics when clergy turn aggressive in the public order. Alexis de Tocqueville saw all clergy in America neglecting dogma and stressing morals as their field of competence, but there now was a moral framework that dealt with private life, not public order. Today that arrangement no longer satisfies (Tocqueville 1969, 448–449). But clergy who are commenting on and observable in public order have to be ready to acquire and be measured by norms belonging to that public order.

Alongside differentiation we have mentioned choice. Peter Berger, drawing on the Greek word "choice" behind *haeresis*, has spoken of "the heretical imperative" as characteristic of modern life (Berger 1979). American clerical standards and practices were born and developed in an epoch in which choice kept becoming ever richer, more alluring, and demanding all at once. Ministers are seen by the public (and probably by themselves, even in an interfaith and ecumenical age) as fundamentally acting out their roles within patterns of competition. They evangelize, proselytize, or at least advertise, in the hope of drawing converts and congregants, presumably from out of secular ways of life but practically, in most cases, from other pools of potential converts or actual congregants from elsewhere. The historical documentation on this pattern goes back to colonial beginnings and then to the First Awakening, when a minister would invade the territory of established clergy and question or denounce them.

Much of the denunciation meant attacks on the morals of the "settled" or competitive clergy made by dissenters, upsetters, innovators, and proselytizers; whereas the establishment, or privileged, clergy in turn pointed to the moral excesses or ambiguities of these itinerants. The competitive clergy found it difficult in a situation of free choice to agree on moral and ethical standards and norms or to follow those that were already presumably there. Today that trend toward competition on moral grounds grows in some sectors, most publicly and notably among television evangelists, from whose example much of the public draws conclusions about the moral shape and intentions of all clergy.

American clergy were necessarily projected as a moral force and are up for examination. When Tocqueville talked about the moral specialization of the undogmatic clergy, he was pointing to a pattern both chosen and imposed on ministers. A secular, pluralist society, one that legally subordinates religion, does not expect clergy to contribute "dogma" on which society should agree in its search for truth. The public despairs of seeing the clergy even finding consensus among themselves. But citizens do seem to expect clerical contributions to morality and ethical decisions. Tax exemption itself is sometimes justified for churches and synagogues on the ground that clergy produce moral good in the society.

In such a situation, when clergy either act or think in ways that radically depart from the norms that society believes they have inherited and that are time-honored, this is perceived as intellectually and morally scandalous. Thus, in the 1960s, when some American clergy began to speak up for a "new morality," for "situational ethics," in ways that the public interpreted as mere relativism, such formal statements of ethics and the clergy who made them were generally repudiated.

Even more scandalous is unethical action by the clergy. The ability of mass media of communication to probe and give publicity to ministerial confusions or lapses therefore complicates the moral claims. When one measured clergy by what one's own minister said and did, in isolation from competition and the larger context, it was easier to do moral measuring. When publics measure the clergy on the basis of headlines that say "Priest Abuses . . ." or "Evangelist Caught . . ." or "Minister Embezzles . . . ," everyone in the clergy suffers.

When "reverends" or evangelists run for the presidency and are subject to moral scrutiny or the savageries of cartoonists, local and "lesser" clergy take pains to distance themselves from the notion that the visible figures are clergy in the same sense they are. Yet the moral complexity of clerical contexts grows in such a media-dominated society.

Theological accommodation in respect to clerical situations and ethics is a constant and is increasing. In a society where, long ago, a single symbol system officially dominated and provided the theological-ecclesiastical norms for determining clergy ethics and conduct, one kind of theology to back that system was manifest and relevant. Inquiry along its lines continues in all ecumenical or denominational ventures to define the sanctioning of ministry and the credentialing out of which moral discourse flows. Thus World Council of Churches studies of Baptist-Eucharist-Ministry, Vatican preoccupation with clerical celibacy or the ordination of women, or denominational inquiries into the understandings of ministry are not irrelevant—for certain purposes.

However, in the practice of ministry as perceived by congregants, the public, and most practitioners, the contractual-entrepreneurial framework dominates and calls forth fresh theological inquiry. Each new infusion of personnel, each new impingement of situations, each new context demands new theology. By theology we here mean the interpretation of the life of a body of people in the light of God's disclosure. The most dramatic illustration of such change is occurring in our third of a century, when the ordination of women and increasing visibility of women alter the entire hermeneutical situation in respect to texts about ministry and ethics. The religious bodies where theological-ecclesiastical sanctioning was sacramentally formalized—Orthodoxy, Roman Catholicism, and Anglicanism—or where biblical literalism about "women preachers" is most adhered to today, see the most stress. They are not exempt from change forced by contractual-entrepreneurial models. Now it is seen that what is "ethical" in clerical situations differs when women are involved, or when the cause of liberation in the "poor world" has impact on North America, or when clergy choose to move further into the new model or seek to reconstruct older ones.

We are to explore the ethical changes occasioned by the shift in American concepts of ministry as a calling or vocation to one that sees ministry as a profession and perhaps as a career. It is not possible here to go into all the details of what that continuing shift means for ethics, but only to indicate that there are precedents in history for the discussion. Some elements of ethics from the ministry-as-vocation era prove to be enduring. They can be retrieved and might offer possibilities for tomorrow. Some aspects of ethics in the ministry-as-profession approach also demand fresh inquiry.

In either case, there will be seen to be theological implications when ministry is set alongside law, business, medicine, education, and other zones of life that are marked by a profession, for professions bring their own norms. These may or may not be congruent or even potentially compatible with whatever it is in the theological-ecclesiastical sanctioning texts and traditions that prevail in various confessional, regional, denominational, or local-congregational contexts. But it will be futile to talk about clergy ethics as if professionalization had not occurred during the past century.

To take but one example: in a contractual-entrepreneurial era, the various nondenominational agencies ask what each means for understandings of ministerial ethics. In the Association of Theological Schools, the basic language for measurement is that of the believing communities that support the seminaries. In the Association of Clinical Pastoral Education, confessional traditions are "bracketed," or seen as momentarily or partially irrelevant. In the American Academy of Religion, purely academic, nonconfessional discussion of clerical ethics is standard. The Academy of Parish Clergy would define clerical ethics for only one, albeit the largest, differentiated portion of the ministerial profession.

When one accepts the historians' proposition that there were no good old days and that stress on ministerial ethical patterns and conducts is not novel, one is free to retrieve some elements from the past and reject others. Such acts of appropriation and distancing will go on in full public view. There is no place to hide while the contemporary inquiry goes on. The congregants, constituencies, clienteles, and citizenry will somehow make their own way while the clergy and their consultants ponder the new situations. The extensive bibliographies dealing with cases and propositions about clergy ethics suggest that we will be dealing with up-front, front-page, prime-time circumstances. It is not necessary to concur in the notion that less is at stake in a secular, pluralist, privatizing society than in a theonomous, homogeneous, public-ministry culture. We live in a mixed spiritual economy and are likely to continue to do so.

This means that religious institutions are likely to survive, that ministerial professionals will continue to be needed, and that the questions of what ethical basis they should act upon, what happens when they do not do so, and how one measures their actions will not decline into a zone of irrelevancy. The evidence suggests and the bibliographies certify that, if anything, the number of cases and disputes will grow. Much is at stake, and the best scholarly and existential resources will be needed by those who would advance the conversation. It is more than passing strange that sustained, disciplined, intense discourse on this has been rare. In a society where most ministers do not believe that they are "on their own," that they are somehow "called" and are responsive to a call, yet where the public sees them as contractors and entrepreneurs, the conversation should be at the same time threatening and promising, but it should never be dull.

References

Berger, Peter L. 1979. *The Heretical Imperative.* New York: Doubleday & Co.

Cuddihy, John Murray. 1976. *The Ordeal of Civility: Freud, Marx, Levi-Strauss and the Jewish Struggle with Modernity.* New York: Dell.

Tocqueville, Alexis. 1969. *Democracy in America.* Edited by J. P. Mayer. Garden City, N.Y.: Doubleday & Co.
Wilson, Bryan. 1986. *Religion in Secular Society: A Sociological Comment.* Baltimore: Penguin Books.

2

Forgotten Traditions in the Clergy's Self-Understanding

Langdon Gilkey

In seeking to understand the significance, role, and ethics of the clergy as a contemporary profession, it is important not to forget the many traditional interpretations of the clergy that this profession has inherited. This is not to say that contemporary ways of understanding the professions of our time—psychological, sociological, and organizational modes—are not important; they are, and we will not understand what a modern clergyperson as a contemporary professional is about without them. However, we will not understand what the modern clergyperson as a minister or priest is about without including in our analysis the clerical traditions we have inherited. And if understanding the clergyperson as "in some mode" minister or priest is not important, then we may be sure that understanding the profession itself is not important.

The first thing to be said about understanding the clergyperson as minister or priest is that this understanding can take place only in relation to an understanding of the church, the religious community, the *ecclesia*. In religion, and perhaps especially in relation to Judaism and Christianity, the individual adherent—despite many Protestant emphases—must be understood in polar relation to the community. Individuals qua Christian or Jewish literally do not exist without the community; and, however individualistic their piety may be, that same piety has itself been shaped by the Christian community and the tradition in which individuals participate. The same is *a fortiori* true of the leadership of the community. The form, status, and function of the leaders of the religious community are shaped by the religious and theological self-understanding of the community. If they are not (that is, if they are shaped by the self-understanding, say, of the modern corporation), that itself must be understood. Thus ministry is understood in correlation with *ecclesia,* or church—and vice versa, though the institution is logically and historically prior.

This is also true for other professions. Teachers cannot be understood without understanding the relevant form of schools and the standards and goals of education generally. The role of lawyers is not comprehensible without understanding the relevant economic, political, and judicial institutions of corporations, legislatures, and courts. Physicians represent an intelligible profession in relation to the variety of medical institutions; as do executives in relation to corporations. Whether this correlation is more true of religious communities or institutions, we will not for the moment determine. I think it is, and on theological grounds. However, it is clear that there is no understanding of the ministry as representing the leadership of the community without a good look at the self-understanding of the relevant religious community, the relevant form of the church.

If we agree with this correlation of professional and institution, minister and religious community, then the important role of tradition and of traditional self-understanding becomes immediately clear. The self-understanding of a community constitutes its identity. Institutions are in their core or essence what they *think* they are in terms of purposes, goals, standards, and ideas of legitimate organization; although, of course, they are also shaped by other social, historical, economic, and political forces. It is this self-understanding, therefore, that more than all else creates, perpetuates, shapes, and reshapes the tradition of that institution. And as we have just noted, a profession is largely defined and understood in terms of the purpose, shape, and role of the institution it serves. Thus it is in terms of the purpose, shape, and role of the religious community itself that the professional status and function of the leader of that community is conceived and understood.

When the self-understanding of the institutional community is clear and strong—and significant to its members—then the shape of the profession serving that community will be obvious to everyone and will be largely determined by the tradition that interprets that community. In some periods of church history, the sense of what the church was and did, and why, was very strong, and the question of its "nature" very significant; then the character of the minister or priest was determined by the theology, the law, and the polity of the church. When the question of the nature and purpose of the church recedes in importance and thus becomes obscure and vague, then the shape of the leadership of the church will be determined by other, extraecclesial forces. Traditional views of the ministry (and of the religious community) will merely haunt the church's sanctuary, the minister's office, and the parsonage like homeless ghosts with nowhere else to go. But the haunting will as always be a relevant factor in understanding, if nothing else, the neuroses and anxieties of the ministers, and the carpings, complaints, and nostalgia of the congregation.

All sorts of practical pressures, accepted goals, and sensible standards from contemporary society function in determining the roles of the clergy and the criteria applicable to them. These are as indispensable to understanding the clergy as they are to inquiring into any other contemporary profession. But professions do differ significantly, and those differences are also important clues to understanding what each profession is about and why its members do what they do. In understanding the differentiae of a profession, we must go to the relevant institution to begin our inquiry. There we must start with the self-understanding of that institution or community—with the tradition of its self-understanding—in order to see what its leadership is about. For it is the traditional self-understanding of the religious community that shapes, if it does not determine, what the community thinks its leaders are to be or should be, and what the leaders themselves think they are or should be about.

Ecclesiology, Then Polity

There have been several widely divergent interpretations of church or religious community and of ministry or priesthood in our common Christian and our common American history. These differences between interpretations of church and ministry—rather than between ministry and, for example, school teacher or psychological counselor—also have affected and continue to affect attitudes and expectations toward the clergies. In large part, what we call denominational traditions shape the rights and privileges, norms and obligations that support, reward, defend, and beset the clergyperson.

These are still in our day different for a Roman Catholic priest from what they are for a Baptist preacher. It is probably these differences between denominational concepts of the role of the clergyperson, and not differences of theology or ethics,

that have caused, since World War II, the noticeable clerical
movement in the general direction of the Episcopal clergy.
How much these differing traditions of ecclesiology, polity,
and clerical role in the denominations actually affect the patterns of behavior of the relevant clergy is an interesting but
elusive question. Are the clergy in America—from Roman
Catholic to Evangelical, from Episcopal to television country
preacher—more influenced by their differing ecclesiastical
traditions than their commonalities by being American? Are
an American Roman Catholic Church and a Reformed congregation more alike qua American, or is either one more similar
to its European counterpart? We are aware of the denominational differences among us because we fail to notice the American similarities; probably an Italian or Chinese observer,
conscious of common American characteristics that we do not
see, would reverse this judgment. In any case, whatever the
answer may be to the question regarding whether particular
ecclesiastical traditions or the contemporary environment exerts the greater influence, there is nonetheless little question
that ecclesial tradition, the self-understanding of the religious
community, affects to some significant degree the shape of the
clerical profession. It is this in large part that defines the role
of minister or priest—that is, the religious role of the clergyperson—and that aspect of the profession can hardly be called
unimportant. Thus, in setting about to understand the ethics
of the clergy, we must begin by looking at the differing traditions of ecclesial self-understanding alive among the clergy we
seek to understand.

Finally, it is important to make clear that by the "self-
understanding of the ministry in relation to the religious community"—of clergy in relation to church—we mean more than
the polity of the denomination in question. Polity connotes the
institutional structure of the community: its patterns of authority and responsibility, its governing bodies or persons, their
rights and obligations, the institutional roles and functions of
its officers, committees, and so on. It corresponds roughly to
the bylaws of most associations. Clearly, these are important
for understanding the clergy; for example, polity determines
who can hire and who fire a clergyperson, an issue of not
inconsiderable importance! Nonetheless, polity is not what we
have in mind here. Polity implies or is derivative from ecclesiology, the latter being what we have in mind. Ecclesiology
represents the theological interpretation of the church: the
church in its relation to God; the church as the means, or as the
result, of grace; the church as an instrument of redemption;

the church, in other words, as a religious institution. It is in relation to God (or, if the church is nontheist, in its relation to its convictions, norms, and ideas) that the church is or becomes a church and not some other sort of institution. Correspondingly, it is in relation to the divine (or what functions as divine in the church) that the ministry ministers or the priest mediates (note that both words connote a communication of the holy in and through the role of the clergy). Different forms of the churches, therefore, represent different ecclesiologies—different views of the relation of God, of God's grace and of God's call, to the community, and thus different views of the minister as mediator of the divine power or divine call to the congregation. If polity makes any real sense, polity reflects ecclesiology—as do church architecture, church liturgy, and church activities. If they do not derive from ecclesiology, then each of them is merely borrowed, as church buildings may be made to look like banks or be organized and run as if they were production or retail corporations. But then this institution literally makes no sense. It is, therefore, at the differing ecclesiologies of the churches that we must look if we would understand the effects of religious tradition on the profession and comprehend, therefore, the ethics of the clergy.

The Types of Church and Ministry

Let us consider three predominant types of church and ministry, of religious community and its leadership. Clearly, I am indebted here to Ernst Troeltsch.* These forms of the church were more distinguishable in the past than they are now. This is so for the following reasons. First, in the past, religious communities were more aware of and concerned with their religious, and therefore their theological, definition. As a consequence, their actual institutional and communal shape—and with that their clergy—reflected more accurately their ecclesiology. These sharp differences have been significantly blurred by the increasingly secular character of the environing society; churches are now more alike.

Second, the coming to be of the denomination in a pluralistic, social environment (and the mutuality that has resulted) has had as one consequence a vast mutual influence: imitating, borrowing, copying, and so on, among churches. In pastoral

*A more considered and thoroughly argued version of what I present here is found in my volume on the church, *How the Church Can Minister to the World Without Losing Itself* (Harper & Row, 1965).

work, preaching, counseling, organizing activities, and political and economic programs, clergy and their communities have learned from one another and from their common society. All—whether Mormon or Greek Orthodox—have dinners, picnics, committees for political lobbying, committees for liberal works in the community, counseling centers, kindergartens, and parking lots. A common ecumenical theology oriented toward the biblical, toward liberation, and toward healing has only added to these homogenizing effects on the mainline churches. Thus have the secularity and the plurality of our cultural environment, plus the appearance of a more common theological and ethical mind, toned down our traditional differences. However, as the denominations have clustered more together, other powerful groups separated in spirit from them have appeared. The latter have interpretations of clergy and of the clergy's ethics that are correspondingly different, though what these new differences amount to is as yet unclear. Whatever the differences are, they must in part be understood in terms of the groups' traditional ecclesiologies as well as the novel possibilities of television, in addition to the contemporary social environment within which fundamentalism has been reborn.

Despite these strong tendencies toward clerical uniformity, ecclesiological differences generated out of very diverse historical traditions still remain; and even where a common understanding of the clergy is present, that understanding has been itself constituted by the amalgamation of these diverse traditions. For this reason, even in the modern setting there is no understanding of the profession of the clergy without some grasp of historical ecclesiology, of how the dimension of the holy has been and is believed to be present in the church, of how the ministers and priests relate to that dimension, and therefore of how the clergy mediate the holy to the congregation. All of this may be merely a ghostly presence haunting the minister (and spouse) like a set of angry ancestors as he or she organizes and leads the activities of the congregation's life, but still that haunting must be understood if we are to understand the possibilities, the obligations, and the travails of the clergy.

Because so much toning down and intermingling has occurred, each type is more an "ideal type" than an actual description. I will try to indicate where the most important erosion of the pure type has occurred as each has settled into its recently achieved and therefore present status as a denomination, as one form of church among others. Still it will be evident how the religious understanding of the community (ecclesiology) is correlated in each case with a relevant interpretation of the clergy. Clergy may all seem to represent a body of look-alike professionals—except possibly for one or two variations of uniform—at the biweekly luncheon of the local council of churches. But probably even today they and their congregations see the role of each—and therefore his or her ethics—in a significantly distinctive light.

The Sacramental Church, the Mystical Body of Christ

The most obvious type, and probably the oldest (though all claim that honor, interestingly) is that of the Catholic churches. If, as has been suggested, a type is to be discriminated from other types according to the locus of the holy—the place where the divine dwells and is "given" to the members of the community—then for the Catholic churches this locus is in the sacraments, especially in the Eucharist. There for any Catholic consciousness—whether Orthodox, Roman, or High Anglican—the faithful encounter directly the sacred, in fact, receive it into themselves. If you ask a conscious Catholic why she or he attends church, she or he will say, "To take the holy sacrament, of course." Preaching here is largely teaching or instruction *(didache)* about doctrine, about law, about organization. Word hovers around and defines sacrament, not the reverse. Thus the minister is priest, sacramental mediator, not primarily preacher or declarer of the Word. And the requirements or obligations on the clergy are first of all to nurture this role and the institutional structure that preserves, continues, and fosters the sacraments. What makes possible the sacraments (makes them valid) is the apostolic succession, the episcopal line believed to extend unbroken back to the founding of the church. The continuation of that line guarantees the continuation of sacramental power in and through that line; hence no sacrament is valid, or conceivable, if not sponsored by that line. Classically, therefore, the ethics of the clergy is primarily directed at the preservation of this divinely established structure of the church. The clergy is validly ordained and by this ordination is given by the bishops the sacramental power to mediate. The clergy keeps itself fit thus to mediate: it is celibate, "ordered," separated from the world, and taught the necessities of the church, that is, doctrine and law. The clergy is obedient to the episcopal order as the fount of the authority and power that generates the church. The church does not create and so choose the bishops but rather the reverse: the church is there established, and in a papal succession, it is there that the episcopacy is established.

Although more could be said, perhaps this is enough to indicate the way this sort of "ancestor" shapes attitudes, norms, and expectations about the clergy in all Catholic consciousness. One can see clearly here the roots of the authoritarian, dogmatic, legalistic tendencies of much of the Catholic clergy. One can see here also, however, their enviable ability to "accept" the world to themselves and then to the church, to mingle with the worldly world and not feel contaminated thereby. Why should they? The "holy" in the church is objectively present in the succession, in the sacraments, in dogmas, and in law. It is there for all, however tarnished and apparently indifferent they may be. Priests are mediators of it; and so, like any relatively passive mediator, their own modes of contamination, although perhaps deplorable for their own salvation, do not affect their ability to be priests. In the late fourth and early fifth centuries, with Augustine, it was determined that the efficacy of the sacraments did not depend on the spiritual health of the mediator. Thus was the priest—so long as he retained the outward requirement of obedience and order for his role as mediator—free from the burden of total personal sanctification if he was to do his professional task. To many Protestants, all this is shocking, practically pagan, and certainly unspiritual, a radical denial of the holy in the church. They do not see, and would not understand, that the holy is objectively there in the Catholic tradition—in sacrament, doctrine, law— and it is (or hoped to be) subjectively present in the religious orders. This holiness cannot be compromised either by the world or by the worldly character of the church as an institution. The realization that there is backsliding, politics, even greed throughout the church does not prevent confidence that there is also the presence of healing grace. As a human institution, the church is, to be sure, worldly; but the church also has a divine nature, like its Lord. In this regard, it is the Mystical Body of Christ where the divine spirit dwells: in sacrament, in dogma, in law, and in the transforming graces that suffuse that body.

This traditional understanding of church and clergy has received some very hard jolts in the last three decades. The modern concepts of autonomy, of the critical spirit, and of democratic authority have together deeply challenged the locating of all authority "in heaven and on earth"—that is, in religious and moral matters—solely in a tradition defined and declared by an elite body of professional men. More and more, questions circulate such as: What do *they* know of sex? of marriage? of raising and training children? of women's bodies or spirits? Is it really necessary to be a male, to be celibate, even to be properly (episcopally) ordained and authorized in order to celebrate the Eucharist, hear confession, declare the law, or do the Lord's work? What if the bishop is ignorant, greedy, uninterested in the poor, in justice, or in peace? How then can ordination be valid or the church be the true church? What is more significant, the clergy in large numbers share in raising these modern (or sectarian!) questions. The entire authorized understanding of church, clergy, and authority—and therefore the recognized loci of the holy, the sacraments—here seems under challenge. No wonder it was Küng, who raised questions about the *ecclesia,* who was first condemned—not the other theologians who, though more radical than he about nonecclesial matters, raised no direct questions about the church. But note, liberation theology presents us with a very different understanding of the holy in the church, thus of its tasks on earth. It presents us with a different understanding of the means of redemption and hence a different idea of the role and ethics of the clergy. The true clergy are here to side with the poor, where alone the authority and the intelligibility of the gospel lie. The theology of the true clergy, if valid, can grow out of only that identity and the struggle it implies. Correspondingly, they are to struggle morally, spiritually, and politically against oppression; and they are in the end to redeem the social order, to liberate persons from their economic, political, social, and spiritual chains. This represents, for all its demurrers, a very different ecclesiology, a different understanding of priesthood, a different locus of authority and of truth, and a different interpretation of redemption—in short, a very different understanding of how the church and its leaders may become means of grace.

Quite possibly—as with the autonomous, historical, and democratic consciousness—the liberationist consciousness can unite creatively with a Catholic ecclesiology centered on the sacraments, as it is already doing with the mystical element in the Catholic tradition. Nevertheless, the church as the community sent to liberate the world has a different understanding of holiness, a different interpretation of its own religious goals and norms; and so in the end it must recognize a different gestalt of leadership. Thus this "liberationist" conception of church and clergy will endlessly shake and perilously challenge the church as an institution established on and by a hierarchical, authoritarian clergy, an institution possessing the sacred in its changeless sacraments, dogmas, and law, and so in its essence accepting the world as long as the world recognizes the church's religious authority and role therein. Nothing will be more creative—or risky—than seeking new ways to interpret a Catholic sacramental ecclesiology, interpretations that recognize fully the historical, scientific, and autonomous consciousness of the modern as well as the liberationist consciousness of the postmodern world.

The Church of the Word

A quite different interpretation of church and clergy appeared at the Reformation. The holy within the community was no longer the sacramental gift of healing grace; rather it was the presence of the gospel of justification of the sinner and the promise of reconciliation with God contained therein. The Word declared in scripture and proclamation has now replaced the sacrament contained in *ecclesia* as the place where each believer most directly and significantly encounters God—in fact, where Jesus Christ is present in his church.

All forms of Christian churches relate in some mode—or seek to do so—to Jesus at the center of their life; almost none of them recognize this in the others. The Catholic does this in the sacrament of the Eucharist; the Reformation communities in the hearing of the gospel; the sects in obedience in the Spirit to Jesus' law; the liberationist in historical memory, in moral commitment, and in political action for the kingdom. In each, the clergy mediates this relationship. Different requirements, therefore, are entailed in each, different modes of education and different sorts of authority. In the Reformation type, the clergyperson mediates this gift of the Word; but because the gift is so different from that of sacramental grace, the function itself of mediating becomes radically different. Preaching or proclamation of this Word is now the central act of the church, and this is the minister's main task. Here the emphasis is not on the clergy's inner perfection or saintliness, as Luther insisted. What is required now is fidelity to the Word, which requires obedient study of scripture and commitment to the role of obedient proclamation. Because this message is contained and preserved in the scripture, scripture itself replaces the authority of church tradition; it is available to each believer and unquestioned in its authority. The clergy are, therefore, obedient to scripture, not to the episcopus. Their own authority as mediator, and thus their authority in the congregation, depends on their knowledge of scripture and their fidelity to the latter's true meaning. In principle, each interpreter is free to follow his or her own conscience in the interpretation of scripture. In time, however, the interpretations of different communities became normative, and thus the authority of particular traditions and of their confessions comes to dominance, and with that dogmatic controversies reappear.

Because the law as well as gospel has been given in revelation and scripture, the clergy were also authorities in interpreting the divine law and the proper morals for the community of believers. This role increases greatly in the Calvinist churches, in Methodism and derivative churches from Calvinism. The Reformed tradition emphasized, as Lutherans and Anglicans did not, the guiding role of divine law for the whole community. Hence, here the clergy became not only declarers of the gospel Word but moral legislators and executive implementors of the moral rules governing the community. The minister as preacher of truth and upholder of moral good really begins here. In a sense, now, the holy abides not only in Word (and sacraments) but also in the holy community and especially in and through the holy person. One can see this concept heavily dominating Puritans, Presbyterians, and New England congregations, influencing much evangelical life, and even in liberal circles hovering over ministers of Calvinist and "deviant-Calvinist" traditions (Congregationalists, Methodists, Baptists). One sees also that this emphasis on moral perfection has been heavily qualified among Episcopalians and Lutherans by the older Catholic traditions that have lingered on in both of these denominations.

In the premodern era, the clergy so interpreted had tremendous significance for the destinies of all in the community and therefore had vast authority and status (new presbyter is merely old priest, said those disgusted with both). This is the only way we can understand how the clergy equaled, in fact outranked, physicians, lawyers, and teachers in seventeenth-, eighteenth-, and nineteenth-century communities. As is obvious, this authority has also found itself eroded by the "acids of modernity," albeit different acids. And part of the psychological problem for the clergy—if not for their ethics—is to try to understand themselves so as to feel that professional importance once again, even if the world no longer recognizes it. The main acid, of course, has been the gradual secularization of most of life, of life "downtown," and the consequent relegation of religion to the spheres psychologically of subjectivity, and sociologically of Sunday, suburban life. But more precise problems have also been at work. The historical consciousness, relativizing both text and the interpretation of text, has done more unconscious damage here than has the conscious battle of autonomy with priestly authority. For in most churches of these traditions, no text or scripture now possesses absolute authority; and each interpretation thereof is also seen, or at least felt, as relative. Therefore, where have flown the authority to declare the Word and the expectation of hearing it on which the status of clergy had been based? Are educated philosophy (even in graduate school), homely wisdom, humane and practical moral advice, and empathetic counseling equivalent to declaring and expounding the divine Word and the divine law to the community? One may be helped by the professional and human powers of the minister; one is hardly saved through them. Declarers of a divine Word are as ambiguous now about their role—though they may have a good "biblical" theology of church and ministry—as are modern priests chafing under an alien episcopal authority and concerned with ultimates other than sacramental participation. The Word is a category fundamental to modern Protestant theology; but as actual through its proclamation in the church, it leaves the clergy uncertain of their role in mediating it.

It has seemed to me that the acids of modern relativism—the historical relativism of sacred texts; the cultural social, ideological, and gender relativism of preacher; and the partiality of any theological interpretation—these acids have made more precarious the religious role of declaring the Word than the priestly role of mediating the sacrament. Words need not necessarily be more relative and human than are creaturely material symbols, but in modern intellectual culture they seem so; they seem locked in the relative, the historical, and the psychological worlds. Thus scriptural text, theology, and sermon are more obviously nonabsolute, nondivine, relative, merely human, one person's viewpoint—all of this begging more, so to speak, for our critical reflection as we listen, than are sacramental media. Therefore, the former, words, have tended in our century to fly apart in opposite directions. They have tended to become "liberal," human (if wise) proposals from the pulpit for reflective faith and ethical action, thus not mediating immediately the divine at all. Hence is the presence of the holy elusive in mainline Protestant churches. However, if these words retain their absolute status, Protestantism moves into fundamentalism. Many people participate in modern relativism during the week and long for verbal and legal absolutes on Sunday. And good theology, conscious of its own relativity, can hardly provide all the background necessary for effective proclamation. No wonder that for this, as well as for other good reasons, so much of the modern ministry finds its important role in some aspect of liberation, even if for many it is not easy to know what that means for middle-class congregations. Nonetheless, liberation themes and modes of action do relate us to the holy, to "demand," as Tillich put it. They do embody and foster love, and they give a role to the leadership and the community alike that even the best theology cannot give.

Material symbols, tangible, visible symbols encased in the mysterious action of liturgy can, however, mediate something beyond themselves, and they can do this in and to a number of diverse intellectual and spiritual atmospheres. The Eucharist can be taken by reflective consciousness as a mediating symbol in a "liberal way," as modern Catholicism and Anglicanism show. It can also still communicate to those who are not inclined toward reflection, and yet not create the fundamentalist consciousness—or so it seems at present. This is why a reformed Roman Catholic church, the Anglican church, and possibly the Lutheran and Orthodox churches seem better able to retain in a sane way a clear experience of the encounter with the holy and yet avoid fundamentalism than are the Protestant churches. And this is why an enlivened sacramental community directed by liberationist motifs may prove a more effective and lasting mode of ecclesial and ministerial synthesis than will a theological-liberationist synthesis. Perhaps clergy do not think much about all this. If they don't, one wonders how they do understand their task. Nevertheless, almost certainly those who in no small numbers have left liberal Baptist, Disciples, Methodist, or Presbyterian congregations to become Episcopal priests or Roman Catholic lay people have thought a lot about all this.

The Churches of the Spirit

Here we encounter a genuine chaos—a wide variety of types of church life and ministry that have proliferated almost endlessly and are steadily growing. Perhaps the most important forms will emerge out of the black churches, as a new synthesis of spirit-centered churches with a worldly, liberationist task, uniting types now a bit worn out in mainline churches or warped into fundamentalist forms in many evangelical congregations. Along with the Catholic union of sacrament and liberation, these newer modes of black congregational life may be destined creatively to form the vital churches of the future.

Let us return, then, to simpler days to see some of the guiding principles of these churches of the Spirit (Troeltsch's "sectarian types"), for these principles have been vastly important. They have provided the background and so the presupposi-

tions for a good deal of the ecclesial structure of the denomination, and hence of the mainline churches. They form even
more of the ecclesial structure of most of the evangelical and
charismatic churches; and, historically, they have dominated
the self-understanding of the black churches. I have suggested
that the denomination (mainline or evangelical) as found in
America is perhaps most helpfully to be seen as the sect type
within the world—with all the ambiguity of that bizarre com-
bination (for originally the sect *withdrew* from the world).

The word *sect* has been applied to forms of the church that
appeared and flourished in the sixteenth and seventeenth centuries: Spiritualists, Anabaptists, Mennonites, Amish, Quakers,
and so on. These groups seemed to emphasize three things,
each of which sharply distinguished them from the churches
of sacrament and of the Word: subjectivity, transformation
unto perfection, and fellowship.

Subjectivity refers to the vivid, evident, and transforming
presence of the Spirit in the believer. This is to the sect authentic Christianity—not cathedrals, masses, ceremonies, robes,
bishops, creeds, doctrines, learning, or objective law, or even
church buildings. Thus the sacraments were minimized or
eliminated; episcopal or presbyterial status were scorned; and
in some there was no recognized ministerial role. Doctrines,
theology, and scholarship were considered irrelevant, if not a
bit dangerous; church buildings and liturgy were eschewed.
All that is objective was negated in favor of inner experience
and transformation of personal and communal existence. The
church to them is holy not because within it are bishops, dogmas, valid sacraments, and holy law, or even because within it
there is the true revealed Word. It is holy simply because it is
made up of authentic Christians, real believers and real followers who have the Spirit and know they have it, and who follow
its leading. The nondoctrinal, nonliturgical, nonsacramental,
"inward" denominational church is one descendant; the twice-
born evangelical Christian congregation is another; the charismatics another. Also, most black churches represent authentic
survivors of this mode.

The second emphasis was a genuine *transformation* accom-
panied by obedience to the absolute law of the gospel. Thus
Troeltsch defined sect as characterized by the drive toward
perfection; I prefer the name "churches of the Spirit" as a
broader rubric. Here there was originally and still is in principle no distinction between a higher ethic for the clergy and a
lower ethic for the laity, as in the Catholic churches, nor a
distinction of person and vocation or calling, as in Lutheran-

ism. The "leader" has no superior religious status. He or she is
one among the congregation, and so he or she (and often it has
been she) is called only to a leadership role in the community,
not to a special religious role. If anything, the community, not
the clergy, is set apart. Here in principle the whole congregation equally is called to perfection; this is why originally they
left the world, which most of them regarded as wicked
through and through. In less rigorous, modern times, the community has thoroughly reentered the world, in fact, established much of it on our continent. Thus the call to perfection
has been reduced to "respectability," probity in business and
vicelessness in personal life. As a consequence, worldly property, military service, governmental vocations, and imperialis-
tic politics commonly characterize groups that were once
"sectarian." And so far have they forgotten their heritage that
they (for example, Baptists, Campbellites, and Nazarenes) take
this worldly sectarianism—and God's blessing on the United
States—thoroughly for granted. Sects can, therefore, change in
relation to the world and can even turn theocrat, as happened
once or twice in the sixteenth century.

The clergy in the churches of the Spirit are thus ethically
in a paradoxical role. All in the congregation should follow the
law (about alcohol, smoking, gambling, dirty stories, and so on);
but ahead of all of them around the track must be the pastor
and, of course, the pastor's spouse. Thus are he and she called,
so to speak, to *more than perfection.* And when, as in the last
decades, most members of these churches have become full-
time Americans and now drink, smoke, gamble, and get rich—
except when the pastor comes to tea—the minister and
minister's spouse alone uphold the law and will be fired (like
a wayward shaman or a Donatist bishop) if they let the worldly
congregation down. Quite unexpectedly, the clergy here have
become scapegoats, sacrificial victims for the congregation;
they must be holy to make up for the community's lapses.

In these churches, the holy is present as the Spirit dwelling
within the whole congregation, vivifying it and transforming
it. Thus they claim, like the Catholics, to represent the New
Testament Church. In the world, these high, almost impossible
standards generally (though hardly in the black churches) have
been somewhat watered down into an emphasis on freedom
from vice, from swearing, and from obscenity, which we associate with Baptist and old-line Methodist congregations. Now
the holy is even more ambiguous in its meaning and is mostly
lodged in rhetoric and borne by nostalgia, as any visit to a
southern Baptist revival will show. Protestant congregations

that are conscious of being in the world, and therefore responsible to the world, have turned this ethical emphasis in social gospel and liberationist directions. This version of the holy dominates the self-understanding of most responsible Protestant leaders and laity, as it may soon much of Catholicism. For congregations *in* the world, this seems the creative path that must be taken. The older requirements of perfection, once possible because of separation from the world, now can create havoc with the souls of the clergy. Required to be holy and yet in the world, they settle for appearing pious. Pressed into being friendly, warm, frequently gushing and agreeing, they can be—unless they know who they are—terribly lonely, often empty inside, and fearful. As the professor who must pretend to be learned becomes empty and disappears inwardly, so these clergy pretend to incarnate the holy and as a consequence repress everything real about themselves. This is not the hypocrisy of the stern Puritan; it is the modern American hypocrisy of phony love.

The third emphasis of the sect was on *community,* the real fellowship of an actual congregation. The church was not the whole church headed by Christ, the pope or bishops; nor was it loyal to the Confessions and related in various ways to civil government. No one thought of "church" that way. Church was *this* congregation, *this* community of people who knew each other, helped each other, married among themselves, shared the same moral standards, and obeyed the same moral laws. This sense of fellowship, of unity of friendship, warmth, and helpfulness, has blessed—and cursed—the American congregation, and characterizes Lutheran, Anglican, and Roman congregations here as it did not characterize their equivalents in Europe. (In fact, all these sectarian traits have filtered into the other denominations: church suppers, coffee after the service, inviting visitors to dinner, and even teetotalism in the South.) The community of congregational Protestantism was its strongest asset, and possibly could be again. I suspect it fares better now in Catholicism, where the community aspect was for long borne by ethnic communal identity and now still can be real because of a sense of identity as a Catholic people, a small community within the larger community of the whole church. Once the denominational communities of Protestantism entered and found themselves established in the world, they split apart on class and professional lines, or else became suburban, middle-class enclaves no longer welcoming the poor, the non-WASP, the kooky, the unwashed. The sectarian community in the world has had an increasingly hard time.

Many clergy have been deeply torn between their moral obligations to Christian fellowship with all people (all races and classes—inclusivity) and the drive of the church toward social and spiritual unity (exclusivity). "A church is where you meet people like yourself, people your kids can marry, people you go home to dinner with." How often I have heard this, and how much it was this very idea of "warm fellowship" that in a different sociological setting turned sour! Here one sect idea is at war with another: the community of loving *fellowship* versus the community of loving *outreach*.

It is time to call a halt. Clergy are inheritors as professionals and as leaders of churches of very significant and very different traditions, traditions vastly diverse in their understanding of the institution and their understanding of its leadership. How one is a clergyperson religiously and ethically has been differently interpreted. As a moment's thought shows, these traditions are still there and are still effective, albeit all mixed up with pressures from contemporary society, its goals, aspirations, standards, and techniques. Consequently, each tradition is confused, even recessive, but it is there in the self-understanding of each clergyperson as to what he or she is and can be. At least, if we are to understand the problems as well as the opportunities of clergypersons, their neuroses if not their greatness, one must understand the ecclesial traditions in which their communities exist and in which they live out their professional lives.

3

Images that Shape
the Public Obligations
of the Minister

William F. May

A healthy marriage includes both its interior and exterior aspects, both the secrets that pass between two lovers and the further public responsibilities that the couple, still nourished by their inner life, are willing to assume. Lovers seek obsessively to withdraw from the world; but marriage partners have determined to face outward toward the world as they contribute to its public life. We symbolize this doubleness architecturally: a home has its private chambers where two people come to terms with and enjoy one another, but also its public rooms—the dining room and the living room—in which they receive friends and strangers. Middle-class Americans signaled their shift toward a more private understanding of marriage when they emphasized the family room at the expense of the conventional public rooms in a house.

The church similarly lives in two realms. The church enjoys, to be sure, its own interior life, but it defects from its total responsibility if it fails to turn outward toward the world. The church in its relationship to God resembles a marriage partnership more than a love affair. It enjoys through word and sacrament the presence of God, but it hardly leads a disembodied life apart from the world. Indeed, each church faces out toward a very specific external world that partly shapes its obligations and the public duties of its ministers. In our case, that world is American society in the 1990s, a society that suffers chronically from a split between the private and the public, between one's inner life and outer forms and institutions. Huge institutions, such as governments, corporations, hospitals, the media, and universities, seem to interlock, reinforce one another, and persist without touching inner lives.

This state of affairs does not create a discrete social problem of the kind that usually makes the headlines, such as urban blight, unemployment, racial tensions, the arms race, homelessness, deficit spending, and bureaucratic red tape. It constitutes rather what the Germans would call an Ur-Problem, a deep fault that precedes and affects all other problems. This split between inner life and outer forms shapes the way in which we perceive all other problems and fatefully affects proposals for their amelioration.

This chapter explores the church's (and therefore its leadership's) potential contribution, less to solving headliner social problems, than to bridging the split between the interior life of the psyche and public institutions. The church—along with other voluntary communities, such as synagogues, political parties, parent-teacher associations, citizens' projects, and cause-oriented movements—constitutes a distinctive social resource on the American scene. Edmund Burke once referred to voluntary communities as "the little platoons" among us, which are "the germ," as it were, of "public affections" (Burke 1962, 71–72). The sociologists less elegantly name them "intermediate institutions." They occupy a middle ground between the solitary citizen and the "mega-institutions" of state and corporation. Whatever their name, they help bridge the distance between the public and private in a culture that experiences acutely today a gulf between the two. As such, they constitute publics within the public at large.

These intermediate institutions perform two services—objective and subjective—in cultivating the citizen. First, objectively, they open up the citizen to the question of the common good. An orientation to the question of the common good distinguishes such publics from mere interest groups. The Cattlemen's Association orients to its own interests, pure and simple. Presumably, a church or a service organization has its special interests, but it should be walleyed with at least one eye focused on the question of the common good. To that degree, the organization functions as a public within the wider public and not simply as a group oriented to its own self-promotion. The public at large cannot exist as an indeterminate, formless phantom; it must be composed of groups. But it cannot long flourish if it merely consists of overlapping interest groups, because interest groups can underlap, as well as overlap, or exhaust themselves in profitless competition. The public at large depends rather upon determinate publics within it that allow it to focus, however imperfectly, on questions of the public good.

Second, voluntary communities—which function as publics—not only point their members objectively to the question of the common good, but also tutor them subjectively in the art of acting in concert with others. They tease people out of the bottle of private preferences, wants, and interests, and provide them with some experience of community that the mega-institutions only limitedly provide. They acquaint people with what John Adams called "public happiness"; that is, one's right to be seen and heard in public disputation and debate in the determination of ends. The very voluntariness of the community challenges each member to learn how to get along with others, cope with friends and opponents over policy differences, and overlook personal slights and grievances for the sake of common goals.

Such voluntary communities, the church included, face a major difficulty, which this chapter will not attempt directly to address. They depend heavily upon their members for the donation of their treasure and time. But long-term inflation and changing tax laws have threatened their monetary base. Also, their human resources have been dramatically reduced as women have moved into the work world, partly for reasons of their own agendas and partly driven there by inflationary pressures. Thus, women have little time and energy left for their families and still less for service in voluntary communities that previously relied upon, to say nothing of exploited, them for free services. In losing women, the churches have often lost the entire family unit, because the church as a traditional "outlet" for stymied women not only took advantage of their talents, but annexed through them their spouses and children. Justice forbids turning back the clock, but prudence requires the church, at a minimum, to think through theologically and sociologically the design of a church that no longer can rely on sexist patterns in the society at large for its support.

This chapter will concentrate on the specific problems in self-interpretation that lead the churches as voluntary communities either to deny the public dimension to their life and responsibilities or to think of their contributions to the political order as merely direct, and therefore occasional, interventions in specific crises. One thereby either defines the church wholly as a private entity oriented exclusively to the private needs of its members (often chronically exhausted by their marketplace responsibilities), or one envisages only occasional, crisis-driven, public action.

The Church as Mission and Community

The Protestant church, and most particularly the free churches, tend to think of the church in noninstitutional terms. The church, first and foremost, exists as a community, a fellowship. Only secondarily does it organize itself as a structure to perform specific functions. This state of affairs explains the rather episodic, hit-or-miss character of church action. Social action flourishes only as long as a church happens to have a powerful minister concerned with such matters and dies out with his or her departure. The church may need to reverse this relationship between community and function, fellowship and action. Instead of thinking of itself first and foremost as a community to which a variety of activities attaches, the church may need to ask itself, What are the essential functions, the essential activities, of the body of Christ? and, then, let community form around them.

To use an analogy from another field: A powerful sense of community can develop in a theater company that dedicates itself first and foremost to its essential activity—putting on a play. The action exhilarates and inspirits members to the point that a letdown occurs when the curtain comes down on the last performance. Ordinary life seems stale after people have expended their time and themselves around a meaningful action. Conversely, a theater group deteriorates and its high standards and morale collapse when it thinks of itself first and foremost as a society that happens incidentally now and then to put on plays.

Analogously, the very expenditure of the church's energies in its essential activities brings it to life; and it trivializes as a community when it lacks a shaping mission. A complementary and reinforcing, rather than a contentious, relationship can exist between order and vitality, function and power, structure and dynamism, body and spirit. Too often, however, in American church life, liberals, evangelicals, and radicals alike have assumed that structures invariably constrict and oppress rather than supply the forms in which the energies of the people of God can come to life and efficacy. If one accepts a symbiotic relationship between the vital and the organic, then a critical question remains: What are the vital functions of the body of Christ that define the church's public mission and the minister's responsibility?

No enduring answer to the question of mission emerges without appeal to the essential functions or actions of Christ himself. The ancient terminological equivalent for function is "office," the specific forms of which the church derives from the scriptures of Israel. Any serious reflection on ministry must reckon with the three great images for the work of Christ: priest, prophet, and king.

The priestly office of Christ authorizes the church's liturgical action; the prophetic office its teaching function; and the kingly office (as Jesus defined kingship), its service function. The church apprehends God's inner life as self-expending love—Father, Son, and Holy Spirit. The offices of Christ and the functions of the church provide three ways of participating in God's self-expending love: worship, its festive celebration; teaching, its clarification; and service, its sharing. These three substantive actions define the work of the minister. On the principle that form follows substance, we must deal with these images first, and only then subsequently with various further contending images of the minister as leader. The formal articulation of the minister's power and responsibility must follow from and be limited to substance.

The Minister as Priest

In exploring the minister's larger public obligations, it would seem sensible to bypass the activity of worship and concentrate on the minister's "royal" service on the grounds that the latter bears most directly on the domain of politics. The arena of the political would seem the farthest removed from the liturgical. Politics defines a world of means subordinate to ends, of instrumental complexes, of conflict, disputation, and strife. In contrast, the liturgical refers to an action that is an end-in-itself; it offers, at best, some measure of respite from those political conflicts that threaten to tear us apart.

Put another way, men and women worship God, first and foremost, because God is. They corrupt the act if they worship for some other secondary goal: peace of mind, career advancement, family unity, political cause, or moral improvement. Some such goods may follow from worship; but if they become the aim and purpose of worship, the worshiper instrumentalizes God to other ends, which is precisely what God is not. "To celebrate a festival means to do something which is in no way tied up to other goals; [it] has been removed from all 'so that' and 'in order to.' True festivity cannot be imagined as residing anywhere but in the realm of activity that is meaningful *in itself*" (Pieper 1965, 7).

Although worship corrupts if one reduces it to the "so that" and "in order to's" of politics (or the pursuits of the marketplace or psychic health), secondary goods do flow from worship that need to be acknowledged. The Catholic moralist Dietrich von Hildenbrand, in *Liturgy and Personality* (Hildenbrand 1943) once attempted to sketch what the liturgically formed person is like; that is, the person who takes the liturgy seriously, which is to say, who does not corrupt it for reasons of self-improvement or self-advancement. Similarly, one needs to ask what the liturgically formed citizen might look like; that is, the person who takes seriously the sacraments of the Lord's Supper and Baptism and the ordinary prayers of the church.[1]

The sacrament of the Lord's Supper. This central act of Christian worship offers the most convenient point of departure, because it structurally resembles the dominant liturgy in the mass media in recent decades (sporting events excepted)— the terrorist attack. The prominence of revolutionary terrorism (leaving aside state terrorism) from the early 1970s onward exposes at once the insatiable hunger of modern people for the liturgical and the deprivations of a politics that springs from a lack of liturgical substance.

The rituals of modern terrorism parody, in a sense, the sacrament of the Eucharist. Luther once called the Christian sacrament the *enacted* word; modern terrorist action has been called a propaganda of *deed*. The Christian rite centers in a figure who serves at once as high priest and victim. The terrorist action distinguishes the high priest from his victims; but, at the same time, the terrorist must also, in one respect, identify with his victims in that his efficacy depends upon his readiness not only to kill but to die. This double readiness creates the power he exercises over the society that watches raptly on television. Like the traditional act of worship, the terrorist's action lies outside of the ordinary arena of political means and ends. Therefore, politically, the deed often seems counterproductive, self-destructive, and irrational. It doesn't seem to make any sense as a means directed to an end. As the Bogside Catholic MP, John Hume, long ago complained about terrorism in Northern Ireland, "The Provos bombed themselves to the conference table and they bombed themselves away again" (*Time Magazine*, January 29, 1973). The action is ecstatic in the sense that it stands outside of the causal nexus of

---

[1]This section on the minister as priest is essentially more Catholic than Protestant. The Protestant usually asks the question "What is the scripturally formed person like?" The Catholic (and the Eastern Orthodox) believer asks instead, "What is the liturgically formed person like?"

means and ends; it juts out religiously as an end-in-itself. It does not look beyond itself to a further justification. The Shi'ite terrorists express this ecstatic element mythically in their expectation that the martyr will be directly translated into heaven.

Terrorism, of course, offers a festival of death, a celebration that has its own priest and victims, and that carries with it the likely risk that the priest himself will become a victim. Others become concelebrants in this liturgical action through the medium of the media. Thus the media respond to the human thirst for celebration, the need for ecstasy, the desire to be lifted out of the daily round. Through violent death, their horror before it and their need to draw near it, the event momentarily relieves men and women of that other death which is boredom.

The Christian Eucharist, like the terrorist's deed, represents a death, but a death that nourishes love rather than arouses fear; that, taken seriously (here I offer a theological statement, not a sociological claim), builds up community rather than isolates, invites others not to watch at a distance on satellite television but to follow and to share. The Eucharist repossesses the past, but in mercy rather than vengeance; transforms the future, but without deforming the present; and it extends outward to the needy, the stranger, and the enemy, while pressing inward to that dark corner where self-pity and malice fester. This ecstatic event should impel Christians both to come together and to go out to others in self-expending love.

Participation in this event is an end-in-itself; it transcends the political, but it is not far removed from the rough terrain of the political; indeed, it lets surface those problems with which the political order must cope. The same meal in which Jesus takes bread and wine and distributes them to his squabbling, defecting followers fulfills his own indefectible purpose—despite the corruption of public good, outright betrayal, the apathy of disciples in Gethsemane, the deviousness of political leadership, and the fickleness of the crowds.

This central Christian act of worship sets itself down squarely in the human scene; it acknowledges those threats to life to which the dark pessimism of Hobbes and the social contract theorists testified. But it states that the deepest taproot of community among us is not the *Summum Malum* that forces fearful, self-interested men and women into the social contract, but a *Summum Bonum* that breaks and limits the hold of fear upon us and invites us into the covenant of self-expending love.

In a pluralistic society, this covenant cannot directly provide the basis for unity in the society. To impose it on others would be to convert it into what it must not be to be itself—an intrusive creed that divides and excludes. But Christians, among the various publics in the public at large, must take the vision that the Eucharist offers seriously. If self-interest alone holds us together, then self-interest alone can as quickly crumble what it originally composed. The social order needs the leavening of self-donative love.[2]

The sacrament of infant baptism. The folksy sentiment with which we surround the sacrament obscures its daring as a public rite. This sacrament acknowledges, on principle, that the church opens up to the disconcertingly strange nothing less than the next generation, still held in arms and not yet revealed in its squirming uncertainty. The sacrament asks the parents, in presenting their child, to give up their obsessive private hold on their child. The sacrament invites those who are most inclined to deal myopically with the infant, to seek its good at the expense of others, and to crush it to the bosom in apprehensive love, to see the child at a disquieting yet quieting distance; that is, to accept it as a child of God. Taken seriously, the rite requires parents to prepare their child for something more than a domestic meaning and to let the child be free for a public significance.

The prayers of invocation and adoration. These prayers at the outset of the service of worship distinguish the Ruler of the Universe from those principalities and powers that normally attract the human heart and command allegiance. They leave no doubt as to the status of the state, and indeed, all political causes; they are humanly important, to be sure, but not ultimate. The citizen cannot pray to the true God and take the state too seriously. God has provided the state for both the good that it can do and the evil that it can prevent, but, in the setting of adoration:

> Even the nations are like a drop from a bucket,
> and are accounted as dust on the scales;

....

---

[2]Hobbes and Locke constructed a politics based on self-interest. Adam Smith described and recommended an economics based on self-interest. Several more recent economists have suggested that self-giving is more important to economic well-being than we have been willing to concede. See Titmusse (1972) and Schumacher (1973).

All the nations are as nothing before him;
   they are accounted by him as less than nothing and emptiness.

                                                            Isaiah 40:15, 17

God's ascendancy over all political powers establishes as its
subjective corollary the principle of the extraterritoriality of
the person. Yet this metaphysical/political vision should not
result in political detachment. It blocks, to be sure, idolatry;
that is, a religious zeal directed either toward the state or
toward the revolutionary cause. But at the same time, it divests
political leaders and activists of vanity and illusion, and therefore frees them to wield power under God and in the service
of God's creatures. The prayers of adoration help let the air out
of inflationary political rhetoric and ought to cut down on the
violence and divisiveness which that rhetoric tends to inspire.

Intercessory prayer. Usually these prayers, whether in the
setting of the worship service or personal devotions, include
petitions for three overlapping groups of people: intimates and
friends, enemies, and the needy. At first glance, prayers for
family and friends would seem to conflict with the meaning of
public life. They seem to presuppose a kind of deity of the
hearth. They extend the parent's loving hand. The supplicant
asks God to treat preferentially those in the circle of intimacy,
to act like a legislature that passes a private bill or like a president who occasionally suspends general laws to intervene in a
special case. Prayers for those one loves do and should occur,
but Christian intercession, however urgent, takes place within
the Lord's own petition—nevertheless not my will but thine be
done. Such intercession should allow the supplicant to take
those who are nearest and dearest, the beleaguered objects of
one's worry, and to see them at a distance and in a strange
light, and to recognize that their ultimate well-being does not
depend upon one's own efforts to contrive their good. Intercession, so understood, moves those one loves beyond the closet
of the private and into a wider arena. Intercessory prayer
ought to continue what baptism begins as it releases those one
loves for a more spacious life.
   Intercessory prayer has a second public significance as it
compels Christians to pray for their competitors and enemies.
Psychologically, opponents usually preoccupy the petitioner as
much as her friends and family. Their very existence threatens; they become an obsession. Toward his enemies, every
man becomes his own Kremlinologist. He scans their every
move, believes that they command too much respect, occupy

too much space; he wishes them dead. Intercessory prayer forces Christians to see their enemies in a new light, to release them from the grip of suspicion, hatred, and revenge, and to pray for their well-being. This saving release for public life acknowledges that no world and space exists wholly free of competitors. As Freud rightly taught, it takes only three parties—a man, a woman, and a child—to create the conditions for enmity in the world, and the introduction of a fourth, as scripture tells us, raises Cain. Intercessory prayer, instead of denying space to the enemy, concedes him some public space. As Martin Luther King Jr. taught us, this kind of prayer need not lead to a quiescent politics; it contends sharply against the unjust enemy, but always in such a way as to give him some room to turn around.

Finally, intercessory prayer means retrieving for public consciousness those people whom we ordinarily remove to the outer edge of consciousness—the lame, the halt, the blind, the sick, the poor, and the captive. Whereas we fix attention on our friends and enemies, the needy we sequester, we remove from sight. We subject them to a kind of premature burial. Specifically, we segregate the sick, the deviant, the defective, the aged, and the delinquent in total institutions, and designate specially trained professionals to manage them—a strategy that frees the rest of us to attend to our own interests and pursuits. Inmates become what a prisoner once called the "forgotten men." This process whereby we neglect the needy and consign the inmate to oblivion shrinks and depopulates the public realm. It reduces the number of those who can be seen and heard, make their wants known, and participate in public debate. Intercessory prayer for "all sorts and conditions" of men and women requires us to return them from the margins back to the center of consciousness to attend to their well-being.

The prayers of confession. Their location in the worship service before intercessory prayer may provide a clue as to why we neglect the needy. Neglect does not usually result from the fact that we are too smug, too complacent, or too engrossed in our own riches to bother with the bereft. If we examine our excuses for neglect, including our reasons for institutionalization, we discover not so much smugness but anxiety, not self-assurance but a sense of harassment, not riches but a feeling of bankruptcy. The question "What can I do?" is often but a way of saying in despair, "I have nothing for the real needs of another because I cannot satisfy my own. What

help could I possibly be to him? Better to avoid him. To have
to face him would be too depressing. He would remind me of
the emptiness of my own fate." Not all expediency in our
treatment of the distressed derives from gross callousness; usually, we are simply too busy obscuring from view our own
poverty. We consign to oblivion the maimed, the disfigured,
and the decrepit because we have already condemned to oblivion a portion of ourselves. To address them in their needs
would require us to confess to God our own needs. But we are
disinclined to want to accept the depths of our own neediness.
The hidden away threaten us because of what we have already
hidden away in ourselves. For some such reason we prefer,
even at great expense, to have them removed from sight. And
what better way to place them in the shadows and to obscure
our own neediness than to put them in the hands of professionals who know how to make a great show of strength, experience, and competence in handling a given subdivision of the
distressed? Thus we convert the exigent into an occasion in
and through which the community seeks to exhibit its precedence and power over them.

What have these strategies of neglect got to do with the
prayers of confession? The French commentator Michael Foucault (Foucault 1973, 68) offers a clue. He observes that medieval society, except for its treatment of lepers (and religious
minorities), was much less inclined than ours to incarcerate its
own members for reasons of deviancy. But by the seventeenth
and eighteenth centuries, society incarcerated the idle, the
poor, the insane, and the criminal without distinction in the
former houses of leprosy. Foucault believes that the religious
ritual of confession helped shape the earlier medieval attitude
toward deviancy. Confession openly acknowledges the fact of
human imperfection; it thereby implies some confidence that
evil can be let out into the open without engulfing those who
pray. But after the seventeenth century, Western society felt
increasingly "ashamed in the presence of the inhuman." It
assumed that one could handle evil only by banishing it. An
age that aspires to total autonomy finds it more difficult to
include in the mainstream of its life the dependent, the defective, and the irrational. They represent a negativity so threatening and absolute that the society can deal with them only by
putting them out of sight.

Confession invites us to acknowledge evil and fault in ourselves and thus allows us to address the distress of others. Confession makes possible intercession. The faith that shapes the
Eucharist and its prayers of confession and intercession assumes that the negative is real but not ultimate. The quarrels

and the defections of first generation disciples, the sins of disciples in our own generation, and the defects and delinquencies of the race at large are grave indeed, but not so grave as to engulf.

The prayers of thanksgiving. These prayers impel the church toward giving—toward its service function—but with a different motive from that which inspires philanthropic giving. The ideal of philanthropy (which informs so much of the giving of voluntary communities, conscientious professionals, and corporations with a conscience) commends a love of humankind that issues in concrete deeds of service to others. The ideal of philanthropy tends to divide the human race in two: relatively self-sufficient benefactors and needy beneficiaries. It presupposes a unilateral or one-way transfer from giver to receiver. This assumption of asymmetry dominates not only private charity, professional *pro bono* work, and corporate philanthropy, but also the conventional self-interpretation of America as philanthropist among the nations, and the American church as patron to the churches in the Third World. This idealist's picture of a social world divided into givers and receivers, although morally superior to a callous neglect of the needy, overlooks the fact that the benefactor receives as well as gives.

The prayers of thanksgiving, as scripture helps shape them, provide the transcendent setting for an ethics of gratitude that differs from the ideal of philanthropy. Scripture provides powerful warrants for giving but always within the setting of a primordial receiving. The scriptures of Israel urge the Jewish farmer, in harvesting, not to pick his crops too clean. He should leave some for the sojourner, for he was once a sojourner in Egypt. Thus God's own actions, God's care for Israel while a stranger in Egypt, prompts and measures Israel's treatment of the stranger in her midst. The imperative to give rests upon the narrative account of a gift already received. Thus the moral/legal element in scripture (the *halacha*) rests upon a narrative base (the *agada*). Similarly, the New Testament reads: "In this is love, not that we loved God but that [God] loved us. . . . we also ought to love one another" (1 John 4:10–11). The imperative derives from the disclosive event of the divine love.

These passages push the believer toward a different notion of love from the philosopher's principle of beneficence. The rational principle of beneficence presupposes the structural relationship of *benefactor* to *beneficiary,* of a giver to receiver. How shall I act so as to construct a better future for others? But these scriptural passages put human giving in the context of a primordial receiving. Love others as God loved you while you were yet a stranger. The virtue in question is not self-derived benevolence but a responsive love that impels the receiver reflexively beyond the ordinary circle of family and friendship. These sacred narratives about God's actions and deeds do not merely illustrate moral principles derived from elsewhere. They reposition the agent; they open up a disclosive horizon in which the potential benefactor discovers herself or himself to be a beneficiary. One's petty benefactions merely signify love already received beyond one's deserving.

Luther located the political order under the fifth commandment, the duties to one's parents. As such, it fell under the ethics of gratitude. But he mistakenly emphasized the duties therein of citizens to their rulers, earthly father figures to whom one generally owed obedience. He failed to emphasize what should be the primary target of an ethics of gratitude— the power wielders themselves, the ministers and other potential doers of good.

The Minister as Prophet

The ministry constitutes one of the three learned professions, but, more than that, it is a *teaching* profession. That special emphasis derives from Christ's prophetic office. In his discussion of that office, Calvin emphasizes Christ as teacher. Salvation includes not only reconciliation with God and the celebration of God's presence (the priestly office), but illumination. "The purpose of this prophetical dignity in Christ is to teach us" (Calvin 1953, 427). Derivatively, the minister should teach, centrally through preaching, but also through counseling, church leadership, and social action.

The teaching responsibility of the minister connects with our understanding of the church as a public within the public at large, as opposed to an interest group. If the church is merely an aggregate of wants and interests, then it can proceed with a wholly transactional understanding of the professional exchange. "Here are our wants in a minister, can you satisfy our wants?" But the ministry, like others of the helping professions, requires a transformational rather than a transactional understanding of professional responsibility.[3]

---

[3]James MacGregor Burns, in *Leadership* (1978), made a distinction between a merely transactional, as opposed to a transformational, leadership, which I have applied here to two different understandings of professional responsibility.

The practitioner in the helping professions must orient not simply to the client's self-perceived wants but to his or her deeper needs. The patient suffering from insomnia often wants simply the quick fix of a pill. But if the physician goes after the root of the problem, then she or he may have to challenge the patient to transform the habits that led in the first instance to the symptom of sleeplessness. The physician is slothful if she or he dutifully offers acute care but neglects preventive medicine. Similarly, the effective lawyer needs to offer not simply wizardry in the courtroom as a litigant, but effective counseling that keeps the client out of the courtroom in the first place. In each case, the professional may need to edge out beyond a bare marketplace transaction, in which one simply sells the customer what he or she wants, and engage in changing a pattern of life.

The transformations that concern the religious leader are far more comprehensive and deep-going than those that may legitimately concern the physician or the lawyer. Clearly, scripture distinguishes sharply between the merely transactional and the transformational. The prophets of Israel knew only too well that people want a message that gratifies their wants rather than addresses their deeper needs. The true prophets complained of the false prophets who cried, "peace, peace, when there is no peace" (Jeremiah 6:14). Despite these predilections, authentic religious leaders have always recognized that they have a responsibility to their congregations above and beyond the mere gratification of wants. Members of their communities are not just consumers of soothing words but hearers of a word for the amendment of their lives.

The term *transformation,* however, awakens legitimate fears of paternalism. The notion of the physician, the lawyer, the manager, and the political leader transforming habits provokes memories of the overbearing authority figures that haunt the American past. We recall the moral officiousness and cramping paternalism of the Puritans, the overbearing presence of company towns, and the professional who vastly exceeds his or her authority at the expense of his or her client's freedom to decide.

Transformational leadership slips into paternalism unless one reckons with teaching as its indispensable form. The professional who insists on transforming his or her clients, but who neglects to teach them, inevitably relies on managerial, manipulative, and condescending modes of behavior control. Teaching respects the client as a rational, self-determining creature.

No one can engage properly in preventive, rehabilitative, and chronic care medicine without teaching his or her patients. Words are to a prescription what a preamble is to a constitution. They provide the clarifying context that makes sense out of the regimen. Similarly, the lawyer in counseling must teach his or her clients. Counseling is the functional equivalent of preventive medicine in the practice of the law. The rabbi and minister cannot do their jobs without effective teaching of their parishioners. The very word *rabbi* means teacher. The Catholic church defines the magisterial (or teaching) authority of the church as one of its three central authorities and responsibilities. In some Protestant traditions, one calls the minister the "teaching elder" to emphasize the importance of teaching in the church's life.

Unfortunately, the teaching component in the minister's responsibilities has been obscured in our time, and this for two reasons: one, specific to the recent history of the ministry; the other, general to all professions. Too many talented divinity school graduates across an extended period from World War II through the 1960s opted for academic careers in preference to the ministry. Often they made their original decision to go to seminary on the strength of college course work in the field and consequently derived their role models from teachers rather than from ministers. Talented students feared oblivion in the parish ministry. Churches seemed rather more absorbed in building campaigns than in the substance of the Christian life. Jobs, meanwhile, were plentiful in the colleges and allowed young teachers freedom to attend to religious issues. But the field of religious studies had a kind of probationary status in the academy, and, in due course, young teachers distanced themselves from (or altogether abandoned) the church. They tended to disengage themselves from the church as though it were a poor relative that slightly embarrassed the upwardly mobile young academic, eager to do well.

The so-called mainline churches suffered the most from this defecting leadership. In the total economy of the church in America, the mainline churches had the special responsibility to teach the Christian faith with clarity and power. Without strong teaching, the church reduces itself to glossolalia on the left or relatively opaque fundamentalism on the right. Unfortunately, the traditional churches had too few talented young ministers, and they were not always adept in getting the talented and dedicated into strategic positions. Theological instruction in the parish has suffered accordingly.

The teaching component in ministry has been obscured for

a second reason, one common to all the nonacademic professions. The modern professions, in general, have defined their practitioners as dispensers of technical services rather than as teachers. They have tended to restrict the teaching function to the academic professional alone. One assumes that other practitioners dispense technical services based on their expertise; they do not teach what they know. The modern university has structurally reinforced this segregation of the teaching profession. It distinguishes the graduate from professional schools—as though the graduate school did not prepare people for a *profession* and as though other professional schools had no obligation to prepare their students to *teach* what they know.

We need to recover the teaching component in all the service vocations, but especially in the ministry. The pastor's obligation to teach derives from the priestly as well as the prophetic office, particularly as the priestly office embraces the principle of the priesthood of all believers. The notion of the professional as the dispenser of technical services tends to establish a gulf between the dispenser and the dispensed to, but the teacher aims to share and therefore to empower those taught, providing the intellectual base for the priesthood of all believers. At the same time, this emphasis on a teaching component in ministry enlarges the minister's role. Other professions are technically interesting, but the ministry, at a technical level, is only marginally so. The ministry acquires much of its intellectual challenge through its teaching function, as the minister draws on an endlessly rich tradition and relates to the full intellectual complexity of a body of learners.

The priest teaches in the setting of the liturgy through the reading and interpretation of scripture. The ancient division of the worship service into the mass of the catechumens and the mass of the faithful provided an early accent on teaching. The so-called learner's mass defined what remains to this day the basic Protestant worship service: prayers and the reading and interpretation of scripture in homily or sermon. But in the nineteenth century, Protestant ministers often fell into the trap of romanticism and interpreted the worship service as an occasion to induce the congregation into a religious experience. Thereafter ministers aimed chiefly for emotional impact; they became magicians of mood. No longer content to teach the faith and invite the congregation into the horizon that the faith opens up, ministers relied increasingly on the techniques of mood control in sermon and song. This reduction of the faith to religious tonality substantively diminished what the church had to offer in its worship, because it testified, after all, to a Word full of grace and *truth.*

Ministers must also teach in fulfilling the royal office of service, and do this in two spheres. First, they teach in their intramural service to the church's own membership through pastoral counseling and care. As we have already noted, this teaching resembles the teaching that other counselors, such as doctors, lawyers, and social workers, perform. Second, ministers must teach through the congregation's extramural service to the world in the form of social action. This teaching ingredient in social action requires comment before undertaking our more extended treatment of the minister as servant.

Social action of the conventional sort may or may not tangibly benefit its recipients, but at its best, it helps educate those performing the service. Middle-class social action often has this important reflexive impact on those engaged in the action. The ghetto suffers from economic poverty, but the white middle class suffers from a poverty of experience. The city, to be sure, needs social action to ameliorate the injustice of the ghetto, but social action can also help the middle class break out of its ghetto. For this reason, social action does not conform technically to the ideal of philanthropy insofar as philanthropy is defined exclusively by giving. Christian social action is a two-way street of giving and receiving. The interrelationship of giving and receiving marks the human community, and not merely in the setting of the family. Long before Americans discussed a Marshall Plan, they received much of their heritage from the continent. The would-be philanthropic nation receives richly from other nations; and the American church, from other churches. Just so, professionals receive nothing less than their vocation from patients, clients, and parishioners who allow them to practice and therewith to be themselves. And corporations receive their identity and support not only from stockholders who invest their money, but from workers who invest their lives, and from other stakeholders in the enterprise—suppliers, consumers, and neighbors—to say nothing of the state and the society at large, which charter them, grant them protection, and endow their enterprises with a public significance.

In addition to its relatively apolitical service activities, the church engages in politically oriented lobbying or demonstrations designed to influence public policies. Some of these latter activities can have a substantial teaching component. When, however, the church functions as a lobbyist without a teaching ingredient in its action, it accepts the rules of the game according to interest-group politics; that is, it lines up as a pressure group alongside other pressure groups in the society—seeking coalition with some and opposing others. It demands that the church be taken into account as one more organized articulation of wants and interests alongside others—the oil interests, unions, the AMA, the highway lobby, the Cattlemen's Association, and hairdressers—for whatever money and power and votes the churches may control.

First, the church should not be afraid to participate in the arena of interest-group politics if it would insert itself into *this,* rather than some other, world and if it will thereby help make the world a little more humane and compassionate. At the same time, the church deprives itself of its full capacity to influence the society if it lobbies without educating. As a lobby, the church counts to the degree that it controls votes and power. But politicians often discount this limited claim to power, knowing that the leadership of the church (which appoints the lobbyists) has failed to carry along its lay constituency. Because neither the lobbyist nor the leadership speaks for members or controls their votes, the power of the lobby withers.

Second, the church has also engaged in social action through movement-based activity on the right and left targeted on the media. The strategy has sometimes substituted placards and demonstrations for teaching. It exclaims rather than explains, often frightening and angering rather than persuading the viewer and the reader. The action provides believers with the ecstasy of action but not the satisfaction of social reconstruction. Such movements constitute a kind of glossolalia from the right and the left, a speaking in tongues rather than in words that clarify and illumine the fateful choices of the day. A cry of pain gets attention, but it does not, in and of itself, shape the community for remedy. Moans of pain and indignant ejaculations are idiotic in the literal Greek sense of that term. Without recourse to other modes of speech, they remain essentially unshareable.

Thus, these statements end up apolitical and antipolitical except in the rarest and briefest of apocalyptic movements, when politics has been suspended in a country. Politics by exclamation point fails to open up a shareable vision into which all sorts and conditions of men and women can enter. It despairs of politics as the art of acting in concert with others for the common good.

Conservatives, liberals, and radicals in the church differ profoundly in the content of their politics, but they agree about its form, insofar as they rely either on lobbying and demonstrations alone. They thereby pressure for action abstracted from the educational task of the church and the teaching responsibility of the ministry.

The social targets for that educational task are twofold: internal and external. The church needs first to educate its own members; it needs to acquaint the laity with that corrective vision of the social order to which the Christian is obligated, a vision that is connected to its worship life and has consequences for the church's social action. Failing that, the leadership of the church finds itself in the embarrassing position of speaking for no one when it claims to speak as and for the church on a policy issue.

I offer just one qualification on this point. The church must educate its laity, but it cannot simply postpone action to that ever-receding date when the internal task of education is complete. The tasks of education and service concur rather than succeed one another. To order them successively would effectively eliminate action altogether, and it would fail to concede the educational value of action. Liberation theology, to say nothing of the experience of our land grant universities, attests to the intricate connection between theological praxis and reflection. Social action often precedes reflection as its indispensable experiential base, just as surely as the action of worship preceded those creedal formulae of the church that sought to illumine, interpret, and defend the church's liturgical experience.

Further, the church cannot wholly restrict its education to its membership alone as the precondition of its action, as though it had no educational obligation to the society at large. Indeed, to confine its education within the fold of members concedes that outside that membership the church could only act as a pressure group—pushing but not persuading, pressing but not educating legislators and administrators in government. This view of things would already concede the perspective of interest group politics—the conviction that groups cannot deal with other groups at the level of moral conviction and argument and social mission. The attempt then to educate constituencies other than its own exhibits some confidence that the church has more to offer than one more voice added to the clash of voices in the social arena; that it has an obligation to explain, clarify, and explicate both without as well as within.

The church must not, however, teach outsiders condescendingly, as though the church alone transcends the compulsions of self-interest. A society dominated by the ethos of interest-group politics runs the danger of underestimating the degree to which men and women can act and think on the basis of moral conviction. It assumes that the country is simply a collection of interest groups and factions, and not a series of publics within the larger public. The church must act as a public but also reckon with others as having the capacity to behave as publics within the public at large.

Finally, the church has a special obligation to speak with and for those in a society who tend in their powerlessness, muteness, and inarticulateness not to speak for themselves. The Catholic bishops pastoral letter on the economic order referred to this obligation as a preferential option for the poor. This special obligation rests upon the scriptural insistence that God will hear the cry of those whose powerlessness is peculiarly the powerlessness of muteness. Correspondingly, the church must undertake the lawyer's role of advocacy to give a place and voice in the public domain to those who otherwise have no voice. And of these there are always plenty. Whatever its prevailing form, a society usually finds a way of creating room for those who cannot give voice to their pain.

The Minister as Servant

This chapter began with the split between inner life and outer forms and institutions. Debates over the service function of the church reflect this split. The kingly office of Christ (remembering that Jesus defined kingship as service) authorizes the service function of the ministry. But service divides into two parts: the church's service inward toward its own members and outward toward the world. The conservatives in the modern church have chiefly emphasized the minister's internal pastoral function; and the liberals and the radicals on the left and right, the minister's responsibility for social action. Thus the church reflects and exacerbates the split between inner life and outer forms that one already finds in the society at large.

But matters in Christendom were not always so. Saint Augustine respected in his own life and writings the primordial unity of the two realms. He was at once mystic and bishop, master of the interior life and leader of the institution. His most influential works reflected his personal interests—the *Confessions*—and his public interests—the *City of God.* The *Confessions* constituted the first Western autobiography; and the *City of God,* the first comprehensive history of the human race.

On the American scene, the Puritans, the early Roman Catholics, and the Jews oriented both the personal and the communal dimensions to biblical faith. In recent decades, the black
churches, perhaps more than all others, have kept alive both
concerns. Their ministers have accepted responsibilities as
both the pastor of souls and the leaders of communities. White
Protestantism, however, in its various forms—conservative,
liberal, and radical—has suffered a disconcerting separation of
the two activities, splitting the personal and the political. The
majority reduces the faith to the experiential, the intimate,
and the familial; and the minority, to the political without
much remainder.

Conservative Christian lay people often reject external service quite vehemently. A parishioner, representing the basic
complaints of conservatives in her church who were about to
ease an activist minister out of office, once complained: "Father X, I come to church in order to be consoled"—the clear
implication being that he had not dispensed much consolation
since he resigned from the staff of an important government
agency to study for the priesthood. The distinguished conservative Edmund Burke once put the woman's complaint in
more sophisticated terms when he criticized progressive cler-
gymen of his own day in England for busily importing some of
the more fashionable ideas of the French revolution:

> Politics and the pulpit are terms that have little agreement. No
> sound ought to be heard in the church but the healing voice of
> Christian charity. The cause of civil liberty and civil government
> gains as little as that of religion by this confusion of duties.
> . . . Wholly unacquainted with the world in which they are so
> fond of meddling—and inexperienced in all its affairs—on which
> they [clergymen] pronounce with so much confidence—they
> have nothing of politics but the passions they excite. Surely the
> church is a place where one day's truce ought to be allowed to
> the dissensions and animosities of mankind.
>
> (Burke 1962, 23)

The social activists, on the other hand, have argued that no
holiday truce can or should be found for the dissensions and
animosities that afflict humankind. They would define ministry
as a service to a world riven with conflict. The activists further
subdivide into radicals and reformers: the radicals pushing for
more global criticism and action, and the reformers pleading
for somewhat more discriminate criticism and for interventions of a more limited nature.

This division within the church that cuts across denominational lines would not be an evil if either the conservatives or the radicals could faithfully be the church by themselves. But clearly they cannot.

The conservative majority cannot be the church by itself alone. The Lord who served the church called the community to serve others, not merely to self-service. Without social action, the church mocks its Lord who ministered to others; it perverts his pity into self-pity.

The more liberal/radical minority, however, also faces its spiritual dangers. Quick to condemn the apathy of the majority, it recognizes somewhat tardily pride and arrogance in itself. The restless minority is inclined to think of itself as a church within a church—the real church—constituted by those academics who stand aloof from the institutional church or those disillusioned professionals and activists who have written it off, especially the local parish.

Early Christians had a name for the minority's spiritual temptation—Gnosticism. When Christian elitists withdraw from the church to do their own thing, they become religious Gnostics who prove their religious superiority by abandoning the church, the fleshly church of ordinary men and women, in favor of an overspiritualized, disembodied movement. They pretend that they serve the needs of others while exempting themselves from need. Thus the pastoral service to members reminds activists that no one is free from need, least of all the disciples of Jesus who needed to receive all things from the Creator.

Pastoral work is that portion of the ministry that, publicly considered, most closely approximates the services offered by other of the helping professions: law, medicine, social work, and nursing. Tensions inevitably develop in all these professions between duties to clients and obligations to the wider public. The professional promise of confidentiality, for example, dramatically illustrates this tension. The privilege of the confessional sometimes conflicts with the public interest and exposes others to real danger. Thus duties to clients, patients, and parishioners might seem rather far removed from public responsibilities.

But the duties to clients and the public do not conflict simply and directly—at least not in a democracy. Indeed, a public justification exists in a democracy for offering shelter even to those who are at odds with the state and its purposes. Public utility does not fully exhaust the meaning of any given person. The public can be said to have an interest in respecting the aforementioned principle of the extraterritoriality of the per-

son and in extending human services to those whose ignorance, sickness, infirmity, and crimes have pitched them out
beyond the ordinary circles of public life and utility and who
may even be at odds with the state. If the state weeds out the
useless or the hostile, then, at one time or another, we all need
to be weeded out. All of us defectively serve the public interest. (A geneticist once warned that genetic engineering rigor-
ously applied could find four or five reasons for deleting each
of us!)

Thus the helping professions, including intensively the pastoral ministry, perform an important public service in reaching out to the anomic—to those who for one reason or another
are stateless, friendless, and resourceless—and in offering help
and consolation. By this activity, the public recovers and
renews its own perishing life. And without this activity, the
grander schemes for reform and revolution often exploit the
misery of others. (A former Benedictine monk, whose convictions led him to work summers in the civil rights movement,
sensed a profound wariness among blacks toward those northern whites in the movement who they felt exploited them for
the sake of the cause. These blacks expressed to him their
appreciation for those ministers who, in the midst of the urgen-
cies of the movement, showed them some personal and pastoral concern. Pastoral work of this kind renews people at the
deepest levels of their being for a life of public significance.)

Traditionally, the church's external service to the world con-
fined itself to social service; it forswore social/political action.
Under its old terms, the service-oriented church naively assumed that social problems can be solved through personal
charity directed to those stricken by fire, famine, and sickness.
The social gospel and the neoorthodox adherents in Protestantism, the natural law theorists among Catholics, and, more
recently, the liberationists, reacted against this kind of Christian service, recognizing that social problems are too massive
and structural for personal charity to solve.

These well-founded objections to personal charity prompted
the church to respond institutionally through its national leadership and clergy to the social crises of our time—acting as a
pressure group or as an educational force on national issues.
But in the course of time, the national leadership operated out
of one ethos and the laity, by and large, out of another. A
divided consciousness meant a divided church; and well-
founded objections to sentimental works of love helped—even
though unintentionally—to perpetuate that divided consciousness. Without the experience that derives from personal service, the ordinary churchgoer lacked contact with the

structural issues of our time. Increasingly, the leadership oriented to structural issues and lay people to pastoral care.

Surely, personal charity is perverse when it becomes a substitute for humane social legislation, but social legislation and personal works of love need not conflict. Indeed, social legislation will not be forthcoming unless the church engages her lay people in such a way as to create a more favorable ethos, atmosphere, or consciousness in which sensitive legislation can be passed and sustained. When horizons narrow to the circle of immediate experience, people balk at the strange: the mentally defective, the prisoner, the aged, the ill, the young, the culturally alien. But service, even of the conventional kind, helps create experienced men and women whose lives are not merely private, narrow, unimaginative, frightened, and unsympathetic.

What relations should exist between the church as an intermediate institution with the mega-institutions of our time? I have in mind here particularly those huge bureaucracies that currently offer professional services to those in need. At first glance, it appears that these huge institutions have their own self-sustaining life; they do not need the interference of so marginal an enterprise as the Christian church. But appearances are deceiving. We may be in for a period of time in which we sustain a kind of dual social organization. On the one hand, we need the huge bureaucracies, the organizational equivalent of the Egyptian pyramids, massive, formal, geometrical, hierarchical—the corporations, the public bureaucracies, and the like—that help mobilize professional talent. But on the other hand, we have need for smaller-scale, informal, spontaneous communities that counterbalance the organizations of grand scale and design. (Herbert Read, the art historian, noted that the ancient Egyptians instinctively developed more spontaneous, lyrical, naturalistic arts and crafts to compensate for the impersonal, impassible forms of the pyramid.)

In such a dual world, the church can perform five important social functions: supplemental, critical, protective, alimentary, and experimental. It needs to provide supplemental services above and beyond those that the bureaucracies provide; to criticize the bureaucracies for failing to provide what they ought to provide; to stand as an advocate and shelter for those who need an intermediary between themselves and the colossi; and to provide the community at large with sufficient contact with the plight of the deprived and the forlorn so as to help create a more favorable ethos of support for the bureaucracies when and as they do their job.

Finally, the church—against the day that the institutions and

the skyscrapers about us, which look so impassive and permanent, should, in their own right and turn, crack and decay—
must experiment in developing those alternative patterns of
common life that may help give shape to the world to come.

This final experimental task of the church reminds one of the
most promising, but partly neglected, opportunities that the
liberation movement offers the church. Hannah Arendt argued in her comparison of three revolutions—the American,
the French, and the Russian—that only the American Revolution succeeded. It alone had already developed in miniature
those institutions that would shape the future society to come
(Arendt 1965, 34–68). To succeed at the deeper levels of historical change, the negative task of freedom *from* must anticipate
the positive constructions of freedom *for*. Exodus is incom-
plete without Mt. Sinai. Those famous shipboard Puritans
reached some advance agreement as to how they wanted to
live in the land ahead. Liberation theologians today may need
similarly to attend as much to the experimental task of reconstruction as to the work of prophetic criticism. Otherwise, the
movement—at least in its North American forms today—may
end up too rootless, too churchless, too much defined by the
Egypt against which it protests, too little oriented to the specific institutional needs of the land ahead. Liberation theology—like the church at large against which it protests—may
suffer from too little rather than too much praxis.

The Minister as Leader

The three offices covered here describe the minister's substantive activities as they bear on the public life of the church.
They do not of themselves sketch out the formal way in which
these activities coinhere in a particular professional (or group
of professionals) with full-time responsibilities for a parish, or
show how these activities connect with the substantive responsibilities of their parish members, who have their own corre-
sponding apostolate. Lay people ideally constitute, along with
the clergy, a priesthood of all believers, a college of teachers,
and a household of servants with counseling and social action
responsibilities in their own right and turn.

H. Richard Niebuhr and his colleagues, in *The Purpose of the
Church and Its Ministry*, noted the importance of this formal
question about the comprehensive "office" in and through
which the minister makes good on the several offices of ministry. Church architecture in the 1950s provided the authors
with a clue; namely, the expanding space for the church office,

which became the hub of the enterprise. They chose the title "pastoral director" to underscore the modern minister's duties as they spread out into the leadership of an active community. The pastor, in effect, functions as bishop of the local parish, directing the enterprise as the priest of priests, the teacher of teachers, and the counselor to counselors (Niebuhr 1956, 83).

Just how does one understand this executive responsibility? Niebuhr and his colleagues recognized the complexity of this problem when they acknowledged the existence in the 1950s of a perverse understanding of the office of pastoral director. They had in mind the "big-time operator," the busy, successful minister whose prestige increasingly lets him run the church officiously. (The big-time operator resembles the shepherd in Navajo lore who tells the sheep which weeds to eat.) Externally, the big-time operator enjoys symbolizing and representing the church to the outside world and begins to buffer himself (it was overwhelmingly himself then) from parishioners.

But, whatever the perversions, the title of "pastoral director" probably reflects too closely the manic phase of expansion of the mainline churches in the 1950s, with their already settled notion of the activities that the church ought to pursue and the pastor's role as overseer and manager of that pursuit. The image does not take into account the ensuing deep divisions within the church about the substance of those activities—liturgical, pedagogical, and pastoral/social activist. The more recent circumstance of the church argues for the necessity of the deliberative process in the church's life and the minister's role as leader in helping the community reach clarity and resolution about its ends.

What analogy or metaphor, then, helps highlight the minister's leadership role in equipping the church for its proper public goals? Niebuhr's emphasis on the minister's directorial role does make one think of the executive branch of organizations—voluntary associations, corporations, and the government—for an appropriate analogue. Obvious models—to cite the two extremes—include the chief executive officer of a corporation and the executive director of a voluntary association. Since both of these models mislead, a third model, the pastor as leader of a republic, will be explored.

The pastor as chief executive officer. This model apparently offers the most powerful conception of leadership: the CEO leads the organization largely (but not exclusively) by command and obedience. Traditional hierarchical societies de-

pended heavily, but not exclusively, on government by fiat. I
say not exclusively because, to the degree that the commands
enjoyed the reinforcement of myth and ritual, they occurred
within an explanatory horizon that made sense of them. They
didn't simply bludgeon people with opaque imperatives. Nevertheless, authority moved from the top down without the
formal or substantive need to persuade. One sought not inward consent but obedience. This mode of leadership obtains
largely in the modern world in authoritarian governments and
in the modern corporation, where the effort to persuade may
exist but does not constitute the sine qua non of the enterprise.
The city state of Sparta symbolizes in its extreme form this
type of authority. Sparta was a society given to taciturnity; that
is, it relied chiefly upon the bark of command and the grunt
of obedience.

This type of leadership will not work in the church for reasons extrinsic and intrinsic to its life. First, government by
command and obedience will not work in the setting of modern democracies that depend both in their political life and in
their voluntary associations upon the consent of the governed.
But, more inwardly, this type of governance should not obtain
in the Christian churches in that they subscribe to a Lord who
does not merely control externally but who rules the inward
motions of the human spirit. Salvation takes hold of the whole
person, the deliberative processes included. The notion of the
CEO fails not simply for the practical reason that lay people
in democratic countries won't put up with it, but because it
foreshortens the deliberative process and therefore diminishes
the reach of the salvation to which the faith testifies.

The pastor as executive director. This model largely defines
the professional who works today as paid chief of staff for
voluntary communities in the United States. Most voluntary
organizations look, not to their executive directors, but to their
boards of trustees to guide the organization. Legislative, deliberative, or policy-making powers repose in the latter bodies. A
board, in turn, appoints a paid executive director or administrator to carry out the board's decisions and conduct its affairs.

This model stands opposite that of the chief executive officer. Whereas the CEO possesses too much power and the
wrong kind of power, the executive director usually enjoys
too little power, whether of command or persuasion. Executive directors tend to receive their marching orders from
boards that operate above them. Applied to the ministry, the
model would convert the pastor into the "clerk of the works,"

the manager of an institution rather than the leader of a community.

The pastor as leader of a republic. The office of the president in its U.S. political setting combines several ingredients, one of which we may wholly reject as germane to the ministry—the president as commander-in-chief. The pastor has no troops to command and very minimal power of command over subordinates on the executive side to his or her responsibilities. Whereas executive management responsibilities in the larger churches may be considerable, the pastor handles relations to professional and even nonprofessional staff more effectively when they are collegial rather than hierarchical. Although the president of the nation has a very substantial responsibility as head of a hierarchy, the ministry at the parish level entails only marginally such responsibilities.

The more important substantive powers of the presidency lie in the powers of persuasion. In that respect, the powers of the presidential office resemble Athens more than Sparta. Whereas Sparta rested upon the tight-lipped power of command, Athens rested upon the power of the word, the art of persuasion. The *logos* or *rhetor* creates the *polis;* in the absence of the word, a society rests on the noise of weapons, not upon the meaning of words. Historians make much of the tension and conflict between Jerusalem and Athens, but on the centrality of the word these two cities agree—a truly human cult and culture depends upon the word.

The presidential power of persuasion takes two forms: exemplary and deliberative; symbolic and legislative. Put another way, the U.S. president tends to combine in one person two roles, which in the British parliamentary form of government remain quite separate: the queen or king and the prime minister. The crown symbolizes the unity of the people, whereas the prime minister more actively leads the Parliament (the house of words). The American president, however, functions both as royalty and as political leader. Unfortunately, and only too often, the president's skill in performing the royal office has obscured his ineptitude in the fulfillment of his political office; or, conversely, his awkwardness as symbol has undercut his political agenda. When either occurs, one is inclined to envy the British system. No matter how much the crown costs the British people, it seems a bargain compared with the costs of a royally mesmerizing but politically obfuscating presidency.

The two roles reappear in the pastorate. Whether one likes it or not, one cannot altogether dismiss the importance of the pastor as a symbol. The religious, as well as the moral life, so the saying goes, is caught as well as taught. The minister partly leads by example, and certainly he or she undercuts the persuasiveness of that leadership when deeds mock words: when one preaches confidence with a furrowed, worried face; or personal charity with bitterness in the throat; or forgiveness with a pouty, hurt, resentful look. And, as recent events have emphasized, the scandalous minister gets in the way of the true scandal of the cross. Pulpit committees have good cause for concern about their minister as symbol.

And yet a huge danger lurks here. The symbol utterly fails to point to the center of the Christian faith unless it recognizes its utter inadequacy as symbol. Only one person served wholly, fully, perfectly, and all sufficiently as symbol, and that one rejected the description of himself as good saying, "Why do you call me good? No one is good but God alone" (Mark 10:18).

Increasingly today, one may need to emphasize the second, ultimately more legislative, aspect of the president's office and reckon with the responsibility of the pastor as prime minister—if a divided church is to achieve clarity about and equip itself for the performance of its public tasks of worship, education, and service. The manse, to be sure, is not 10 Downing Street, but the minister cannot lead as commander-in-chief nor as clerk of the works, nor as the white-haired or fair-haired symbol of piety. I would shy away from the title of prime minister, but the reality of the responsibility cannot be dodged. As prime minister—as leading minister among the ministering and the ministered to—the pastor must help guide the congregation and shape its policies, and do so largely by persuasion. A church divided and troubled over its ends requires at least this much of its minister if, as a body, nourished by its worship and informed by its teaching, it is to equip itself for its own forms of service to the common good.

References

Arendt, Hannah. 1965. *On Revolution.* New York: Viking Press.

Bate, W. Jackson. 1975. *Samuel Johnson.* New York: Harcourt Brace Jovanovich.

Burke, Edmund. 1962. *Reflections on the French Revolution.* Chicago: Henry Regnery, Gateway.

Burns, James MacGregor. 1978. *Leadership.* New York: Harper Colophon Books.

Calvin, John. 1953. *The Institutes of the Christian Religion.* Vol. I, bk. II, chap. XV, p. 427. London: James Clarke.

Foucault, Michael. 1973. *Madness and Civilization.* New York: Random House, Vintage Books.

Hildenbrand, Dietrich von. 1943. *Liturgy and Personality.* New York: Longmans, Green.

Niebuhr, H. Richard, Daniel Day Williams, and James M. Gustafson. 1956. *The Purpose of the Church and Its Ministry.* New York: Harper & Row.

Pieper, Josef. 1965. *In Tune with the World: A Theory of Festivity.* New York: Harcourt, Brace & World.

Schumacher, E. F. 1973. *Small Is Beautiful.* New York: Harper & Row.

Time Magazine, January 29, 1973.

Titmusse, Richard M. 1972. *The Gift of Relationship.* New York: Random House, Vintage Books.

4

Liberating Ministry

Rebecca S. Chopp

A theology of ministry should provide a framework for understanding the shape and tasks of ministry in the midst of the church and culture. This chapter advocates a liberationist framework for ministry, but it is a framework that is developed out of, and sometimes even in opposition to, the way in which modern ministry has been shaped and formed in the North American context.

Because liberationist Christianity and theology are deeply committed to the awareness of their own context, I need to begin with a brief introduction to my own commitment to liberation theology in the midst of my involvement in modern ministry. My entrance into Christianity as a young adult came in the late 1960s and early 1970s and was related to the civil rights movement, a growing feminist awareness, and questions regarding America's military involvement in Southeast Asia. Time and time again, what impressed me was the action of ministers who were willing to place their bodies on the line for what they believed, who offered words of grace and hopefulness in the midst of critique and despair, and who consistently reached out to those who opposed them with acts and words of fellowship and reconciliation. I saw in those years what I would only much later learn to label, in the terms of liberation theology, a mystical-political faith, a way of being in the world where spirituality and action were intertwined for the sake of representing God's grace in the world.

As I entered seminary in the early 1970s, liberation theology was already established as fundamental in the curriculum. Indeed, my first assignment in theology was to compare the methods of Schubert Ogden, a North American process theologian concerned with the reality of God, secularization, and metaphysics, with Johannes Baptist Metz, a German political theologian reflecting on issues of the Holocaust, Latin American poverty, and bourgeois apathy in the culture and churches of the Western world. In such a manner, modern, Euro-Anglo theology and liberation theology collided *and* blended during my theological education. During and since that time, I have lived in a parsonage family, as either the minister or the minister's spouse. I have worked intimately with churches in rural communities in Kansas and Washington State, in the urban environment in Chicago, and in establishment churches in the South. These congregations contained charismatics combined with middle-of-the-road Methodists; black, white, and Asian Americans of middle and underclass folk; conservatives, evangelicals, and radical social activists. In all of these churches, I experienced in various ways the connection and collision of liberation theology and modern, Euro-Anglo theology. True, I brought this connection and collision with me, but it was also present in the lives of individuals, in the nature of community, and in the struggle for programming and witnessing. In all of these churches I found concerns about the church as a structure of bureaucracy, and in all of these churches I found persons seeking desperately for existential meaning—all of which I want to suggest defines modern Euro-Anglo Christianity and modern ministry. But in all of these congregations, liberationist Christianity and theology also were present: in the critique of modern America's consumerism and destructiveness; in places where racial issues were struggled with and occasionally worked through to new levels; in the struggles of women trying to define their lives in new ways and to hold together job, home, families, and church; and in the dreams and hopes for new forms of human flourishing that would integrate a praise-filled celebration with a committed witness in the world. Liberation theology, throughout these years, has provided me with the framework for understanding the frustrations and limits of modern Christianity and ministry, as well as a framework for constructing a new vision of church and ministry in relation to God's activity in the world.

An Introduction
to Liberationist Christianity
and Liberation Theology

Perhaps my experience with ministry in the United States, as lived with both modern Christianity and liberationist Christianity, is because, in some sense, liberationist Christianity arises out of modern, Euro-Anglo Christianity. Modern Euro-Anglo Christianity has long been concerned, as has the modern Western world, with the idea of freedom, especially what it means to say that individuals are free, authentic beings. Correlative to this notion of freedom and equality in modernity is the idea that free persons can make meaning and can create meaningful experiences as they exercise the choice of self-expression through their work, their partners, their religion, their leisure, and their government. This opportunity to choose, and thus to lead meaningful lives, became linked with the modern notion of historical progress, with the promise that with each generation things would get better and better. In the North American context, this was the westward dream— that we could expand across the continent and continually increase our material and moral prosperity, thereby developing a new land of promise. But these ideas were deeply connected, in reality, to certain social structures and relations of power that divided the world into persons and nonpersons (America and her colonial peoples), owners and slaves (America and her history of slavery), American citizens and American dependents (men and women).

Liberationist Christianity, in the North American context, emerges out of and calls into question the relation of such ideas of freedom, equality, meaning, and history to the structures of power that distinguish between the persons and the nonpersons, the owners and the slaves, the citizens and the dependents. For example, in North America and in her neocolonial partner, Latin America, liberationist theology arises when the nonpersons, the "others" of history, begin to speak in their own voices of freedom, meaning, hope, and suffering. The single most important condition for understanding liberationist Christianity is the respectful recognition that the other speaks in her or his own words of faith, freedom, hope, suffering, life. For anyone defined and structured as a nonperson—as "the other"—the power to speak, to say "I am," is the justifying grace of God who affirms and makes new life in spite of social-cultural realities. James Cone, in his *God of the Oppressed,* talks about his own experience of growing up in Bearden,

Arkansas, where, six days of the week, the culture worked to tell him he was not a human. But on the seventh day, in the midst of worship at Macedonia African Methodist Episcopal Church, Cone says he "encountered the presence of the divine Spirit, and my soul was moved and filled with an aspiration for freedom" (Cone 1975, 1). For "the other" of history, it is not merely the ideas of modernity that overthrow the structures of power, but God's grace working through liberating relations and communities to reform those ideas of modernity as concrete realities of emancipatory transformation for all people.

For anyone defined and structured as a "person" in modern history (and many reading this text are so defined and structured in one dimension or another: class, race, sex, and/or heritage), hearing the voice of the nonperson is also an experience of grace. True enough, grace is experienced as judgment, as those privileged with a certain color of skin, or class background, or preferred sexual makeup have to confront how those luxuries have enmeshed them in forms of domination and how such structures and luxuries have constituted them as individual human beings. Judgment is necessary and vital, for the good news of judgment is that grace not only corrects and critiques, but heals and reconciles. Thus grace, in listening to the other, may also lead to recognizing new ways of relating; new ways of structuring churches, educational systems, business practices; new ways of making up our identity; new ways of defining our humanness. And between the judgment of grace and the new life of grace emerges the possibility for discerning and mourning the limits that our dominance has forced on us, the faultedness of our belief that we are superior, the boundaries of rage that our power is now questioned.

The goal of liberationist Christianity is to discover and create new ways of being human that are not dependent upon structural and ideological divisions between white and black, men and women, rich and poor. It is not merely a political project of social revolution, nor a new quest for a more equitable distribution of resources, that distinguishes the shape and nature of liberationist Christianity. Rather, liberationist Christianity is a way of being Christian in the world, a way based in a faith experience of the gratuitousness of God working for emancipatory transformation for all people in history. Liberationist Christianity is a kind of structural horizon for those theologies arising out of black churches, Latin American basic Christian communities, women's experiences in traditional congregations and in women church, and those forms of Christian praxis in North America that seek new ways of being human in the midst of God's gratuitous activity of emancipatory transformation.

It is at this point that important differences arise between liberationist theology and modern theology: the particularity of the voice in liberation theology as compared to the stance of common human experience in modern theology, and the question of suffering and transformation as compared to the question of the reasonableness of God and the authenticity of existence. Actually, I'm not sure the phrase "compared to" really functions well, for liberation theology differs substantially from modern theology in terms of what it tries to address, how it interprets Christian symbols, what forms of rationality and warrants it invokes, and even how it sounds. (For modern theology, liberation theology often sounds too practical or political; yet for the liberationist, modern theology sounds suspiciously abstract or out of touch with human subjects.) So even though liberation theology is related to ideas of modern theology, it must also be understood as quite different from, even incommensurable with modern theology (Chopp 1986, 149–153). Liberation theology asks questions of suffering and speaks of how God moves and works for emancipatory transformation. Its anthropology bears the face not of the anxious bourgeois subject, but of the poor campesino, the drug addict, and the homeless in North America, the woman who has been silenced in culture and the church, the black who bears the scourge of the victim of America's racism. The point of liberation theology becomes not to make sense of God for the nonbeliever or to explain some kind of religious yes to existential angst, but to speak out of the deep experience of the others of history and to guide emancipatory transformation within history.

Interpreting Modern Christianity and Ministry

From this perspective, then, liberationist Christianity and theology address the shape and tasks of modern ministry. The standard discourse about modern ministry, an appropriate place to begin our reflections, borrows heavily from the model of the modern professional (Lebacqz 1985; Campbell 1982; Glasse 1968). The practice of ministry is organized as a profession: ministers are trained in professional schools; they join professional organizations; they read professional journals; they have professional job descriptions. Ethics, understood broadly as the philosophical understanding of the basis of one's decisions for action and morality, is used in the clergy profession to consider the role of conduct in the profession, patterned after the use of ethics among lawyers and doctors. Note that by ethics we no longer mean, as was the case at the turn of the century, the morality of the minister, or even, to use Nolan Harmon's 1928 title, *Ministerial Ethics and Etiquette* (Harmon 1928, 1987). Now we mean the use of modern ethics in and of the ministerial profession. Professionals need rules of conduct, for to be a professional means, first and foremost, that the guild enforces certain limits of excellence and degrees of conduct. To be a professional, after all, is to have responsibility for making decisions and judgments that require a certain character, principles, and commitments. In theory, there is nothing here to quarrel about. Who does not want the doctor or lawyer or business executive or therapist or social worker or teacher or minister to have standards of excellence? Indeed, from the perspective of liberation theology, the employment of professional codes of ethics in modern ministry may well function as an important corrective against any possible excesses allowed in power relations of modernity. The question liberation theology poses is, rather, What is the locus of understanding ministry as a profession? That is, to the liberationist, the problem is not *that* ministry is seen as a profession but *what* it is as a profession, both in the sense of what ministry thereby professes and what it professionally entails. Liberation theology asks not about the specific principles of professional ethics, but about the assumptions behind the current discourse of ministry as profession, about the shape and form of ministry in modern Christianity. To say it differently, liberation theology focuses not so much on specific ethical principles in the profession of ministry, but on the ethos, or terrain of modernity and modern Christianity, that shapes and forms ministry into a profession with certain set tasks and limits.

There are numerous ways to articulate a liberationist interpretation and critique of the ethos of modernity and modern Christianity. I will draw on the resources of feminist theology, German political theology, and Latin American liberation theology. With the turn to modernity, bourgeois society established the identity of leading citizens, white middle-class Euro-Anglo men, by making them autonomous individuals in the public sphere. The public sphere was, as a result, the realm of Euro-Anglo men—the realm of reason, exchange, and scientific objectivity. The private sphere was the domain of otherness—feeling, subjectivity, and irrationality. Whatever was not objective, scientific, value free was placed in the private realm—religion, tradition, art. This was the realm upon which white, Euro-Anglo males depended for their physical sustenance and through which women, blacks, and Latin Americans were figured as different, as naturally subservient, as lesser in intelligence, as controlled by emotions (Chopp 1989). This kind of division runs through the ideas of modernity, but also through the cultural, political, and psychological structuring of modernity.

Modern Christianity, perhaps in order to survive, accepted this ordering, though, as we shall see, not without some critique. Modern Christianity was located in the private realm, and religion was considered a voluntary activity. Religion is outside the realm of the ordinary, so the modern theologians asserted; and certainly religious knowledge, usually talked about in terms of feelings or special, privileged claims of knowledge, is radically different from objective, scientific knowledge. Modern theology cooperates with modernity by making an anthropocentric turn, locating the relation with God within the individual and suggesting that religion contributes to the existential well-being of the individual. Religion makes good persons better and in this secondary way contributes to the upholding of civilization. It is interesting to note that the same values and shape given to religion in modernity are also assigned to women; indeed, the destinies of women and religion are intertwined as they are assigned the task of building up the private morality of men and thus, in a quiet, nonpublic manner, contributing to the public good. Religion and women temper the primary competitiveness of the public realm by giving secondary virtues and moral character.

Jürgen Moltmann, the famous German political theologian, has suggested that in this context the church is assigned three tasks: (1) the cult of subjectivity, where private individuals are dealt with on interior, existential levels; (2) the cult of cohumanity, where individuals flock to associate in life-style enclaves; and (3) the cult of the institution, where the church constructs itself as a modern, bureaucratic organization (Moltmann 1967, 304–338). Because Moltmann defines the cult of cohumanity as the place lonely individuals come for at least some superficial fellowship, I want to place that particular task, for now, as a variant of the cult of subjectivity. By focusing on the dual character of the church as individual, existential, personal, and as an institution, an organization, a locus of management practices, we can determine that ministry, as a profession, is, on the one hand, "service oriented," and on the other, "management oriented."

Moltmann suggests that the first and most important role for religion in modernity is "the saving and preserving of personal, individual, and private humanity" (Moltmann 1967, 311). From philosophical explanations to common expectations of the laity, it is assumed that the religious locus of Christianity is in the individual. The church seeks to give meaning and value to existence underneath, beyond, and around the busy day of the public marketplace. For many people, the pursuit of exchange and money translates into rather boring, meaningless activity, and religion functions to secure persons' subjecthood. When they come to church on Sunday morning, they want to be assured of their meaningfulness and value, to be given an "ultimate concern," to be granted a meaning outside of the historical conditions in which they live.

What is essential for ministry in the modern, American context is that the minister finds ways to fill the individual needs and wants of her or his parishioners. What this usually means is that the minister's role is to provide parishioners with the gentle assurance of the correctness of their life-style enclaves and to offer them professional care when life is broken through disease, disruption, or death. Surely, none of us would want to deny the necessity or importance of this understanding of ministry: ministers are there to help individuals. Yet the particular shape of this individual, need-centered view of ministry bears examination. Americans believe that one doesn't have to go to church to be a good Christian. One goes to have children nurtured, to express one's faith, to meet with like-minded people. According to the role of religion as the cult of subjectivity, the church itself is not constitutive of Christian experience. Because the religious relation is secured existentially in the individual and God, and because the church serves the needs of this individual, ministry is shaped by a kind of care-oriented, service-minded mentality often resulting in the assumption that ministers need to be first and foremost popular with their congregations.

As an organization, the church exists, in modernity, as a bureaucratic institution, which in the United States is called a denominational organization. Christianity organizes its collective and associative face into a bureaucratic institution defined through modern rationality, using modern technology and employing professional workers. The role of the church is, like any other bureaucratic institution, to protect itself, to establish its policies, to preserve its ways. The minister finds his or her energy consumed with answering to the bureaucratic structure, filling out reports, attending meetings, raising money, judging colleagues, and so forth. From ministerial journals to expectations for salary increments, ministers are urged to be good managers and executives, to care greatly about numbers, development, programs, and buildings.

Between these two roles—the role of serving individual subjectivity and managing the corporate organization—the minister is both caught and pulled. She or he is caught because the minister is a professional in an organization that, by its own definition in the modern church, is not constitutive of religious experience; she or he is pulled because the demands of meeting the needs of people as a responsible service provider and serving the requirements of an organization as a competent manager leave hardly any time or energy to form the church as a constitutive community (see the definition by Sandel below). The form and ethics of modern ministry are prescribed by modernity and modern Christianity in what is at the same time its best and worst model—the professional. The model is best because it offers standards of excellence and responsibility; worst because it threatens to suffocate ministry with bureaucratic rationality and technical service.

Liberation theology argues that the limits of modern ministry are the limits of modern Euro-Anglo Christianity. Modern Christianity is organized through a problematic division between public and private, knowledge and feeling, in which modern religious experience is assigned a private, internal, even existential basis. The church, located in the private realm, directs the shape and tasks of ministry in two basic directions: ministers serve the needs of individuals who choose whether or not to "attend" church, and ministers run the organization like their counterparts in other bureaucratic organizations.

The Liberation of Christianity

Within the critique of modern Christianity, including the critique of modernity, liberation theology also offers a challenge to modern Euro-Anglo Christianity, its churches and ministers. Can the churches become centers of emancipatory transformation in our culture? Liberation theology provides a framework for understanding Christianity as representing God's activity of emancipatory transformation in history. In this framework, churches are not merely organizations or care stations, but rather constitutive communities of emancipatory transformation that present God's grace in the midst of history. There are, I think, at least three important aspects of the challenge that liberation Christianity offers to modern Euro-Anglo churches: (1) Can the churches become constitutive communities of emancipatory transformation in the culture? (2) Can the churches sustain an open dialogue with the "others" of history, including learning from them their visions, images, desires of human flourishing? and (3) Can the churches interpret Christian traditions, including resistance to culture, in order to offer new symbols, discourses, relations of emancipatory transformation?

Earlier in this chapter I subsumed Moltmann's second task for the church in modernity, the longing for community, under the first task, the cult of subjectivity. Moltmann argues that in modernity the longing for humanity is longing to find others like ourselves. Yet this longing for community so widely experienced in modern Christianity contains within itself the subversive possibility that churches can become constitutive communities of emancipatory transformation. Churches exist as places in our culture where words of hope and freedom are read, where relationships of trust and faith can be experimented with, where moral inquiry and education can occur, where experiments of celebration and critique can happen. The term *constitutive community* is one coined by Michael Sandel and expresses well the understanding of community in liberationist Christianity: "To say that the members of a society are bound by a sense of community is not to say that a great many of them profess communitarian sentiments and pursue communitarian aims, but rather they conceive their identity— the subject and not just the objects of their feelings and aspirations—as defined to some extent by the community of which they are a part" (Sandel 1982, 147). A constitutive understanding of community can be opposed to instrumental and sentimental senses of community. In the instrumental sense, individuals agree to cooperate only to meet their needs; in the sentimental sense, individuals associate because of some motivations, both benevolent and selfish, shared in common. Modern Christianity, organized to focus on individualist needs and bureaucratic organization, mitigates against constitutive community.

There are three tasks of forming the church as a constitutive community of emancipatory transformation. First, a theological understanding of the church as a sacrament of God's grace in the world must be developed. Gustavo Gutiérrez, father of Latin American liberation theology, refashions Vatican II's notion of the church as sacrament in order to suggest that today the church is a visible sign of God's invisible grace (Gutiérrez

1973, 260). In liberation theology, the church, not the individual, is the locus of Christian reality in the world. Second, a new relation must be forged between liturgy and witness in the churches. Liturgy, according to liberation theology, is performative action of Christian praxis—the embodiment of God's Word in the world that leads to and is fed by ongoing Christian witness. The center of church activity is the ongoing living out of grace in the world through Christian praxis. Third, the church cannot be a sacrament of God's grace in the world, enabled through its liturgy and service, without itself being constructed as a community of justice and reconciliation, of caring and discipleship. Hence the community must become structured, through justice and reconciliation, as itself the living out of grace.

If the church is to be a sacrament of God in the world, if it can work toward emancipatory transformation in our culture in relation to both psychic destructiveness and physical destructiveness, then it must recognize that the voices of the others of history are the voices through whom God speaks today. These voices are "outside" many modern, Euro-Anglo churches. For instance, in worship, the Euro-Anglo church needs to hear and perhaps even receive the power of worship that Cone hints at. The modern, Euro-Anglo church has much to learn from the others outside the church: the power of imaginative hope, the walk with Christ in the midst of the suffering of the world, the resurrection of new life in the midst of sin and oppression. But the other is not only outside the church; the other is inside the church, in the lives of women. The church belongs to these women; and today the church—from patterns of leadership, to images of God, to how the Bible is interpreted—must be transformed in light of women's changing lives. The openness to the other is itself an act of transformation, a living out of justification by grace, within churches that have been constructed as merely a life-style enclave. In this respect alone, the church can model new ways of being human to the surrounding culture.

Finally, the church can become a community of emancipatory transformation by reexamining its tradition—its scripture, church teaching, popular piety—for new visions and ways of being human. Cultures live by images and practices, discourses and structures; and the church exists as one place to form and experiment with such images and practices. Two examples will suffice for description of what this might mean. The first is a theological example, drawn from modern theology, which, though it accommodated itself to modernity by accepting the anthropocentric turn to thought, almost always resisted the narrowing of knowledge to objectivity or scientific fact. Theologians from Friedrich Schleiermacher to Karl Barth to Reinhold Niebuhr to Jonathan Edwards always pointed to the "something more" of knowledge. Today, a similar criticism is made in feminist theory, in the careful analysis of how knowledge was structured and defined away from feelings and affections. Can the church formulate a critique of knowledge in our culture, drawing upon the history of theology and contemporary feminist theory, to question the division between objective knowledge and subjective feeling?

The second illustration is seen in the role of liturgy as the performative action of the dangerous memory of Christ and as a reenactment of transformation through God's grace. Every Sunday in our churches, we reenact with our bodies and our words what we as Christians take to be the central meaning of the world: the praise of God, the opening of our lives in confession, the healing reception of forgiveness, the giving of new words of emancipatory transformation to ourselves and to the world, the going forth in freedom to represent God's activity in the world. Christian traditions of liturgy provide a rich set of resources for the embodiment of God in the world, for the constant rehearsal of grace and transformation, for the reevaluation of the body as the meeting place of grace and faith. The Christian liturgy continues to stress the importance of embodiment, of nourishment, of the celebration of elements, of the physicality of God's grace.

Implications for Ministry

The most striking implication for ministry in liberation theology is to work not primarily for individual needs and bureaucratic organization but for transforming the church into a community of emancipation. I will conclude with four specific ways in which liberation theology might shape ministry, but I recognize that such shaping will take place in the process of bringing to bear the lens of liberation theology upon the people's present struggles and the anticipatory signs of emancipatory transformation within them.

The minister as artist. In a time when new images of human flourishing desperately need to be created and discovered, our imaginations need to be stirred and enlivened. One of the central places in the culture that this can take place is in our churches, and one of our richest resources is the wealth of possibilities in Christian tradition and experience. The thought that persons might go to church to have their imagination stirred may be a bit startling, and yet surely God works through imaginations, feelings, and desires to create new ways of being human.

The minister as community builder. Central to the argument of this chapter has been the insistence of liberation theology that modernity has failed at developing substantive community and that persons in our culture deeply desire new forms of community. Even the language for such substantive community in a highly pluralistic, transient culture has not been developed into a formula. We need to develop images of community that one does not have to be born into, or for which one does not need the right social status or physical abilities. Perhaps these images may be born out of our experience of communion with God at the table. Practices of community must be developed, practices such as moral inquiry and discussion, but also practices of community where persons can celebrate and fellowship. Women church, black church, and basic Christian communities all provide resources for each other and for the broader Christian community in developing new images and practices for forming substantive communities of emancipatory transformation.

The minister as prophet. This is not a surprising image for liberation theology, but what I mean most pointedly about minister as prophet is the role of moral leader both in the congregation and in relation to the larger context. Christianity, at least in liberation theology, lives decidedly to represent God in the world, to serve and liberate God's creation. Thus ministry's focus must be not on the church for itself but on the church for the world (West 1982). The minister must both act prophetically and support others in the church community and the community as a whole in order to critique dominant practices of oppression and destruction. The minister must also imagine and build new ways of human flourishing.

The minister as teacher. Central to liberation theology is the role of education as a spiritual activity of naming one's world, one's freedom, one's desire. Through dialogue with the scriptures and the breadth of Christian traditions, ministers equip the church with their power to think, to dream, to sing God's praises in the world. In liberationist Christianity, education is a liberating activity as it is used to form human freedom and agency. Latin American liberation theology, for instance, is heavily influenced by the pioneering work of Paulo Freire, in which education as conscientization emerges through a process of critically thinking through a concrete problem—a process that involves social analysis, biblical engagement, and theological reflection (Freire 1970). Latin American liberation theology has built on this process of conscientization to name the activity of faith as the constant engagement between scripture, life, and social situations. In this role, the minister can combine a critical engagement of Christian traditions with liberation theology's insistence on conscientization as the practical activity of forming and enacting faith in history.

Conclusion

The ethics of ministry that liberation theology seeks is one of emancipatory transformation within both the church and society. This is a very difficult task: ministers must resist that which feeds them and transform that which tells them that they are acting responsibly. But the liberationist asks ministers to be *in* the modern church but not *of* it, and in this ministers will find willing co-workers among the laity. There are innumerable ways to speak of the tasks of emancipatory transformation: encouraging new aesthetic visions, learning to be a deliberative community, working for changes in laws, supporting alternative life-styles, addressing the sins of our times in words and deeds. In these tasks, many forms of ministry and ethical principles will be employed, but they will be employed in the *how* and *what* of a Christianity that professes solidarity with God's gratuitous activity in the world.

References

Campbell, Dennis M. 1982. *Doctors, Lawyers, Ministers: Christian Ethics in Professional Practice.* Nashville: Abingdon Press.

Chopp, Rebecca S. 1986. *The Praxis of Suffering: An Interpretation of Liberation and Political Theologies.* Maryknoll, N.Y.: Orbis Books.

———. 1989. *The Power to Speak: Feminism, Language, God.* New York: Crossroad.

Cone, James. 1975. *God of the Oppressed.* San Francisco: Harper & Row.

Freire, Paulo. 1970. *Pedagogy of the Oppressed.* Translated by Myra Bergman Ramos. New York: Herder & Herder.

Glasse, James D. 1968. *Profession: Minister.* Nashville: Abingdon Press.

Gutiérrez, Gustavo. 1973. *A Theology of Liberation.* Maryknoll, N.Y.: Orbis Books.

Harmon, Nolan B. 1928, 1987. *Ministerial Ethics and Etiquette.* Nashville: Abingdon Press.

Lebacqz, Karen. 1985. *Professional Ethics: Power and Paradox.* Nashville: Abingdon Press.

Moltmann, Jürgen. 1967. *Theology of Hope.* Translated by James W. Leitch. New York: Harper & Row.

Sandel, Michael J. 1982. *Liberalism and the Limits of Justice.* Cambridge, Mass.: Cambridge University Press.

West, Cornel. 1982. *Prophesy Deliverance! An Afro-American Revolutionary Christianity.* Philadelphia: Westminster Press.

5

Clergy Ethics
in Modern Fiction

James P. Wind

An appropriate way to begin discussions of clergy ethics is with a line from Walker Percy's *The Thanatos Syndrome:* "This is not the Age of Enlightenment, but the Age of Not Knowing What to Do" (Percy 1987, 75). Percy's aphorism seems so apt for our age of ethical uncertainty. Politicians, scientists, physicians, business leaders, everyday citizens, and our clergy increasingly find themselves in situations where they really do not know what to do. As a result, ethics has become a boom industry, and moral failure a regular front-page phenomenon. Conventional wisdom seems glaringly inadequate in the face of our environmental, technological, political, economic, and social situations.

The purpose of this chapter is not to compile a list of perplexing quandaries, although they have become part of the fabric of all of our lives, thanks to our interdependence. Nor is it to paint one more broadbrush description of our modern ethical situation. Such lists and portraits abound elsewhere. Even within the more circumscribed terrain of clergy ethics, such lists and portraits exist, and it seems doubtful that we gain much by adding one more.

Instead, I want to move the discussion of clergy ethics in new directions. First, I want to discern how clergy look beyond the pale—beyond the borders of their guilds and primary communities. To do so I turn to an unconventional source for ethics—American fiction—where we will see how we look from the outside. Through the eyes of Walker Percy, J. F. Powers, Andrew Greeley, and John Updike, we will see what we can learn about the contemporary ethical situation of American clergy.

This turn to fiction is made for several reasons. First, the arts have distinctive disclosive capacities. They help humans see things about themselves that remain obscure or hidden in everyday or scientific experience and reflection. The painter, sculptor, poet, and novelist provide us with fresh and powerful ways of seeing who we are and what is really happening in our comings and goings. They make it possible for us to see ourselves differently.

Second, as many in theological and religious studies have recognized, narratives, whether they are based in fact or fiction, tell us powerful locating types of truth. As we read or listen to someone's story, we enter the world of a text that reveals insight about human character, about life in community, about the meaning and purpose of life. Sojourns in these alternative worlds alter our imaginations and send us back to our everyday lives with transformed vision and wider ranges of possibilities.

Third, although clergy have always had a place in literature, little attention has been given to the existing tradition of writing about them. As individual works have appeared—for example, Willa Cather's *Death Comes for the Archbishop* or Sinclair Lewis's *Elmer Gantry*—much discussion of particular portraits has often occurred. But the larger story of clergy in fiction remains untold. What it is that has caught the novelist's eye over the generations, how these portraits have changed, and what the import of this growing body of literature for ministry might be remains untapped. This chapter begins at the near end of that tradition, with contemporary portraits. But works of Nathaniel Hawthorne, Oliver Goldsmith, and others from earlier periods need to be revisited to set the ethical situation of the late twentieth century into a more complete and helpful context. That larger task will have to wait for another time.

Nonetheless, from these contemporary literary descriptions I intend to distill a basic shape for the modern ethical situation of clergy. Taken together, this small selection of portraits suggests an ethical quadrilateral that constitutes the moral shape of many clergy situations. I have chosen the geometric image of the quadrilateral because of its malleability. A four-sided object, the quadrilateral does not have to be a perfect square or a neat rectangle. Rather, this geometric form can take numerous shapes, with its four sides consisting of various lengths. Its pluriformity is congruent with modern ministerial experience, which may find these four dimensions present in varying proportions. The quadrilateral image gives us a rough, or approximate, structure at the same time that it allows for the diversity of individual ministerial situations.

On the first side are extreme cases, those rare moments of truth that lead clergy to bold outcry and disruptive action. These impel clergy to risk livelihood or jail to stop a war, integrate a university, or close an abortion clinic. On the opposite side of the quadrilateral is the everyday world of the institutional leader who must raise funds, attend Rotary Club or Women's Society luncheons, plan worship services, balance the budget, and build membership. Whether they inhabit congregations or some other sort of institutional setting, few clergy escape the humdrum, nuts and bolts side of institutional maintenance. These tasks are the rent the clergy pay to fulfill their callings. More than that, they provide the occasions and raw material for most ministerial action.

Another pair of dimensions provide the second and fourth or top and bottom sides of the quadrilateral. At the top is the network of personal relationships that constitute the minister's lifeworld. Family, colleagues, friends, lovers, parishioners—these people make countless individual claims upon priests, rabbis, and pastors. They add color, concreteness, and complexity to the minister's ethical situation. The bottom side of the quadrilateral, its ultimate side, is where clergy most directly feel the pressure and presence of the sacred, of God. Here is where they face what or who matters most to them, where they struggle for authenticity, identity, and purpose.

Before turning to the colorful portraits provided by these novelists, a few disclaimers need mention. The world of modern fiction is enormous, and my selection of four authors does not represent its breadth and diversity. I have chosen authors who have provided recent, prominent, and interesting accounts of modern American ministerial experience, and who bring the contours of our moral situation into view. Readers will certainly think of other authors who can amplify and sharpen this initial sketch.

Second, I do not make my living interpreting modern fiction, so my readings will have more of the feel of the amateur—the lover of literature—than the critic. Other more expert interpreters can provide many nuances and layers of interpretation to qualify these portraits. But my somewhat naive readings of these texts may have their own kind of usefulness. Instead of forcing these novelists into larger critical debates, I hope simply to hold up their portraits and see if we can recognize our situation within them.

Third, none of these novelists set out to discuss clergy ethics. I will focus on features of their works that relate to this agenda, asking questions that may—or may not—have been peripheral to the authors' interests. I will not attempt to deal with the place of these portraits in the larger fictive worlds these authors construct; that is a topic for another time. Rather, I will isolate these portraits and see what they tell us on their own. Despite these limitations, I believe that important angles of vision on the modern ministerial situation can be provided through these modern literary windows.

Ministry in the Extreme Case

As the aphorism in the opening line of this chapter portends, Walker Percy's *Thanatos Syndrome* is an apocalyptic tale about the dire straits of late twentieth-century America. The book presents an extreme case—one that Percy tells with characteristic exaggeration and wit. The case chosen is a timely one, filled with bioethical and social-policy questions. The plot develops from psychiatrist Thomas More's discovery of a covert medical experiment upon the citizenry of Feliciana, a Louisiana community. A group of well-intentioned but fundamentally misguided medical researchers has slipped a Sodium 24 ion into Feliciana's water supply. The drug has made a measurable impact upon all deviant behavior in the community. By inhibiting certain cortical activities in the brain, the odorless, tasteless, invisible drug has caused significant declines in crime, the spread of AIDS, substance abuse, wife battering, child abuse, and teenage suicide. Unfortunately, this magic bullet has side effects: flatness of affect, dramatic linguistic and sexual aberrations. The Felicianans may be better behaved, but the price of their improvement is the loss of distinctive human characteristics.

With his tongue firmly planted in his cheek, Percy is calling into question a cultural mind-set that fails to question the logic of its technological and scientific developments—especially within the field of medicine.

For our purposes, that too brief description of *Thanatos Syndrome*'s story line will have to do. More important here is the priest who plays a prominent role in the novel. The reader discovers Father Simon Smith perched, like a postmodern Simeon Stylites (the fifth-century saint who witnessed to his fallen society by climbing a pillar and staying there), in a fire tower on the outskirts of Feliciana. Father Smith has fled to his fire tower in despair over the success of the Qualitarian Movement, which advocates quick and painless deaths as the solution of choice for the suffering encountered in our hospices and hospitals. Once a hospice director, this priest has given up on conventional attempts to halt our cultural dash to mercy killing and other attempts to protect the quality of life by removing all traces of suffering.

Instead he opts for an absurd act in the desperate hope that someone might ask why. When Dr. Thomas More finally does ask, the priest responds with a jeremiad reminiscent of the great Old Testament prophets and the Puritan divines of the seventeenth century:

> "You are a member of the first generation of doctors in the history of medicine to turn their backs on the oath of Hippocrates and kill millions of old useless people, unborn children, born malformed children for the good of mankind—and to do so without a single murmur from one of you. Not a single letter of protest in the august *New England Journal of Medicine.* And do you know what you're going to end up doing? You a graduate of Harvard and a reader of *The New York Times* and a member of the Ford Foundation's Program for the Third World? . . . You're going to end up killing Jews."
>
> (Percy 1987, 127–128)

On another occasion, the priest elaborates on his message: "Do you know where tenderness always leads?" "To the gas chamber." Facing a problem so extreme that he likens it to the Holocaust, the priest proclaims, "More people have been killed in this century by tenderhearted souls than by cruel barbarians in all other centuries put together" (Percy 1987, 361).

Impassioned rhetoric like these priestly words cannot help but set off many debates. Some will argue with the priest's Holocaust analogy, concerned that such a rhetorical move trivializes the experience of Jews under Hitler at the same time that it inflames our debates about abortion and euthanasia. Others will point to the extended suffering produced by modern medicine and suggest that compassion requires providing relief, even in the extreme case of bringing suffering life to an end. Those debates are important and are increasingly a part of the clergy ethics terrain. But for the moment, it is important to set aside these debates in order to attend to what this priest's behavior—intentionally caricatured by the author—tells us about our ministerial moment.

From Percy's vantage point, our situation is an extreme case. His priest is not found at Mass, in his study, or in a pastoral counseling setting. Instead, he first makes a ridiculous protest—reminiscent of Jeremiah or Jonah—and then joins Dr. More in hand-to-hand combat against the medical experimenters.

Percy's portrait of clergy ethics draws a bold and long line on the "extreme case" side of the quadrilateral. In his portrait, the other three lines are much shorter and less distinct. In the 1980s, when Percy wrote *Thanatos,* such ministerial action was much less in vogue than in the 1960s, when clergy were frequently found in protest marches and other forms of advocacy. The fact that Percy makes his priest so pronouncedly one dimensional suggests how serious our modern situation had become for this author, how terminal the Thanatos Syndrome seems to be.

Ministry in "Everyday-ishness"

A very different view of ministerial reality is offered by J. F. Powers in *Wheat that Springeth Green.* Unlike *Thanatos Syndrome,* where Father Smith is a supporting figure to the protagonist, the priest in *Wheat* is the central figure. Another striking contrast between Percy's and Powers' novels is the place where we find these priests. Percy's priest is completely cut off from his ecclesiastical context; he operates as an estranged individual. Father Joe Hackett, on the other hand, is deeply enmeshed in the institutional reality of the church. By and large, his ethical challenges come from within his ecclesial reality, not beyond it.

We first meet Hackett, not in the midst of prophetic action, but as an infant growing into a priestly vocation. We watch him come of age physically and sexually and then follow his spiritual formation in seminary. Serious enough about his pursuit of God to don a hair shirt (except at night) and then to serve as de facto spiritual director of a little band of fellow students who wanted to be more than "time servers" on the way to priesthood, Hackett learned an early lesson about life within religious institutions:

> The seminary was a community, and a tight little one at that, and just wasn't the place for all-out mysticism, for growth in holiness beyond a certain point—a low point by the standards of saints. No place he'd ever be, no parish, would be the place for that. And just this, for him, knowing what he did about the life of the spirit (not much but something) and not being able to give himself to it—wouldn't that be a hair shirt of sorts?
>
> (Powers 1988, 55)

Leaving behind a physical hair shirt for one woven of institutional fibers, Hackett encounters the daily dilemmas of the parish ministry. At the Mass celebrated immediately following his ordination, he collides with a wily priest whose pursuit of the dollar dismays him. Informed that he must take a special collection celebrating his new priestly status, Hackett tries to protect the liturgical integrity of the Mass by offering to write a personal check that will more than offset the loss of the anticipated collection. The older cleric accepts Hackett's check and then announces the offering from the pulpit. Hackett walks out of the service in outrage, feeling betrayed. An hour later at the next service he complies, having learned how the institutional game is played.

A month after his ordination, Hackett meets with his classmates and hears one say, "We have to make a distinction, Joe, between following the counsels of perfection and doing the job" (Powers 1988, 70).

The rest of the novel rings the changes on this tension between the demands of the ministerial soul and those of the religious job. In his first parish, we watch assistant pastor Hackett retrieve an old prie-dieu from its use as a plant stand. There he seeks to grow in faith—while he answers the phone on his knees. His career takes him next to a diocesan office where he serves first as assistant director and then director of charities. There he covers for incompetent superiors and masters the games of bureaucracy. In 1968 he is called to a new suburban parish, the Church of Saints Francis and Clare, Inglenook, California. As pastor of a congregation, he meets his moments of truth in decisions about furniture purchases, choices about how to respond to threats of public criticism for his failure to pray for certain political causes, and official disapproval of his approach to fund-raising.

Exhausted by duties as bookkeeper, bulletin-typer, and phone-answerer (especially answering the question dreaded in every rectory or parsonage on Saturday night, "What time are Masses tomorrow?"), Hackett finally "succeeds" in landing a curate who wears T-shirts, does not keep regular office hours, and cannot type. Instead of feeling relief from his administrative burdens, Hackett faces extra work finding things for the poorly equipped curate to do. Besieged by the relentless demands of running a parish, Hackett warns his young curate: "This—*all* this—isn't my idea of the priesthood. But this is how it is, Bill, and how it's going to be. This is *it*, Bill—the future. I'm sorry" (Powers 1988, 175).

Estranged from lay people who want their rights, from fellow clergy who leave the priesthood, and from a younger generation of priests who do not share his commitments, Hackett presses on in his ministry. Faithful to his vow of celibacy, Hackett copes with his situation via traditional clergy defense mechanisms—alcohol and rich food. Likening the priesthood more to a sack race than to a 100-yard dash or a mile run, Hackett keeps going through the motions of ministry, defending the confidences of a young conscientious objector, posing with a group of cheerleaders to keep the archbishop happy, making his too frequent liquor runs to a store remote enough from his parish to offend no one. In these and countless other little choices, Hackett seeks to maintain "the separation of Church and Dreck," which he still believed "was a matter of life and death for the world" (Powers 1988, 270).

Powers' admiring, if at times sardonic, portrait of the modern priest is almost a polar opposite of Percy's. Instead of raising the extreme-case side of the ethical quadrilateral to prominence, Powers makes the everyday-side his dominant line. Here and there ultimate concerns break through—a shorter line. And once or twice we get a glimpse of an extreme case, but such are always handled in savvy, everyday fashion. Father Joe Hackett reminds us how much of ministry is ordinary, tedious, even boring. Yet a conversation between the priest and the young conscientious objector he defended reveals what is at stake in the everyday choices of ministry: " 'Do me a favor,' Gregg said. 'Sure. What?' 'Keep it up.' 'What?' Joe said, though he knew what. Gregg just looked at him. 'We'll see,' Joe said then and drove away" (Powers 1988, 333).

Ministry in the Web of Relations

Of the four authors under consideration in this chapter, Andrew Greeley may be the most surprising choice. Some may doubt that this sociologist-priest belongs with established novelists like Percy, Powers, or Updike. My reasons for including him have little to do with issues of membership in the contemporary literary canon. Others can debate Greeley's place in modern fiction. Here it is important to note that Greeley has written a trilogy of best-selling novels in which priests are very prominent. His novels give prominent attention to another side of the quadrilateral.

In what he calls *The Passover Trilogy* Greeley shows us priests who are tangled in dense webs of relationships. Sean Cronin, the central figure in *Thy Brother's Wife*, for example, is a son following a vocational map drawn by his powerful father. As he does, Cronin is never free from the claims of his powerful, wealthy family.

Assigned a depressing inner-city church for his first call, this priest encounters the underside of the ministry: clergy who envy his privileged family background; long days of hard work with few tangible results; spiritual torpor. Even as he climbs the ecclesiastical ladder—study at the Gregorian, appointment as vice chancellor of the Chicago archdiocese, elevation to monsignordom, eventual appointment as titular bishop of a Roman church, and then a cardinal's red hat—he searches for a glimpse of faith and invests himself in human relationships. Part of Cronin's burden was the way the church rendered his relationships with the world dishonest. *Humanae Vitae* "was a catastrophe for the Church and would appall, insult, and infuriate American Catholics. Yet as a churchman he had to loyally honor it. To be a good churchman meant that you be a good hypocrite" (Greeley, 120–121).

Finally deciding to leave the priesthood, Cronin confesses his love to Nora who, while sharing his love, refuses to see him as less than a priest. Their clandestine love affair functions sacramentally to renew the would-be ex-priest's vocation and enables him to go on in service to the church.

The second priest in Greeley's *Trilogy* is Hugh Donlon, who in many ways mirrors Cronin's experience. Again a son is set aside for the priesthood by his father, and again a young man enters the priesthood in search of salvation. A stint in another backwater parish follows, and then graduate school and the promise of greater service in the church.

But at this point, Greeley twists the plot line, making *Ascent into Hell* a different story. Donlon has an affair with Sister Elizabeth Ann, who becomes pregnant. The fallen priest then asks for a dispensation and marries his pregnant lover. A career as sociologist at the University of Michigan leads improbably to a wildly successful career as a stockbroker, which leads more improbably still to an ambassadorship and then to prison after a stock scandal. Here, too, an affair saves a fallen priest, who experiences the forgiveness of God from a lover who accepts a clergyman after his fall.

At times, Greeley's novels read like installments of *Dallas,* and it is tempting to ignore important things he has to say about ministerial life because of some of his less than plausible plot lines. But note how in this novel, too, it is human relationships that matter.

Early in his priesthood, Donlon found meaning in the human side of ministry:

He loved the work of the parish and was good at it. Sick calls early in the morning, the weary old faces smiling when he came into the bedroom; visits to grammar school classes to joke and laugh with the smart, bright-eyed kids; hospital calls to bring a little light to the anxious and depressed; counselling young people whose hopes could still be salvaged; instructing young couples before marriage and rejoicing in their discovery that the Church could be more than negative in its impact; reconciling older lovers who were tired and bored but still in love, even if they didn't know it; cheering for the grammar school football and volley ball teams and showing tall, taciturn teen-agers that he was still better at basketball than they were; instructing adults in the new, postconciliar Church, adults who were eager to understand and to act; helping business and professional men to think through the difficult ethical problems they faced in their work. Mass, sermons, anointing the dying, wakes, funerals— Hugh loved it all.

(Greeley, 256)

When the institutional realities of the church overwhelmed these human relationships, Donlon left the priesthood searching in vain for more adequate ones outside the church. Finally, an illicit love affair (a favorite Greeley device) brings epiphany, forgiveness, restored vocation.

Before turning from Greeley's novels, it is important to note one or two themes. His priests are all people bound up in a thick Roman Catholic familial culture that both confines and sustains these clergy. Their routine ethical decisions involve relations with people in this culture, and their major dilemmas involve questions about leaving or following their calling.

Further, in spite of their loss of faith, their moral failings, and their decisions to leave the priesthood, the priesthood does not leave them. In *Ascent into Hell,* Donlon continues to pronounce absolution, say the last rites, and even offer Mass long after he has married and become a commodities broker. He does not continue his priestly ministry because of abiding faith but because others continue to see him as a priest. He is held in place by the web of relations that is American Catholicism. He remains a priest forever, in spite of church rules.

Moreover, salvation for these flawed priests comes not from the official channels of grace but from women who love and accept and make possible new life. Relationships are where grace is to be found. This is especially true in Greeley's third novel of the trilogy, *Lord of the Dance,* where teenaged Noele Farrell frees an entire family from the results of their priest-son-brother's twenty-year deception. Her truth telling makes possible a new start for the priest and all his relatives.

Those familiar with Father Greeley's hobbyhorses will find many familiar echoes in these novels. (His send-ups of the liturgical experimentation of the 1960s are not to be missed!) And they will find much to debate about his assessments. But here it is important to focus on what his novels tell us about the ethical quadrilateral. To be sure, Greeley gives us many glimpses of institutional "everyday-ishness" and the clerical search for ultimacy. But the bold line in his novels is the human relationship side of the quadrilateral.

Ministry in Ultimate Context

Regarded by many as the premier novelist of our time, John Updike provides the lone Protestant voice in the quartet I have chosen. His *Roger's Version* provides a picture very different from those of our first three authors. Roger Lambert is not an apocalyptic prophet, a loyal preserver of a flawed institution, or a seeker after intimacy. Instead, this New England divinity school professor seeks to proclaim the truth about God and care for the suffering.

In *Roger's Version,* those classic ministerial tasks take new forms. First, the Methodist clergyman-in-good-standing, who left the parish after divorcing his first wife, does battle with a graduate student who is convinced that "God is showing through" the discoveries of the New Physics (Updike 1986, 10). In response to the mind-numbing statistical proofs for the existence of God offered by this conversation partner, Lambert invokes classic themes from the Christian tradition:

> "The church preaches, I believe, and the Old Testament describes, a God Who acts, Who *comes to us,* in Revelation and Redemption, and not one Who set the universe going and then hid. The God we care about in this divinity school is the living God, Who moves toward us out of His will and love, and Who laughs at all the towers of Babel we build to Him."
>
> (Updike 1986, 22)

At stake in Professor Lambert's neo-Barthian response to this scientist's attempt to make God one more fact among many is ultimacy, truth about God, the Christian tradition. This minister makes it his primary concern to battle in pastoral conversation for the truth about God. To do so means shaking misplaced faith, welcoming doubt so that blasphemy may be exposed. Relentless in his attempt to shake his student's bad faith, Lambert raises ultimate questions that disturb and unsettle: "If God is so ingenious and purposive, what about deformity and disease? What about the carnage that rules this kingdom of life at every level? Why does life *feel*, to us as we experience it, so desperately urgent and so utterly pointless at the same time?" (Updike 1986, 87).

Pastor Lambert, however, is anything but a proselytizer. When his niece asks him if he is in the religion business, he responds, "Not distribution. You might call it quality control" (Updike 1986, 63).

Simultaneous with his battle against science for the truth about God are Lambert's attempts to help his young niece, Verna Ekelof. The young woman has a new baby, no income, no husband, and no support from her parents. Lambert responds to her needs with conventional liberal wisdom. To overcome her bleak job prospects, he encourages her to take a high school equivalency test. He tutors her in literature. When she becomes pregnant, he encourages her to have an abortion and then pays for it. When she injures her first child in a fit of rage, he tries to help her cover up her crime and then takes the abused child into his own home. When the niece responds to his care with sexual invitations, he resists the first two times but then succumbs.

The pastor's reflections after intercourse with his niece are part of a neoorthodox ethos that counts blasphemy the great sin and relativizes all other failings:

> When I was spent and my niece released, we lay together on a hard floor of the spirit, partners in incest, adultery, and child abuse. We wanted to be rid of each other, to destroy the evidence, yet perversely clung, lovers, miles below the ceiling, our comfort being that we had no further to fall. Lying there with Verna, gazing upward, I saw how much majesty resides in our continuing to love and honor God even as He inflicts blows upon us—as much as resides in the silence He maintains so that we may enjoy and explore our human freedom. This was my *proof* of His existence—the distance to the impalpable ceiling, the immense distance measuring our abasement. So great a fall proves great heights. Sweet charity invaded me.
>
> (Updike 1986, 280–281)

In Updike's version of ministerial existence, the institutional side of the ethical quadrilateral is almost invisible. The church is an abstraction, a bad memory from earlier parish ministry days. Major ethical dilemmas emerge neither in everyday ecclesiastical routines nor dramatic extreme cases. Instead they occur in theological discourse and in needs of the neighbor. One issue norms all others, idolatry. In Updike's rendering, then, the dominant line of the quadrilateral is the ultimate bottom line. The other sides are smaller and much less weighty. Regardless of whether we agree with his theological stance vis-à-vis the ultimate line, Updike renders it prominent, unavoidable.

Conclusion

This preliminary exploration of current literary depictions of ministerial situations only begins to assess the significance of modern literature for clergy ethics. But even this limited initial probing provides a rough framework for looking at our varying clergy ethics contexts. Moreover, it shows us that, far from being irrelevant to the larger social context, clergy ethics is of great interest beyond the walls of organized religion. These authors are among our nation's most read. That they pay this kind of attention to ministerial behavior suggests that our clergy may not be as marginal as they think they are.

Further, even though each of these authors highlights one of the four sides of the quadrilateral, it makes more sense to see the four as related parts of a larger ethical context. One feature may be more prominent in any individual case, but all four merit attention and reflection.

These authors have, for the sake of their own larger literary purposes, distorted the quadrilateral in different directions. Although some clergy may find their own ethical situation leaning heavily toward the extreme-case side, and others may find themselves almost completely shaped by institutional, relational, or ultimate pressures, most clergy will find their situations taking more conventional shapes. In Percy's and Updike's stories, for example, the quadrilateral initially seems to collapse because of the absence of ecclesiastical pressures. Yet most clergy in America will find that the institutional side is as present and demanding as are the other three.

None of these novelists proposes strategies for reshaping the ministerial quadrilateral. None sketches an ideal shape; would it be a square, a rectangle, a parallelogram? But what they offer in their portraits of distorted or unbalanced clergy situations are sharp shocks of recognition, pictures of the kinds of pressures that clergy face. The fact that one or more of these portraits find resonance in clergy readers' lives suggests that distortion and lack of balance may be more than fictional invention. These portraits, along with concerns raised elsewhere in this book, suggest that clergy are faced with the choice of either accepting such misshapen existences or reshaping their ethical situations into more healthy ones.

If they choose the second option, what should they do? Perhaps without intending, these novelists provide clues. In one way or another, each of the clergy portrayed reaches back to elements of larger ministerial traditions for help. Percy's Father Smith appropriates the watchtower tradition of Habakkuk and the pillar saints. Powers' Joe Hackett regains his moorings in a breadline, where he steps back into a fundamental tradition of care for the least of these. Greeley's priests search for new manifestations of a sacramental presence that is at the heart of Catholicism. Updike returns his cleric to the "Barthian nugget" of the experience of the gap between God and the human, which stands, of course, in a tradition reaching back to Calvin and through him all the way back to Moses.

Taken individually, each of these solutions seems to further the distortion even as each attempts to respond to it. But the common strategy of reaching back holds promise nonetheless. When we place these four modern accounts next to each other and see the complexity of the ministerial situation—its multi-sided and multidimensional character—we see that single-handed reaching back will not reshape things. Instead, a much wider reappropriation, making use of more of the traditions of ministry that have been fragmented and distorted over the centuries, is needed. Thus these novelists, without calling for it in their writing, push us into new collaborative searches across the history of ministry for resources.

Perhaps because these novelists are American, perhaps because the novel is an essentially solitary medium, it is striking how individual centered these portraits are. These clergy, despite their location in familial, ecclesial, and other social structures, tend to respond to their ethical quandaries as ministerial lone rangers. Never do we see the church or any other institution serve as a communal resource for these troubled loners. A correlated phenomenon is the pronounced anti-institutionalism in all of these portraits. In each case, the church appears as problem, burden, inhibitor, complicator. We must ask why that is. It may be that there is an American shape to clergy ethics that our novelists have successfully captured. In the presence of such readings, we cannot avoid asking if that shape is adequate or healthy. Our answers to that question may set us off in directions as surprising as those pursued by the fictional clergy of Percy, Powers, Greeley, and Updike. But we also have the option, having entered their worlds, of setting off in new directions, together.

References

Greeley, Andrew. 1982. *The Passover Trilogy,* including *Thy Brother's Wife, Ascent into Hell,* and *Lord of the Dance.* New York: Crown Publishers.

Percy, Walker. 1987. *The Thanatos Syndrome.* New York: Farrar, Straus & Giroux.

Powers, J. F. 1988. *Wheat that Springeth Green.* New York: Alfred A. Knopf.

Updike, John. 1986. *Roger's Version.* New York: Alfred A. Knopf.

6

Clergy Ethics and the Professional Ethics Model

Paul F. Camenisch

The field of applied ethics, including business and professional ethics, has virtually exploded in recent years. It is therefore natural that any systematic attempt to address clergy ethics will have to confront the question of the professional ethics model. Some will see this model as a blessing, because it provides a general structure for considering clergy ethics and offers the benefits of the prior reflection invested in formulating and assessing that model. For others, this model is at best a mixed blessing and at worst a curse, because it either misrepresents the situation and standing of clergy and subsequently distorts clergy ethics, or it is simply fundamentally inappropriate for application to the clergy. Rebecca Chopp's characterization of professional ethics in her contribution to this volume as our best and worst model reflects both of these responses to this model. (see Chapter 4).

In order to assess the professional ethics model as a tool for "doing" clergy ethics, we will first have to establish what we mean by "profession", whether the clergy is indeed a profession, and what the professional ethics model is. We will then have to weigh the considerations that support and those that challenge the application of that model to clergy ethics.

There are at least two distinguishable but finally inseparable ways to approach our first two questions. One is predominantly historical and descriptive; the other is predominantly contemporary and analytical. The first looks at the development and interaction of the two realities that concern us—the clergy and the concept of a profession—over a period of time, to see how they were linked by observers and by the clergy themselves. Given that across time the two entities will vary, a clear and unequivocal verdict about their relation is hardly to be expected from history. At the same time, the greater complexity of history and its ambiguous answer are crucial checks on the possible abstractness of the second approach.

The second approach is contemporary in that it examines the clergy in its current form and situation. It is analytical in that it begins its examination of the question of the professional standing of the clergy by stating as precisely as possible what we mean by "profession."

It should be clear why these two approaches should not finally be seen as separate and totally independent. On the one hand, what the contemporary analytical approach offers us can be seen from one perspective as only the most recent but by no means the final form of what the historical approach attempts to understand through time. At the same time, it should be clear that in one sense what the historical approach at its best attempts to do is to become contemporaneous with the various historical stages in the evolution of "profession" and the clergy, and the relation between them. It does so in the attempt to offer a kind of running analysis of the observed data as they evolve. One might liken the contemporary/analytical approach to the photograph that permits careful examination of the images framed by the camera at a given moment in time, but that offers only hints of the past out of which those images came, the future toward which they move, or the vital forces that propel them on their way. The historical approach, on the other hand, is more like a movie, which usually does not permit such careful examination of its individual images and scenes, but which through its greater scope and more dynamic portrayal gives us a knowledge of and a feeling for what we see that are qualitatively different from what the photograph provides. An additional reason for not trying to construe them as two absolutely different approaches is the fact that the current understanding of "profession" and "professional" yielded by the contemporary/analytical approach is to a significant degree the product of the evolution the historian studies.

One question any critical historical approach must be aware of is whether the concept of the profession to be applied to the changing forms of the clergy is to be the understanding of "profession" that prevailed during the period being studied, or whether it is a contemporary understanding of profession being projected back into an earlier time. Both approaches have their uses. The major mistake would not be to choose the wrong approach, but to be unaware of the differences between the two approaches and between the kinds of information they yield.

In the following brief historical sketch, I will assume a contemporary and rather general understanding of "profession" that I believe to be widely, although not universally, shared. Although this understanding of profession will be elaborated later in the contemporary/analytical section, for the moment it can be summarized as follows: a profession is an organized group (a) whose members possess specialized skills and knowledge widely believed to be useful, even crucial, in the pursuit of highly valued conditions or states of affairs such as justice, health, and spiritual well-being; (b) who have certain kinds of control over their professional work; and (c) who usually claim to be, and are expected to be, motivated in their professional activities by more than personal gain.

The Historical Approach

It is clear not only that the clergy in America have not always conformed to the professional model, but that other models have also helped shape it. Martin Marty suggests:

> Three broad, chronologically sequential yet overlapping and not displacing forms of the clergy profession . . . emerged in the United States. First, from 1492 to the 1830s, the ministry can be seen chiefly as a *public* role in a congregational-territorial context, its soil being that of church establishment. The second period remembers the public dimension but produces a new professional context, the *congregational-denominational.* It remains strong and institutionally it even dominates, but cultural shifts have worked to produce a third model. This one took shape during the rise of the other professions in America, and builds on the congregational-denominational. The emergent accent for the past century at least has been toward the *private clientele* setting and expression.
>
> (Marty 1988, 76–77)

The current professional model was least influential in the early centuries of America's history, with significant changes becoming evident in the early 1800s. For this early period, our best evidence comes from Donald M. Scott's study of "the New England-based and -derived Congregational-Presbyterian ministry" (Scott 1978, xiii). Scott acknowledges that the image or model on which he focuses, that of "clerical public guardianship," was most fully developed among Congregational ministers during the period of establishment (xiii). No such limited group can adequately represent the great variety of American clergy from the 1700s to the present. However, the importance of New England in the nation's early history and of Congregationalism in its early religious history suggest that this group's experience may well reveal dynamics crucial to the clergy of other denominations and faiths, of other regions and times.

During this early period, the Congregational minister of New England was not just a religious leader serving a congregation of believing, practicing Christians. Because of the establishment of the Congregational church and because of the role of religion and theology in the total life of the community, he was as much the holder of a public office as the church in which he preached was a public building for nonreligious as well as for religious assembly.

The major element in the standing and authority of ministers in that time and place was the simple fact of their occupying that position in the town or parish (Scott 1978, 11). There were two major dimensions of that occupancy that granted the minister authority and standing. First, the occupancy was determined locally. Only the local body, according to Congregational polity, could elect a pastor, and it did so owing neither obedience nor even explanation to any body beyond itself. Reflecting the public nature of the minister's office was the fact that, although the church and its active members took the leading role in identifying a new minister, ordination and installation followed only after a majority of the voting inhabitants of the parish endorsed the selection (3).

The second crucial factor, possibly more significant than the first, was that occupancy of the ministerial position presumably was, and often in fact was, for life. Of the graduates of Yale College from 1702 to 1775, 79 percent spent their entire professional lives in a single pastorate. Only 7 percent changed pastoral charges more than once (Scott 1978, 4). We have here not a professional temporarily employed in a given place, but a publicly elected, permanently situated pillar of the community. The minister was not here temporarily as one step in a career of personal professional advancement, but as a response to a calling of God through these people to a public office in a community (9). By presiding over and preaching at various public rituals, such as election day, fast days, and thanksgiving days, by the delivery on these and other occasions of jeremiads calling the community back to the proper path lest it suffer God's wrath, by frequently calling to account those engaging in antisocial behavior and helping to adjudicate disputes among parishioners, "the ministerial office in eighteenth-century New England . . . [became] inseparable from the fabric of the New England towns that contained it" (12). Thus the minister was a major bearer and agent of the values and dominant culture not just of the church, but of the community itself. Magistracy and ministry were, Scott suggests, much more kin than they were ever again to be in the American experience (9).

Of course, the dominance of the "public office" image did not mean a total absence of other themes and dynamics that would later take center stage with the emergence of the professional model. Parallels with other "professions" did not go unnoticed. In 1656 Richard Baxter, in *The Reformed Pastor,* "assured his readers that the minister was the 'counselor for their souls,' just as a lawyer was the counselor for their estates and a physician for their bodies" (Holifield 1983, 36–37). The minister's standing in the community derived in large part from his being seen as God's "ambassador," or as God's appointed "shepherd" for this flock—two of the most frequent images of the New England minister (Scott 1978, 7). But the fact that, of colonial Massachusetts' one thousand preachers, 90 percent were college graduates in an overwhelmingly unschooled society should not be ignored in assessing the grounds of their authority (Holifield 1983, 53). As early as the first decades of the eighteenth century, a tentative step away from the absolute autonomy of local congregations and toward a regional denominational structure and possibly toward a professional association was taken when neighborhood ministerial associations began to emerge that examined and licensed candidates for the ministry and responded to inquiries from local churches about possible candidates (Scott 1978, 2).

But whatever seeds of the future professionalization of the clergy can be found in those early stages of American ecclesiastical history, and whatever dynamics were at work there to bring those seeds to maturity, the church—including both lay people and clergy—was also part of the larger society and subject to the forces shaping its evolution. Burton J. Bledstein has persuasively argued that a number of such forces at work in American culture from early on led predictably, perhaps almost inevitably, to the professionalization of practically everybody. At work here were simple and immediate human drives such as the desire to better one's situation in a social hierarchy strikingly flattened and open compared with that of Europe. Professional training and the subsequent rise in status were the most accessible ways of achieving this, which accounts in part for the humble origins of many early ministers.

But also at work here, according to Bledstein, were deeper, more complex drives: "Mid-Victorians would structure life, its space, its words, its time, and its activities. And professionalism with its cultural rituals, ceremonies and symbols satisfied this need" (Bledstein 1976, 105). This national trend toward professionalization can be seen in a number of developments; but probably most indicative of what happened during the 1800s to theology, law, medicine, dentistry, pharmacy, and veterinary medicine is the growth in the number of professional schools. During the period of 1801–1825 there were thirty-five such schools, with eighteen of them being theological and twelve being medical. During the following three-quarters of a century, the total number moved up so that by 1900 it had reached 283. Although divinity, or theology, had led the way in numbers until 1875, by 1900 it was only 47 of the total 283, being exceeded by medicine (86) and law (50), and equaled by dentistry (Bledstein 1976, 84).

Although such general trends were evident in the larger society and by no means left the clergy untouched, there were also developments peculiar to the clergy that pushed it closer to the professional model as currently understood. One of these was the shifting, we might even say the declining, role of religion and church in the society itself, which tended to diminish the role of the minister as public officer. But there were also more positive developments that pulled the clergy toward the professional model. These had to do primarily with the emergence of causes or campaigns to which the clergy felt called, but which clearly transcended the local parishes from which they had hitherto drawn their standing and authority. The two major such causes in the experience of the New England clergy studied by Scott were the abolition of slavery and the evangelization of the country (Scott 1978, chaps. 4, 5). Once ministers began seeing their calling in terms of such translocal movements, and seeing themselves as having responsibilities and audiences larger than their local parishes, they predictably thought increasingly in terms of their connections with professional colleagues with whom they took up these new and larger battles. Some such coming together of increasingly "professional" colleagues happened in emerging denominational structures, and some through the various voluntary associations founded to further those larger causes now competing for clerical attention.

Such a shift in the role and the nature of the clergy caused considerable unhappiness in parishes accustomed to the older pattern, but the transformation proved unstoppable. "Of the 162 Yale graduates from 1795 to 1815 who entered the clergy, only 39, or 24 percent, held one pastorate while more than half had three or more pastorates and 29 percent had four or more positions" (Scott 1978, 74). Clearly, the idea of one's own career was replacing that of ministry as a local public office. The emergence of the theological seminary in the form of Andover Theological Seminary in 1808 as an institution distinct from the undergraduate college meant a significant further step in the professionalization of training for the ministry. At the same time, increasing concern about special canons or codes of ministerial manners and conduct made clear that the evolution of the ministry as a profession in the modern sense was well on its way (63–64). As Scott writes:

> In short, by the 1850's, in institutional terms, the clergy had become a profession, a coherent, self-conscious occupational body, organized and defined by a set of institutions which were outside lay or public control, which controlled the special learning needed to become a clergyman, and which possessed the power to determine who could enter the clerical ranks.
> (Scott 1978, 154–155)

Thus did what Martin Marty (Marty 1988, 76–77) called the congregational-denominational stage emerge, a stage that in many ways still dominates and so will be central to the analytical/contemporary section that follows. But developing both within and alongside of that stage is the third form, also reflected in the contemporary situation of the clergy, which Marty (Marty 1988, 77; cf. Scott 1978, 128–130) calls the private clientele stage. This stage relied on and required increasing specialization in those services the clergy could offer private, often individual, clients. It relieved clergy of many of their remaining public or societal duties and offered more and more opportunities for ministry without a congregational base (Scott 1978, 128–130). Whether or not Marty is correct that this mode of ministry crested in the 1960s (Marty 1988, 84), it is clear that it remains part of the currently complex and ambiguous situation of the clergy.

The Analytical Approach

The second approach to our question of the professional status of the clergy is the analytical and contemporary one, which begins with the attempt to state as clearly as possible what we mean by "profession." In the absence of a universally accepted definition of a profession, I suggest that full-fledged professions are distinguished by four characteristics (Camenisch 1983, chap. 2). The question of how many of these characteristics an occupational group must exhibit to be a profession, and whether they must be exhibited in precisely the form specified here, seeks a precision that current usage will not sustain.

1. Members of a profession are distinguished by the possession of *specialized skills and knowledge* not possessed by the population at large. These skills and knowledge currently are almost invariably acquired by extended formal education and rest on a theoretical base also known to the professional. Knowledge of the theory enables the professional to apply such skills and knowledge in novel situations.

2. A profession and its members enjoy *professional autonomy,* which encompasses both self-governance, or regulation, and liberty of professional action. Such autonomy is seen in (a) the profession's general insulation from assessment of its professional performance by any but members of that profession (that is, insulation from lay assessment); (b) the profession's control over the preparation and admission to the profession of new members; (c) the profession's power, whether exercised or not, of continuing oversight of its members and their professional activities; and (d) the right to admit to and expel from membership. This autonomy is established and protected by the larger society through legal statute, usually in the form of licensure or certification laws, and sometimes results in a legally enforced monopoly in some areas of professional activity.

3. A profession pursues with and on behalf of its clients and/or the larger society *a distinctive goal* that may involve the use of products and which includes services, but that is essentially a state of affairs (health, justice, knowledge, spiritual health) generally highly valued by the client and by the larger society and is widely seen as linked to our fullest well-being as human beings. This state of affairs often needs to be established or protected in crisis situations and is such that the client is usually unable, or at best is questionably able, to attain alone.

4. Finally, professions and professionals have traditionally exhibited, and at their best are still expected to exhibit, in their professional activity an *atypical moral commitment* to the interests and well-being of the client, and possibly to those of the larger society as those interests relate to the distinctive goal of that profession, a commitment that we do not normally expect of other economic agents and that may on occasion be in tension with the professional's own self-interest.

Status, power, and income level have not been mentioned

because these are derivative and are not essential to what it means to be a professional.

Just as there is currently no universally accepted definition of profession or professional, so there is none of professional ethics. I therefore propose the following statement as capturing the key elements of professional ethics as it is currently understood. Professional ethics consists of a number of

1. behavioral guides and
2. supporting basic values or general principles that may be expressed in
3. professional oaths, codes of conduct, statements of purpose, mottos, and/or more general kinds of literature such as essays and speeches, and that are sometimes elaborated and applied in authoritative pronouncements by agencies of the profession, violation of which is at least potential grounds for disciplinary action,
4. that are intended to guide or inform the conduct of members of the profession toward the client, toward professional colleagues, and toward the society at large,
5. that derive their content from (a) standards of common decency and acceptable conduct prevalent in the society at large; (b) the significance, including the moral significance, of what it means to be a professional; and (c) the significance, including the moral significance, of the specific profession in view, including its distinctive goals or purposes as a profession (such as health for physicians, justice for lawyers, knowledge for the professorate, spiritual health for the clergy),
6. and that are thought by many to be essential to being a profession and a professional in the fullest sense.

This brings us to the question of whether the clergy constitutes a profession as defined (Camenisch 1985). Our brief historical excursion above has already given us some sketchy data on this matter. But given that we now wish to address the question head-on, it will be most helpful to approach it on the basis of the above characteristics. Clearly, many clergy do have specialized skills and knowledge acquired during extended formal education, which do rest on a kind of theoretical base that the well-prepared clergyperson has mastered.

However, three qualifications must be added. Although some specialized skills and knowledge can often rightfully be claimed, many clergy, especially those holding a congregational charge alone, find they are expected to be a jack-of-all-trades, including properly clerical, but also administrative, counseling, financial, managerial, and other more general kinds of tasks. This situation breaks down the rather sharp focus professional activity usually aspires to and can undercut the clergy's sense of being practitioners in a specialized, professional field.

Second, not all clergy can claim mastery of such skills, knowledge, and theoretical basis because there are no clear and universally enforced standards of admission to the clerical profession. Various religious bodies establish and enforce their own standards. Predictably, these vary widely with regard to formal preparation, in some cases being positively antithetical to such educational requirements, predicating admission into the clergy on a more confessional or experiential basis. This fact raises a significant challenge to the professional standing of the clergy that will have to be faced under professional autonomy below.

The third aspect to be noted about the skills and knowledge of the clergy is that they will not be as consistently valued and respected throughout the larger society as are those of other established professions such as law and medicine. This results in part from the regard, or lack thereof, some segments of the society have for organized religion, its goals and practitioners, including its professional leaders. Many clergy may be indifferent to this societal assessment of their qualifications. Nevertheless, to the extent that it is the larger society that finally grants professional status, this fact is quite germane to the question of the clergy's professional standing.

The question of the professional autonomy of the clergy is more complicated yet. Some clergy do enjoy some elements of professional autonomy as defined above. However, most such elements, including insulation from lay assessment, control over preparation and admission of new members, and continuing performance review and discipline of one's professional colleagues will in the American situation apply at most to the clergy of a given religious body as provided for by the polity of that body, and not to the clergy as a whole.

In this area, however, the largest difference from most established professions is that the larger society does not license or certify members of the clergy except for very limited aspects of their professional activity, such as performing marriages. This raises the question of whether an occupational group whose members are certified by a limited, self-defined group within the society for practice primarily if not exclusively within that group, rather than by the society at large for practice throughout the society, is a distinctive sort of profession, or is no profession at all.

Given this fact that the clergy are ordained by their own communities of faith, there is certainly no legally enforced monopoly over any services, except possibly within a specific community.

This brings us to the question of the distinctive and highly valued goal of professional activity that distinguishes other professions and that helps determine the content of each profession's distinctive ethos and ethics. Can the clergy lay claim to such a goal? Often the purpose of the clergy is presented as identical to that of the religious community it serves. For our present purposes I will let that equation stand. I assume that the religious community and its leaders, the clergy, can indeed claim to have such a goal, even if it is not universally recognized or valued.

We need not here settle the question of precisely how that goal should be defined. However, we must at least note some of the most obvious possibilities. Gaylord Noyce suggests that for the clergy, the ultimate value served—an expression that seems identical to our "distinctive professional goal"—is faith (Noyce 1988, 22–23). In other contexts, one might have said that the goal is salvation, or, in possibly more contemporary terms, spiritual health or wholeness, or in H. Richard Niebuhr's terms, "the increase among men [*sic*] of the love of God and neighbor" (Niebuhr 1956, 31).

In some contexts, it would be useful to determine which of these goals, or which expression of the one goal, is most appropriate to the clergy as a whole or to certain groups of clergy. But this imprecision poses no special problem for our investigation of the professional standing of the clergy. Similar debates rage even in the paradigmatic professions of medicine and law. Is the goal of medicine health? Long life? The reduction of pain, disability, and disfigurement? The return to the patient of autonomy and control over the patient's life? For law, is it justice? The resolution of conflict within the law? Protecting the rights of the client? Fulfilling the wishes of the client within the limits set by the law? Seeking the most workable and defensible compromise among the competing interests of the adversaries and the larger society? Or assuring the client's freedom and autonomy?

However, we should note that whatever expression we adopt for the distinctive goal of the clergy, it is unlikely to find the nearly universal approval in the general population that is accorded to health and justice. It is, in part, this lack of a broad social consensus about the precise nature and the value of the goal of the clerical profession that makes the society relatively uninterested in licensing and thereby legitimating the profession or in involving itself in the other internal affairs of the clergy.

Do clergy aspire to or actually exhibit the atypical moral commitment to client and/or society ascribed above to the established professions? Such a commitment is in fact a significant part of the public's expectations of the clergy and of the clergy's own self-image. What clergyperson would ever feel entirely comfortable refusing professional services to a client simply on the basis of inability to pay or because such services involved some risk for the clergy? In fact, I would suggest that one reason the clergy has been slower than the other major professions to develop its own distinctive ethic is that this atypical moral commitment was assumed to be so central to the profession that many thought it insulting to suggest that specific rules and guidelines were needed to require it.

Professional Standing of Clergy

The above observations lead to no clear, easy verdict concerning the professional standing of the clergy, nor to the related question of the appropriateness of the professional ethics model for doing clergy ethics. A brief summary of the relation of the clergy to the suggested professional model will lay the groundwork for addressing this second question. Counting against professional standing for the clergy are (a) the variation—among different religious traditions and the denominations within them—in requirements for admission to the clergy; (b) the resulting absence of a comprehensive and reasonably homogeneous professional community bridging these lines between traditions and denominations to establish and enforce professional standards for clergy; and (c) membership in the clergy being granted by a number of discrete, limited communities and not by the larger society. Complicating the clergy's professional standing by at least making it a distinctive profession is the clergy's claim to be in the service of some transcendent reality or set of norms, which may on occasion rightly claim precedence over all other claims upon the clergy, including any deriving from professional considerations.

It is increasingly clear that we cannot answer the question of the professional standing of the clergy definitionally, that is, by a careful examination of the definition of "profession" followed by an equally careful examination of the characteristics of the clergy to see if they qualify. This approach is defeated by the imprecision and variety of definitions of "profession" and by the variety of the clergy themselves.

It may therefore be more helpful to consider these two questions—the professional standing of the clergy and the applicability of the professional ethics model—simultaneously by looking at the most frequent answers given to them and the reasons supporting those answers.

One possible answer to the questions is that the professional model for the clergy and the professional ethics model for clergy ethics are totally inadequate and unacceptable. This would appear to be simply one way of asserting that the clergy is not a profession. This assertion can arise from two quite different perspectives. On the one hand, it may be made by those who do not think the clergy measures up to other professions such as law and medicine. Often speaking from outside the religious communities, these persons might maintain that the skills and knowledge of the clergy are not equal in precision, in social usefulness, or in some other important respect to those of the other professions, or that the clergy rightly lacks other crucial characteristics of a profession, such as professional autonomy and societal licensure.

On the other hand, a seemingly similar denial of professional status to the clergy may come from members of religious communities, even from clergy themselves, who may argue not that the clergy does not measure up to the other professions, but that to group the clergy with the other professions would diminish the clergy in unacceptable ways. This group does not mean to suggest that unprofessional clerical conduct is acceptable. The clergy should be skilled and knowledgeable, committed to their "clients," and serious about their "professional" activities.

Why then is the professional label thought inappropriate for the clergy? Some of the reasons derive from this society's current ambivalence about the professions. Many parents want their children to be professionals; countless occupational groups aspire to professional status; we all want "professional" performance from the persons with whom we deal. At the same time, there is a growing uneasiness about the professions in society. Many are not sure that the rather high moral view of the professions presented here is at all realistic. There is growing concern that professional skills and status are used as much to serve the self-interest of the profession and the professional as they are to serve the crucial interests of the client or the society; that professional autonomy is used as much to protect professional territory and maintain a monopoly over certain crucial services as it is to facilitate serious self-regulation and to assure competent professional performance (Larson 1977). There is also growing concern about the dangers of an overprofessionalization of society in which professions simultaneously wield too much influence over public policy and individual lives and, by cultivating dependency on themselves, disable us for taking care of ourselves (Illich 1970; 1977). And of course there is the persistent resentment about the income of the members of established professions such as law and medicine. It is not surprising that many clergy and their supporters would like to avoid associating the clergy with these problems.

In her contribution to this volume (chapter 4), Rebecca Chopp offers additional reasons for not seeing the clergy as professionals, reasons that seem to underlie her reference to the professional model as our best and worst model. She seems to suggest that to adopt that model is not just to adopt a neutral language and model for understanding the clergy, but is to buy into a substantive and problematic way of seeing the clergy and the religious communities they serve. Increasingly, professionals work in and for institutions, often as the administrators of those institutions. To the extent that this increasingly dominant shape of professional reality informs our use of the term, we are, in considering the clergy professionals, signing up for an institutional view of religious communities and for an administrative/managerial view of clergy and their roles. This exists in some tension with Chopp's and others' conviction that religious communities should be much more than, or, should even be something other than, established institutions lodged comfortably within the existing social matrix, administered by competent, well-trained professionals—the clergy. Such an institutional-professional view obscures other dimensions of religious communities, primarily the prophetic, challenging, discomfiting view of the calling of religious persons and communities. Institutions and established professionals, she seems to suggest, seldom make good prophets.

The prophecy needed, however, is not just the crying out against blatant social and economic injustice, but prophecy against the prevailing values of the culture, values that are often embedded in and reinforced by institutional and professional models. One element of these values that concerns Chopp is the individualization of so many dimensions of contemporary life, including religion. This development obviously correlates with that third stage in the development of the American clergy that Martin Marty sees as being distinguished by its relation to a private clientele (Marty 1988, 76–77). Thus do the privatization and individualization of religion in America, the increasing orientation of many clergy to a private

clientele, and the professionalization of the clergy all become
mutually reinforcing elements in the current picture of American religion.

An additional related reason for being circumspect about
the professional model can be extrapolated from Langdon
Gilkey's contribution to this volume (see chapter 2). Gilkey
suggests that scripture and the various ways it is mediated to
us through our traditions, for our particular purposes, especially through ecclesiology, decisively shape the *religious* roles
of the clergy.

But then other factors in the larger society, such as pluralism
and secularism, and other factors in the church's own situation
add other roles the clergy are expected to fulfill, such as counselor, therapist, manager, and political leader. These latter
roles seem to be the ones Gilkey suggests might *help* the laity,
but are not likely to *save* them. In terms of the clergy's current
situation and our concern with ethics, the following extension
of Gilkey's thought seems plausible. As the clergy's distinctively religious roles and the theological/ecclesiological foundations that supported them lost their clarity and some of their
authority, these other non- or less religious roles took over
more and more of the clergy's time and energy, and increasingly shaped the laity's and the clergy's view of the clergy.

It is reasonable to suggest that the concern with clergy ethics
arises primarily in relation to these latter roles. After all, helping roles make the clergy look more like other professions in
terms of the functions served and the training required. And
if these other professions have their ethics—codes, oaths, and
so forth—shouldn't the clergy also have theirs if they are going
to be real "professionals"?

This analysis may also suggest why clergy ethics, as that term
is now used, was relatively late in emerging and why tradition-
alists who give priority to the religious roles resist construing
the clergy on the professional model. With regard to the religious role, it might be said that the major questions are not
ethical in any narrow and focused sense, but are primarily ones
of competence; that is, knowledge of the relevant tradition,
skill in its proper proclamation and/or its enactment through
appropriate rites, and fidelity and personal commitment to
that tradition. Of course, competence is also an issue in professional ethics, but with significantly different connotations than
in the context just invoked. This analysis explains the neglect
of clergy ethics in the contemporary sense as long as the religious role of the clergy prevailed. But once the clergy move
to these other helping roles, where religious/theological tradi-

tions are less directly informative about proper conduct than they are with regard to the religious roles, we—clergy, laity, and academics—naturally begin looking for other appropriate standards to guide conduct in these new roles. Behold! Clergy (professional) ethics!

An even more serious possible implication of this analysis is that these various influences at work in the larger culture coming to bear on laity, clergy, church, and religion as a whole not only provide the clergy with roles additional or alternative to the religious roles, but that they help erode such religious roles and so reinforce the felt need to identify some "useful" functions the clergy can serve. If this is the case, and if I am correct in suggesting that clergy ethics has special relevance, maybe even has relevance *only* for these other "helping" roles, then the more we emphasize clergy ethics, the more we collaborate in the displacement of the religious roles by these other roles that we now try to legitimate and enhance by making their execution ethically appropriate and professionally respectable.

At the very least, this should make us open to the possible contributions of those who resist the professional and the professional ethics models for clergy. Such resistance may reflect a refusal to bring religious faith and leadership into line with contemporary culture and its increasingly professionalized ethics. But it may also represent a refusal to risk diluting or even subverting important elements of their faith, and possibly of religious faith as such, as reflected in their understanding of the nature and practice of religious leadership.

Conclusion

What can we conclude about the appropriateness and helpfulness of the professional ethics model for use in clergy ethics? There is no simple answer. I have suggested that both the concept of "profession," or "professional," and the derivative idea of professional ethics are constellations of factors. There are enough similarities between the clergy as generally perceived and the professions as defined above, that to some extent the clergy can usefully be seen as a profession. On the other hand, there are enough divergences between the two to caution us against subsuming the clergy completely under that model. The similarities are seen in that the clergy generally claim to have and are expected to have skills and knowledge not possessed by most laypersons; that they do aim in their professional activity at a distinctive sort of goal for clients, or the society as a whole (or at least the community of faith) that is seen by many as essential to human well-being; and that they claim to have an atypical moral commitment to those they serve. Needless to say, they probably fall short of the ideal performance on all these matters with roughly the same frequency as do other professions. But that is not the question here.

The clergy most conspicuously fall short of the professional model in the area of professional autonomy. They do not, at least as a total group (that is, spanning various faiths and denominations), have the same control over preparation for and admission to the profession as do other more unified professions, nor are they licensed and thus societally authenticated as are other major professions.

This puts the clergy in an unusual situation in relation to other established professions. Those characteristics of professions that the clergy most clearly share—distinctive goal, atypical moral commitment, and, perhaps somewhat less universally, special skills and knowledge—are precisely those that both undergird and give specific content to a truly professional ethic. In a sense, these characteristics—especially the potential compromising of self-interest in light of the atypical moral commitment and the often expensive acquisition of those skills and knowledge—can be seen as the debit, or the costly, side of being a professional. They make demands on the professional and call for sacrifices so that the high calling of the professional can be attained.

On the other hand, that professional trait in which the clergy are most often deficient—professional autonomy—has quite a different relation to professional ethics. Professional autonomy, rather than being one of the professional characteristics that undergirds and lends content to professional ethics, is at best one aid in implementing professional ethics—for example, by making self-regulation possible not only in matters of competence, but also of integrity and morality. But beyond that, professional autonomy carried too far, or even positively abused, potentially undermines professional ethics by insulating the profession from accountability to external parties by permitting, even tempting, professions and professionals to abuse the monopolies that some forms of autonomy make possible.

Furthermore, professional autonomy, although a many-faceted reality, is in general not the costly side of being a professional. Instead, it is part of the payoff. It is in most of its manifestations a privilege and power society grants the professions as a reward for exhibiting the other three more costly characteristics. It represents the privileges of insulation from lay interference, of control over training and admission of new members, of self-regulation, of defining appropriate professional practice, of—in some areas and some cases—establishing a virtual monopoly over certain important services, and of enjoying the increased income and status that often accompanies such a monopoly.

If this analysis is correct, one might say that with regard to the usual costs and benefits of being a profession, the clergy pay most of the costs and reap relatively few of the benefits.

In light of all of the above, I would argue that the professional ethics model is useful and appropriate for the clergy as far as it goes. Seen positively as the standards that guide professionals in their relations to clients and the larger society in light of the special skills and knowledge they claim to have, the distinctive goal they pursue in their professional activity, and the atypical moral commitment they aspire to, professional ethics sets a floor below which the clergy ought not fall. Where their activities overlap or coincide with those of other professionals, their conduct ought not fall below that of those other practitioners.

But seen, as they sometimes are, as the way professionals decide unilaterally how they will deal with clients, reflecting the power professionals wield over their clients (Veatch 1981, 6), professional ethics ought to be eschewed by the clergy. Furthermore, those dimensions of the clergy's calling that derive not from their acquired skills and knowledge, nor from the more or less empirical dimensions of the professional goal they pursue, but from the transcendent source of their ultimate authority as religious leaders, will have to be guided by standards deriving from sources other than some societal consensus about what it means to be a professional, or from some consensus of professional peers about what it means to be a professional of this specific sort. Clergy true to their calling will have to be open to the possibility that the higher ethic of the clergy, like that of the believer and of the community of faith itself, may on occasion call them to forsake all the security, the predictability, the prestige and other rewards of being a professionally ethical professional in contemporary society, and to stand outside, even stand over against a society that would seduce the clergy from their high calling by granting them professional status with all its perquisites. Professional status and the professional ethics attached to it may be a boon to the conscientious clergy in many ways. But they may also become a temptation, a seduction against which the clergy must be on

guard if it is to remain faithful to the distinctive commitment
that is at the very heart of its being.

References

Bledstein, Burton J. 1976. *The Culture of Professionalism: The Middle Class and the Development of Higher Education in America.* New York: W. W. Norton.

Camenisch, Paul F. 1983. *Grounding Professional Ethics in a Pluralistic Society.* New York: Haven Publications.

———. 1985. "Are Pastors Professionals?" *The Christian Ministry* 16, no. 4 (July): 12–13.

Holifield, Brooks E. 1983. *A History of Pastoral Care in America: From Salvation to Self-Realization.* Nashville: Abingdon Press.

Illich, Ivan. 1970. *Deschooling Society.* New York: Harper & Row.

———. 1977. *Medical Nemesis.* New York: Bantam Books.

Larson, Magali Sarfatti. 1977. *The Rise of Professionalism: A Sociological Analysis.* Berkeley: University of California Press.

Marty, Martin E. 1988. "The Clergy." In *The Professions in America,* edited by Nathan O. Hatch. Notre Dame, Ind.: University of Notre Dame Press.

Niebuhr, H. Richard. 1956. *The Purpose of the Church and Its Ministry.* New York: Harper & Brothers.

Noyce, Gaylord. 1988. *Pastoral Ethics: Professional Responsibilities of Clergy.* Nashville: Abingdon Press.

Scott, Donald M. 1978. *From Office to Profession: The New England Ministry 1750–1850.* Philadelphia: University of Pennsylvania Press.

Veatch, Robert M. 1981. *A Theory of Medical Ethics.* New York: Basic Books.

Selected Additional Works

Bayles, Michael D. 1981. *Professional Ethics.* Belmont, Calif.: Wadsworth Publishing Co.

Behrman, Jack N. 1988. *Essays on Ethics in Business and the Professions.* Englewood Cliffs, N.J.: Prentice-Hall.

Boyajian, Jane A., ed. 1984. *Ethical Issues in the Practice of the Ministry.* Minneapolis: United Seminary of the Twin Cities.

Browning, Don S. 1983. *Religious Ethics and Pastoral Care.* Philadelphia: Fortress Press.

Campbell, Alastair V. 1984. *Professional Care: Its Meaning and Practice.* Philadelphia: Fortress Press.

Campbell, Dennis M. 1982. *Doctors, Lawyers, Ministers: Christian Ethics in Professional Practice.* Nashville: Abingdon Press.

Harmon, Nolan B. 1928, 1987. *Ministerial Ethics and Etiquette.* Nashville: Abingdon Press.

Lebacqz, Karen. 1985. *Professional Ethics: Power and Paradox.* Nashville: Abingdon Press.

Reeck, Darrell. 1982. *Ethics for the Professions: A Christian Perspective.* Minneapolis: Augsburg Publishing House.

7

Ethos, Incarnation, and Responsibility

M. L. Brownsberger

Perspective depends on where you stand . . . or sit. For the past twenty years I have been sitting on the other side of the pulpit.[1] Six of those years were spent working in higher education and for a human rights commission. For the last fourteen years I've been in business. Included in these years are five in which I have engaged in part-time, tent-making ministries. Even including the four years in full-time, pastoral ministry, I have sat in the pew longer than I stood in the pulpit. It is from this perspective that I write about clergy ethics.

Everyone makes a living, a home, or both. Occupying forty to sixty hours a week, our work is the most powerful and pervasive organizing principle of our lives. It determines when we get up; when we eat; what we worry about; our life-style; our public identity; our family patterns; the form and content of our productivity, ambitions, and dreams; our health (to some degree); our voluntary memberships; and when we go to bed. Our work exerts a greater influence over the time, quality, and content of our lives than our family, our church, our politics, our cultural and aesthetic interests. Our work can even shape our moral posture on current issues. Our work is our public life, where what we do is "seen and heard by everybody" (Arendt 1958, 45), where we are paid to act, not simply

---

[1].Some of the material in this section has appeared in two articles by M. L. Brownsberger: "From the Other Side of the Pulpit," *The Christian Century* (August 27–September 3, 1986): 746–784; "Christian Faith and Business: A Story," *The Chicago Theological Seminary Register* 79, no. 4 (Fall 1989): 746–748.

to cope; to perform, not reform. And the work of a majority of pew sitters involves conducting the transactions of American business.

But in my years as a pew sitter, I have rarely heard a sermon, participated in a liturgy, heard a prayer, or repeated a confession that in any way recognized or affirmed or celebrated or commiserated with the work performance that engaged the majority of my waking life. Indeed, I don't recall a pastor talking with me about what I do to make my living. Perhaps that's part of the problem. It's difficult for anyone to respond to questions that don't have an occasion to be asked. I did hear sermons and liturgies and prayers dealing with the arts, with family, with politics, with church, with theology and ethics. However, these sermons, liturgies, and prayers tended to be more therapeutic or prophetic in "accent" (Stackhouse 1987, 162), focusing not on what I did forty to sixty hours a week but on those dimensions of my living that my work tends to dominate and support. My work constitutes a substantial portion of my "manner of life" (Phil. 1:27). Granted, I am more than what I do, but what I do is critical. This silence could be construed as a failure of vocation and as such is a topic for clergy ethics. What follows is a reflection from the pew on this silence.

The story is in two parts: one critical, the other constructive. Critically, I'll offer some anecdotal evidence presenting views from the pew about the silence of the pulpit regarding the manner of life of people in business. I'll suggest that this silence implies a discontinuity between the knowledge embodied in religious communities and the knowledge embodied in economic communities, a discontinuity not apparent in the pulpit's use of other bodies of knowledge such as sociology, history, political thought, or psychology. There seems to be an unspoken criterion of selectivity operating, which, in itself, implies an assumption of discontinuity.

Constructively, Alasdair MacIntyre's notion of a social practice with its internal and external goods provides a model by which the actual operations of clergy and business managers may be addressed. This model can provide a pastoral, if not ethical, link between the manner of life characteristic of both religious and economic practitioners, and can overcome any selective discontinuity. That "link," I will suggest, is an ethic of responsibility—a manner of life embedded in the ethos of our culture, one "worthy of the gospel" and of business activity. It is a manner of life clergy seek to incarnate in the lives of their people through their ministry; it is also a manner of life business people seek to embody in their structures and organizations. Both clergy and business practitioners are committed to and involved in making the ethic of responsibility live in the people they serve. If this is what both are doing, then for clergy, whose vocation includes preaching of the Word, the notion of responsibility can be an organizing principle for engaging the pew in what I will call the "ethics of the Word."

The Silence of the Pulpit

I received the first hints of the consequences of the pulpit's (and my own) silence on matters economic in a business ethics class I taught in a mainline Protestant church. Most of the participants were business people—top executives, middle managers, entrepreneurs. I opened with a couple of questions.

The first question: Do you feel any conflict between your understanding of Christian faith and what you do forty to sixty hours a week?
Some responses:
"No. I compartmentalize. If I had to worry about that on top of everything else, I'd never get anything done."
"No. There's a difference between family stuff and business. Church is family stuff."
"Every time a preacher tries to say something about business, I become more convinced he doesn't know what he's talking about."

The second question: Is the church—in its preaching, teaching, community life—supportive of what you do at work?
Some responses:
"No. Well, some of the guys around here are helpful, but generally, the church focuses on my personal life and on the social issues I should be concerned about. That's the way it should be. I don't want a preacher telling me how to run my business. There's no more a Christian way to run a business than there is a Christian way to pave a street."
"I agree. Some of the guys around here are helpful. But I don't talk to (my pastor) about my job. I don't think he's ever been involved in a corporation. What can he say that would be helpful?"

These responses reflect a rather low level of expectation on the part of the pew toward the pulpit about matters other than the therapeutic and the prophetic. They seem to echo the observation of Max Stackhouse: "Most contemporary pastors and theologians simply do not know what to think about [corporations], and their witness on economic matters is not believed by the laity who have accepted the corporation as the proper basis of economic life" (Stackhouse 1987, 122). The people in the class readily identified the therapeutic and the prophetic accents of the clergy and accepted the assumptions of the community's culture, but literally did not see the relevance of that model to their work nor the place of their work in that understanding of ministry. On the other hand, perhaps neither had been taught otherwise.

A comment of their pastor confirmed the lay people's perceptions and the operating assumptions of the community. When asked by one of his "corporately active" parishioners why he didn't preach on issues facing business people, especially because at least half of his congregation consisted of people involved in business corporations, he replied: "If I was interested in business, I wouldn't have gone into the ministry."

Again, the understandings of the lay people appear justified. It is echoed by William Diehl, a former executive of Bethlehem Steel: "My church really doesn't have the least interest in whether or not I minister in my daily work" (Diehl 1976, v). In spite of the lack of interest his church shows, layman Diehl is concerned; he has spoken and written on the subject of ministry in the workplace. This expectation and concern is again echoed by William Weiss, Chairman and CEO of Ameritech, in a talk at Fourth Presbyterian Church, Chicago, in 1986: "A well-known Chicago CEO said that, in all his time of faithfully attending church, he had perhaps only once heard anything remotely of use to him in his work. We need to hear more in the church about our vocation in the world of work. . . . Many [business people] felt their churches and synagogues failed to provide support for their vocation in the world of work."

I tried to do just that recently in a series of sermons relating Christian faith and ethics to work. The idea was simply to introduce some notions, including work as our public life and responsibility, that could be explored in greater depth should the interim period I was filling be extended. The response confirmed the above comments: "We've never heard that subject addressed from the pulpit. It should be done more often." "I've never heard anyone talk about Christian faith that way. Interesting." "When are you going to publish it? I want to send it to my son." And from a young man on a very fast track: "You are hitting close to home. I need to hear this stuff. Thanks." Before this experience, the relation of Christian faith to work was somewhat abstract, limited perhaps only to my own frustrations and influenced by the response of the class. After this series and other one-shot efforts, I am now convinced that pew sitters are as hungry as I was for the Word and the words addressed to the manner of life they live at work.

If people are hungry for this kind of word, how can churches and synagogues feed them? Gaylord Noyce may provide a clue. A few business people talked with him about some issues that were troubling them. His later comment: "Neither of these men had a *rationale* that could help him *morally integrate* his work, his faith and his idealism. . . . Neither had an *intellectual handle* or a community of moral support and criticism to help him cope with his schizoid experience in a capitalist economy" (Noyce 1981, 802. Emphasis mine.). Stated positively, the vocation of clergy is to assist people in "morally integrating" all dimensions of their lives. The traditions provide a range of "rationales" that can function as the "intellectual handles" needed for faithful living.

All this suggests that some lay people do not expect the pulpit to address the nontherapeutic and nonprophetic issues of their public working life; that preachers feed this expectation with their silence, if not spoken attitudes; that some people wish it were otherwise; and that when their public life is addressed, they are most appreciative. Further, these comments and responses suggest that clergy may be ignoring a substantial portion of the 'ethos' of their own congregations. It is ironic that, although some pastors may be "prophetically" critical of insider trading, fee skimming, work in the nuclear industry, industrial pollution, South African investment policies, and so forth, a number of pew sitters may be asking for guidance through the "moral mazes" (Jackall 1988) of their corporate employment and are being ignored. A cynic might get the impression that there is more psychic satisfaction in being "prophetic" than in listening to the people.

If there is one job clergy of all traditions share it is that of assisting their people to morally integrate their living in the light of those traditions. If that is not happening, then we have an issue for clergy ethics: clergy are failing at one of the basic jobs that is part of their calling.

If moral integration of faith and work in business is an aspiration worthy of pursuit, an assumption of continuity between and among all bodies of human knowledge is necessary. Otherwise, there is nothing to integrate. The notion of continuity lies at the heart of liberal theology (Cauthen 1962, 6). Without such an assumption, the bodies of psychological, sociological, scien-

tific, political, anthropological, archaeological, legal, and other
bodies of knowledge would be irrelevant to the "supernatural"
knowledge of religious communities. Nevertheless, much of
current theologizing is informed and influenced by just these
bodies of knowledge.

However, when we come to the economic knowledge that
undergirds such activities as wealth creation, deal making,
bureaucratic organization, trading, exchange, profit making,
money making, markets, and the consumption that drives it
all, the silence of the pulpit implies an epistemological discontinuity, at least in this arena. Clergy do speak and help people
cope; clergy do speak and urge people to be agents of reform.
But clergy simply don't seem to know what to do with or say
about the pattern and dynamics of economic organization that
has been emerging—and is emerging now on a global scale—
since the Civil War: the corporation (Chandler 1988, 202–225).
In not knowing, they may be failing to help the participants in
these historical dynamics achieve some degree of moral integration in the context that has become a fact of their work life.
To be unable or unwilling to deal with these facts is to imply
a discontinuity in knowledge and expectation that makes religious faith irrelevant in these organizational settings.

But, the church and its clergy have historically been in dialogue with their immediate culture. Indeed, because of that
dialogue, the churches have not only survived but flourished.
This process was not unique to the church. Virtually every
community, institution, or organization that survives its founding must engage its mission with that of the forces external to
it. Virtually all human communities are embedded in and
share the same dynamics of development. None live in a co-
coon uncontaminated by the forces external to them. To do so
would be to die. Each community must find its "market," must
discover the needs in the external environment to which its
internal mission can be effectively addressed.

In so doing, elements of that external environment are inevitably incorporated into its internal mission. By dealing with
and responding to the interplay of internal missions and the
forces and needs in the external environment, communities
are continually seeking to find a point at which both the internal and the external are brought into some kind of operation-
ally effective and functionally beneficial balance. Through the
processes of adaptation, assimilation, and, one could add, co-
optation and adoption, communities tend to acquire some of
the tints constituting the palette of the surrounding culture,
providing their own tints to that palette while simultaneously

and self-consciously maintaining their own distinctive coloration. In the pluralistic collage of our culture, the dynamics of development would also seem to be the dynamics of survival.

Religious communities have functioned no differently. They have taken rationalities, structures, and processes from the "external" culture—whether philosophical, scientific, political, social, or economic—and placed them in the service of the Word. After being so adopted, adapted, and transformed, those assimilated resources were returned to their origins different in hue, tone, and texture to become positive, integrating additions to the mixes that make up the cultural palette. By so doing, religious communities created, maintained, and improved their "niches" in the "moral ecologies" (Bellah et al. 1985, 40) of our civilization.

Religious communities and leaders may need to (1) reassert the practices that got them into their current positions in the first place; (2) seek access to the culture and ways of being accessible; (3) use the knowledge, techniques, and language of that culture in the development and propagation of their internal missions; (4) create new alternatives for self and social perception in the light of conditions as viable options for choosing; and (5) provide the resources for so choosing while maintaining and improving and clarifying the standards of the community of faith.

For communities to open themselves to the forces and dynamics that surround them is to risk becoming tainted by those forces. Religious communities, with their internal patterns of moral integration, may be especially sensitive to the valuational mice the external cat might drag in. It is out of such sensitivity that discontinuities begin to be built. This may be especially so in relation to the economic, deal-making, money-focused "mice" being dragged into the more altruistic theological house. But those mice are being dragged in by pew sitters. The mice are the values they live with and live by. Because religious communities may have forgotten how they established and maintained their integrating niches in the first place, they need to reassert these processes of adoption and adaptation, taking the risk of seeking to integrate and transform the mixes of the economic palette that paint the lives of pew sitters. If ethos is "that subtle web of values, meanings, purposes, expectations, obligations and legitimations that constitute the publicly operating norms of a civilization" (Stackhouse 1987, 114), then this is the content of the palette religious leaders must seek to understand.

My argument to this point is simply this: The silence of the pulpit about economic activity and toward the people who engage in such activity is based on an implicit belief in epistemological discontinuity. A consequence is a failure in the vocation of moral integration. By reasserting the historical patterns of engagement and continuity with the external culture that have rendered religious communities effective in the first place, this vocation can be reaffirmed. The solution is already sitting in the pew. The "terrain" of clergy ethics is that point at which the organizational rationalities and values and publicly operating norms of the social practices of both religious and nonreligious communities intersect. Ironically, that point is in the sanctuary where the pulpit and the pew are located. As such, it is the point from which all the issues of clergy ethics should be addressed.

During one of the seminar sessions from which this volume grew, I mentioned my concern about the silence and told the story about the pastor mentioned above who wasn't interested in business. One of the pastor members of the seminar said to me, "Bud, tell me. What do you do every day? I can learn from you." I was moved. That was the first time any pastor had ever asked that question. I told him, briefly. He asked more questions. I responded with some of my own about what he did. We both learned.

It occurred to me later that just by asking that question, this pastor was doing what good managers do: they ask their staff questions, share information, develop alternatives and choices, indicate standards, identify resources and commitment. It was a first step in my moral integration. The rationales and the values undergirding the social practices of pastors and managers of people are not that much different. There is much that is shared: a sense of obligation, values, purpose, expectation. The missions of our organizations are different, but so are the missions of different businesses and religious communities. I was reminded that business people fail in their vocations and for similar reasons: overlooking or ignoring the values of various groups and markets. That is an issue for business ethics. Clearly, there was a continuity of experience present in our conversation. The values we shared were out there for all to see. They were and are public.

It also occurred to me that the pastor had done what clergy have historically always done. He invited himself into my commercial life, thereby implicitly inviting me into his theological life. There was no discontinuity in the relationship. Our lives merged through our words and understanding. Two lives created a "third" (Buchler 1955, 80). That is what happens in dialogue. However, that such dialogue with the "corporately active" pew sitter is not a clearly identified good internal to the practice of ministry is what I am suggesting is a critical issue for clergy ethics.

Internal and External Goods

There is a continuity between the activities of the manager-business practitioner and the clergy. Both engage in social practices that have goods internal to their operation by which those practices are defined. For Alasdair MacIntyre, a "social practice" is

> any coherent and complex form of socially established cooperative human activity through which goods internal to that form ... are realized in the course of trying to achieve those standards of excellence which are appropriate to, and partially definitive of, that form of activity, with the result that human powers to achieve excellence, and human conceptions of the ends and goods involved are systematically extended.
>
> (MacIntyre 1984, 187)

On this definition, throwing a football, even skillfully, is not a social practice; the game of football is. Planting a tree is not a social practice; gardening is. Preaching, calling on people, singing with people, praying with people are not social practices; the work of ministry is.

For MacIntyre, two kinds of good are possible in any social practice: internal goods and external goods. Goods *internal* to a practice can only be achieved through engagement in one specific practice; can only be specified in terms of the practice itself; and can only be recognized by the experience of having participated in the practice (MacIntyre 1984, 188). Goods *external* to a specific practice are only derivative and contingently related to it; can be achieved through a variety of other ways; and "always" end up as "some individual's property or possession" (190). Examples of external goods for MacIntyre might find parallels in the temptations of Christ—money, fame, and power.

The distinction is helpful. For example, I was a manager in a pharmaceutical business. The goods internal to my operation were technical competence, promise keeping, employee support, profitability, product quality, customer satisfaction, internal and external reporting processes, governmental compliance. Internally, all these processes and forces had to be kept in some kind of balance if the internal mission of the corporation was to be fulfilled—profitably manufacturing safe, effective, high-quality pharmaceutical products. The goods external to this social practice are profit dollars, prestige, power, personal wealth. For MacIntyre, both internal and external goods are good. The distinction is helpful in assisting in the specification of those goods that are absolutely essential if there is to be a social practice at all, and those readily available goods that are not specific to the practice but do occur as a consequence of effectively performing the internal goods.

The distinction is also helpful in that it specifies a line the crossing of which violates the integrity of the goods internal to the practice. In my business, if I become more concerned with profit dollars than with profitability, I may engage in activities—legal and illegal—that might quickly produce those dollars, but in the process may violate the internal goods of business practice. The useful point is that when an external good (for example, for preachers, celebrity) crosses over the line and becomes an internal good pursued as if it were essential to the practice, other internal goods must be violated (activities that enhance celebrity use time needed for pastoral counseling and calling).

But although generally helpful, there are some problems. First, Jeffrey Stout (1988, 266–292) argues that the distinction, as drawn by MacIntyre, is too rigid. It cannot adequately account for the mediating positions of institutions. On the one hand, institutions do trade heavily in external goods, allocating money, fame, and power. To do so, they must establish and meet criteria of merit, desert, fairness, justice—standards that are internal to the practice of institutional allocation. This is management. On the other hand, extending Stout's insight, institutions, by virtue of their trading in external goods, provide the positive incentives and conditions by which the practice of the internal goods is created, maintained, improved, and perpetuated.

Three comments are in order. First, one of the basic jobs of a business manager is to organize the various technical and administrative resources so that the goods internal to the enterprise can be approximated. Part of that job is to establish the policies and procedures (practices) by which everyone is focused on doing just that. This is done according to criteria relevant not only to the goods internal to the technical practice of pharmaceutical manufacturing but also according to the goods internal to the practice of sound management. In our company, a dual focus is required to meet the goods internal to both pharmaceutical manufacturing and management.

Second, within the same organizational arrangements, goods external to one social practice may be internal to another. For the chemist, the practices of facilities development, equipment acquisition, finance, and production scheduling are not goods internal to the practice of chemistry. They are goods internal to the practice of business management. However, when these presumably external goods are not adequately met, the chemist is likely to raise the question, "How can you expect me to practice good chemistry if . . . ?" In these circumstances, both he or she and the manager become quickly aware of the "conditions providing" function of management and, hence, of institutions.

Third, and perhaps of more importance, by defining external goods as only "some individual's property or possessions," MacIntyre fails to see that few "things" exist independent of some kind of organizational arrangement (practice) set up for their allocation. What MacIntyre's distinction between internal and external goods amounts to is simply the differentiation between "performance goods" and "reward goods," with the former embedded in a practice but not the latter. Clearly, performance goods adhere to a practice. But surely, so do reward goods. Money, fame, and power are not some kind of magical manna dropping from heaven; they are allocated by some kind of system which, by definition, is a practice. It is difficult to conceive of any kind of good existing independent of some kind of social practice and hence, independent of some kind of organizational or institutional arrangement.

Stout is correct in pointing out MacIntyre's failure to appreciate the mediating function of institutions. Because institutions as such do not mediate, but their managers do, the focus then is on goods internal to management. The social practices of management and their goods enable a particular practice to in fact happen. Managers see to it that the practitioners have access, knowledge, alternatives, choices, resources, standards, and organizational (if not cultural) commitment by which the goods internal to those practices can be achieved and proper rewards or sanctions allocated.

The practice of management does not require the technical mastery of the internal goods to be effective or to be competent in the evaluation of outcomes. One doesn't need to be a Ph.D. chemist to organize a pharmaceutical firm; a layperson doesn't need to have an M.Div. to evaluate the effectiveness of a pastor; a pastor doesn't need to have an MBA (although a touch of economics would not hurt) to appreciate and speak to the work of commercial practitioners. What is required at the intersection is a sensitivity to what is going on in the mix—the ethos, the public norms operating among this people, at this time, in this place, with this history. Hence, I suggest "opportunity" or "mediating" goods be inserted between performance goods and reward goods.

If the notion of opportunity goods and practices has merit, then these are the goods that obtain at the intersection of the internal and the external. The purpose of the internal is to perform a practice with a high degree of excellence; the purpose of the external is to provide the incentives necessary so that the fundamental practice can be performed; the purpose of the opportunity goods and practices is to structure and organize the occasions and conditions by which the latter is balanced with the former so that something in fact happens. The job of the manager is to create the conditions by which the abstract becomes concrete. The job of the manager is to create sets of relationships, an organization, through which the pluralism of internal goods can be effectively practiced and the goods external to those practices judiciously allocated. The mediating position of the manager then requires not a dual but a trinitarian vision: goods internal to various practices, goods external to various practices, and the opportunity goods of managing the practices at the intersection. In the mix is both discovered and created the various publicly operating norms—the ethos of the organization.

From these norms the mediator/enabler is able to construct a framework that assumes the specific internal and external goods but whose purpose is to create a "third" that encompasses both—a third set of goods through which all the various goods become reality. The criterion of this "third," I suggest, is the principle of "incarnation": the processes by which abstract, disembodied practices and goods are enabled to become concrete and lived.

Such language is indigenous to the religious communities. In some sense, all claim that God has acted and is acting in history with empirical consequences. For Christians, Jesus *is* in person, *is* in human form, God's Word, will, and Son (Küng 1980, 685). If this is not true, "our faith is in vain." The calling of the clergy is to be an instrument of the Spirit by which God's Word in the person of God's Son abides in the lives of pew sitters. The job of pastor requires a trinitarian vision—conjoining the internal goods of the gospel with the external goods of the pew, and through the mix discovering and creating the ethos of the organization that enfolds all. On some views, the ongoing incarnation of God's Word is the church.

This language has operational value in economic organizational behavior as well. The job of the managers of such organizations is to bring ideas to the marketplace. Business managers make economic ideas become flesh in the economy. In this sense, it could be argued that "incarnation" is the practice, the purpose of organizations. If so, the principle of incarnation is a value shared by both clergy and business practitioners; it is part of their publicly shared ethos; it constitutes their respective responsibilities.

Responsibility

Responsibility is an ethical notion embedded in the American ethos; is a notion that both descriptively and normatively speaks to the process of incarnation; and as such, is a notion that indicates how we get from here to there. Ethos and incarnation define the terrain of clergy ethics; responsibility is its moral content.

The notion is relatively new (McKeon 1957). It was first used by John Jay in the *Federalist Papers,* "On Treaty Making" (#64) in 1787, a full seventy years before receiving any philosophical treatment.[2] The context of its use is significant. Americans had spent 180 years wresting physical places out of the undifferentiated spaces of the "wilderness." In the course of claiming this space (Sellers 1970, 22–25), they developed patterns of meaning and value—a subtle web of publicly operating norms—that rendered such phrases as "all men are created equal," "inalienable rights," and "We, the people" revolutionary in their historical and existential power. Having declared themselves independent of an absentee government, Americans now had to so constitute themselves domestically that all the many and various publicly operating norms and social practices could be shaped into a distinctive political, economic, and social entity suitable to the new context. But along with the domestic structures, the new government had to create mechanisms by which answers could be given to the complex international questions required of all nation-states—the regu-

---

[2]Some of the material in these paragraphs is drawn from M. L. Brownsberger and Dennis McCann, "Doing Business: A Theocentric Approach to Business Ethics," a paper presented at the January 1988 meeting of the Society for Christian Ethics. The model of responsibility developed here relies heavily on the work of Herbert Spiro, *Responsibility in Government: Theory and Practice* (New York: Van Nostrand Reinhold, 1969). To the five conditions Spiro outlines, Brownsberger has added "access" and "standards".

lation of trade and commerce, weights and measures, currency—so that the reciprocal relations and expectations that underlie all such political and economic practices could be made clear and reasonably predictable. Hence, treaty making—the formation of those international expectations—was an appropriate context for the introduction of the concept of responsibility.

The assumptions underlying treaty making highlight the three dimensions of responsibility: the internal, the external, and the reciprocal. Internally, a person acts, responding to circumstances out of his or her public role (for example, as an agent of a state or organization), contributing thereby to a course of events according to an internalized set of publicly accepted norms. Externally, by so acting, the agent expects a response that reflects the interrelated legal, economic, and political realities of the situation for which, on both counts (his or her action and the response received), he or she will be held accountable. A result of this activity is a structure of action and a structure of accountability, both of which bind the parties in a continuing reciprocal structure of obligation. The internal, external, and reciprocal dimensions of responsibility correspond, then, to responsibility as cause, responsibility as accountability, and responsibility as obligation. Therefore, responsibility means that people are responsible internally as to the beliefs and attitudes that inform and shape their interpretations of "what is going on"; are responsible externally as to social expectations and the responses their actions evoke; and are responsible reciprocally in assuring an obligatory congruence between the two. In other language, to be responsible is to feel the obligation to care about how the consequences of your actions have affected and will affect the interests of others as well as your own.

In this context, the phrase "we are all responsible for our own fate" makes some sense. The notion of "We, the people" covenanting together, pledging "our lives, our fortunes, our sacred honor" to create a government whose legitimacy is based on the "consent" of the governed, makes no sense unless there is consenting action taken by the governed for which the actors are mutually accountable and obligated. Being responsible for one's own fate has become a descriptive and normative "ought" adhering not only to our political life but also to our economic, social, and personal lives. Being responsible is an ethical assumption that lies at the heart of the American ethos.

If this is the case, we must ask an empirical question: What conditions must exist if a consenting people in fact are to be responsible for their fates and to be able to effect the reciprocity of interest? If I am to be able to insert myself into a course of events, make a "causal contribution" to those events, and be held accountable for that action, I must have *access* to those events and to the structures through which they are likely to occur; I must have *knowledge* of what is going on, of what needs doing, of what is expected of me; I must have real *alternatives* so I can do this and not that, be able to do otherwise; I must have the *capacity to choose,* the capacity of actually opting for this and not that, with the reasonable expectation of affecting the course of events; I must have the *resources* with which to effect choices and make a contribution; I must have *standards* by which to measure the outcomes of my choices; and I must have the *commitment* of the institutional system— whether political, economic, social, or personal—to assure provision of these conditions.

If I am to be responsible in any and all of the three dimensions of responsibility, I must have access, knowledge, alternatives, the capacity to choose, resources with which to effect my choices, standards, and the committed obligation of the institutional arrangements to provide this necessary substance. When all of these conditions are in reasonable balance, I am in a *fair situation of responsibility.* If they are not, I am not unlike black people in the period prior to and, to perhaps a decreasing extent during, the civil rights movement. At the very least, this was a movement to gain access to all manners of life so that choices could be expanded, resources garnered, and commitments made by which blacks could in fact have greater control over their individual and collective fates. "I have a dream," if nothing else, was the cry of the black community to be provided with some organizational (political) commitment whereby their aspirations could be linked with the American ethos. If nothing else, the civil rights movement was a quest to realize the conditions of responsibility within not only the black community but within the ethos of American life itself. It was and still is a demand for the right to be responsible. It may be arguable whether the movement succeeded. What is not debatable is the fact that the quest is now embodied in the structures of law and government. What is not debatable is that the quest is now incarnate in the behavior, if not values, of a large majority of American people. In pursuing their quest, the black community made Americans generally more responsible.

Descriptively then, these conditions must exist if I am to be responsible for my own fate. Because I need the support of the institutional arrangements for the provision of these conditions, I cannot be responsible for my fate alone. Hence, the descriptive conditions become a normative (prophetic?) imperative: *create, maintain, improve situations of responsibility for yourself and others.*

The "and others" in the imperative sharpens the focus. We are not human alone. To be human is to be in relation. It is in relation that the values, meanings, and so forth, of a culture's ethos are created, maintained, and improved, and that people are enabled to continue to consent to being responsible for their fate. To exercise responsibility is to empower others and therefore one's self so that reciprocally each has the capacity to act and each can answer to the other for outcome. The individual dimension of action and the corporate dimension of accountability combine in the reciprocal dimension of the obligation to the "and others." In effect, we make each other responsible by creating, maintaining, and improving situations of responsibility for ourselves *and others.* The civil rights movement made us all more responsible.

We can now speak directly to the principle and process of incarnation. God has acted in our history, our ethos, creating situations of responsibility for the Divine Life and others. By Word and by Spirit, God creates by organizing, directing, and focusing the unorganized, the misdirected, the undifferentiated powers of chaos into organizational and relational systems formed around the conditions and norms of responsibility. The conditions and norms of responsibility constitute the moral ecology of creation; they are the conditions and norms of covenant; they are also the conditions and norms of reconciliation. Through God's activity among us, we have been granted at least the seven conditions of responsibility and, in varying ways, have been called to exercise faithfully the subsequent imperative ("do unto others . . . "). We occasionally remember—but more often painfully forget yet are nevertheless reminded through sacred writings, traditions, reason, and experiences—that we are not responsible alone. As God has acted toward us, we act toward each other, covenanting to make each other responsible as per the imperative. We thereby participate in God's ongoing acts of creation, of incarnation.

To do so is to participate in the formation of the structural means that embody the conditions of responsibility, the organizational arrangements that constitute any covenant-based community. Incarnation requires a theology of institutions, a theology that links religious communities who seek to embody their traditions in people and other organizations who seek to do the same. Both contribute to the palette of culture, linked by the ethos—the publicly operating norms that already exist as a consequence of God's action, the content of which is, in part, the conditions of responsibility and their imperative. In short, as two or more organizations or people are gathered, there is created a "third" reality—the relation itself, its life and its outcomes. What may have existed only in the abstract or in the imagination of potential participants is now concrete in this new "third." For this new entity to continue to be viable, the conditions of responsibility are necessary prerequisites. The emergence of this new "third" is incarnation.

The content of the intersection of the religious and the economic is the subtle web of values that constitutes the ethos of a culture. Incarnation is one way to describe the processes by which the new "third" is formed out of dialogue. Responsibility—its conditions and imperative—sets forth the descriptive and normative process of embodiment as well as its controlling ethical purpose. A concept of ministry that entails all of the above broadens the definition of "professional" and specifies its application.

Ministry as a Field-Encompassing Practice

If ministry occurs where the various elements of the "subtle web" converge, then clearly ministry embraces a broad spectrum of virtues and values and aspirations that are integral to an equally broad spectrum of social practices. Each of these practices has its own generally accepted principles and procedures (GAPPs) for establishing the lived truths, the lived meanings, the lived values that constitute and are specific to that practice. Within these GAPPs are patterns of argument, criteria as to relevant evidence, and procedures for organizing that evidence into a practice-specific pattern of meaning and behavior. Each practice then generates its own "field of argument" (Harvey 1966, 49–65) that contains the essential constructs, processes, and procedures specific to that practice. These fields of argument become "force fields" that obligate the practitioners to obey not only the rules that govern the practice but also the ethos in which those rules are embedded. To the degree that ministry, in pursuing the historical processes of adoption, adaptation, and assimilation embraces the practices of the external environment and their "fields of force," ministry, in the words of Van Harvey, is a "field encompassing field."

Harvey, following the analyses of Stephen Toulmin (1986), likens the practice of history to the practice of law. Like a lawyer, a historian will deal with a variety of fields—psychology, economics, sociology, linguistics, diplomacy, archaeology—to arrive at an explanation not only of what happened but why. Each of these fields has its own GAPPs that the historian must mold into patterns appropriate to the GAPPs of the practice of history. Clearly, the practices of history and law are "field-encompassing fields." To law and history could be added the field-encompassing fields and practices of medicine, accounting, and, I would suggest, management.

From this point, it is possible to go in two directions in discussing the question of "profession" as it relates to clergy practice. On the one hand, if GAPPs are used as a primary measure for how professional knowledge is generated and used, clergy practice would not fit this criterion. GAPPs represent an operational consensus formed around a body of knowledge that serves some ultimate values. These values are embodied in a set of standards enforced by a peer group of practitioners within an institutional matrix. If this is the measure, then clergy practice is not a profession. For underlying the GAPPs is an "if-then logic" in which there are subsets of GAPPs by which the "if" can be determined, a subset by which the move from the "if" to the "then" is governed, and a subset for implementing the "then." In medicine, the field-encompassing knowledge by which the "ifs" of diagnoses are established leads to the consensus "thens" of treatment. In ministry, however, there is no such general consensus on either the "ifs" or the "thens"; there is no agreement on the defined meaning (as opposed to usage) of the principle by which its practice is organized; there are no GAPPs. On the knowledge criterion, clergy practice is outside one of the fundamental measures typically used to define a profession.

On the other hand, if the notion of field-encompassing practice were added to the standard criteria by which a profession is defined, clergy practice would join, unambiguously, with medicine, law, accounting, engineering, and management as a professional practice. Clearly, ministry is a practice that encompasses many fields in dialogue. To preach a sermon on, for example, abortion, may entail dealing with the truth claims and conclusions from a variety of fields: biblical criticism and interpretation; "official" positions of the religious communities; political, legal, and social histories relating to the status of women; psychology and sociology of sexuality and sex education; issues relating to medical practice, not the least of which

is definitions of "life." Whether the focus is on preaching, counseling, pastoral calling, administration, or the public pursuit of
social issues, there is little in the practice of ministry that does
not encompass a broad spectrum of force fields and practices.
By this criterion, ministry is clearly a profession.

It is in this context, then, that the notion of the "ethics of
the Word" makes some real world sense. All religious communities claim that the Word to which they respond is an
all-encompassing Word, a Word that embraces all of life.
("Neither death, nor life . . . will be able to separate us . . ."
[Romans 8:38].) In other language, the Word is field and practice encompassing. Indeed, it was and is on this assumption
that religious communities have adopted, adapted, co-opted
elements of the ethos encountered at the intersections of
fields, placed them in the service of the Word, and so survived and grew. They did so by asking, What is going on?
(Niebuhr 1963, 60) and by acting so as to create, maintain,
and improve situations of responsibility for themselves and
others.

Therefore, the ethics involved in the terrain of this profession, so understood, is focused on something other than what
should be commonsensically assumed about any practice. For
clergy, faithfulness to the scriptures, traditions, religious rea-
soning, and experiences of their foundations; faithfulness to
the person involved in the counseling relationship; loyalty and
integrity and trustworthiness in relation to colleagues are all
reflective of those responsibilities that adhere to the role and
its social expectations, and of goods internal to the practice of
ministry (Noyce 1988). However, it does not take a moral genius to know that one who stands under the discipline of the
Word in preaching should not use the pulpit for propagandiz-
ing one's own opinions; to know that one should not violate the
counselee either verbally or physically; to know that it is generally a good idea to establish positive relations with one's
colleagues. But it does take considerably more moral sensitivity to ask after and to develop the practice-specific definition
of the ethical and the practice-specific reasons therefore. It
does take considerably more energy to discern what is going
on than it does to jump into the rule-asking question, What
should I do? To discover what is going on requires engagement
in conversation—in dialogue with practitioners of the practices that constitute what is going on and the subtle web of
values that make up the ethos of both our culture and our
religious communities. And in our culture and communities, the energy driving our living is the force fields found in

the economic organizations in which most pew sitters are employed.

The ethic of the Word, then, begins with the ethics of conversation, the basic conditions of which are the conditions of responsibility and its imperative. Sermonically, therapeutically, prophetically, relationally, it seeks to provide access when access has been denied; it seeks to know when knowledge has been kept hidden; it seeks to find and provide alternatives when hope has been abandoned; it seeks to enable choices when that freedom has been constrained; it seeks to provide resources when vulnerability diminishes the capacity to control one's own fate; it seeks standards that are not only right and good but, of more importance, fitting; and it seeks the reciprocity of love and support that humans are obliged in faith to give one to another.

To be a responsible pastor is to be an agent of reconciliation. A mediator/helper in dialogue with the various fields of force and their various internal and external goods seeks through the Word to form a "third" by and through whose mediation all may participate in the ongoing incarnating and opportunity-creating spirit of the organization. Ministry is asking, "Bud, what do you do? I can learn from you," as did my colleague in the Clergy Ethics Seminar.

Ministry, then, is a field-encompassing practice, embracing within its vocation the intention to create, maintain, and improve situations of responsibility for its own practices and the practices of others. It is a profession that creates opportunities for both pew sitters and pulpiteers to be responsible internally as to the beliefs that inform their interpretations of "what is going on"; externally as to social needs and expectations; and reciprocally in assuring a congruence between the two. It is a vocation of enabling the creation, maintenance, and improvement of the structures of human conversation and organization so that people are provided the means for being responsible for their own fates and effective in the performance of the goods internal to their practices. It is the work of creating the conditions by which something can in fact happen. It is the work of incarnating responsibility, which is perhaps what God did in the first place and in whose name ministry is to be effected. The practice of ministry, then, is the practice of the ethic of the Word.

References

Arendt, Hannah. 1958. *The Human Condition.* New York: Doubleday & Co.

Bellah, Robert N., Richard Madsen, William M. Sullivan, Ann Swidler, and Steven M. Tipton. 1985. *Habits of the Heart: Individualism and Commitment in American Life.* Berkeley: University of California Press.

Buchler, Justus, ed. 1955. *Philosophical Writings of Peirce.* New York: Dover Publications.

Cauthen, Kenneth. 1962. *The Impact of American Religious Liberalism.* New York: Harper & Row.

Chandler, Alfred D., Jr. 1990. *Scale and Scope: The Dynamics of Industrial Capitalism.* Cambridge: Harvard University Press, Belknap Press.

———.1988. "The Organization of Manufacturing and Transportation," in *The Essential Alfred Chandler: Essays Toward a Historical Theory of Big Business,* ed. Thomas K. McCraw. Boston: Harvard Business School.

Diehl, William. 1976. *Christianity and Real Life.* Philadelphia: Fortress Press.

Harvey, Van Austin. 1966. *The Historian and the Believer.* New York: Macmillan.

Jackall, Robert. 1988. *Moral Mazes: The World of the Corporate Managers.* New York: Oxford University Press.

Küng, Hans. *Does God Exist?* Garden City, N.Y.: Doubleday & Co.

MacIntyre, Alasdair. 1984. *After Virtue.* Notre Dame, Ind.: University of Notre Dame Press.

McKeon, Richard. 1957. "The Development and the Significance of the Concept of Responsibility." *Revue internationale de Philosophie* 39 (1): 3–32.

Niebuhr, H. Richard. 1963. *The Responsible Self.* New York: Harper & Row.

Noyce, Gaylord. 1981. "The Dilemmas of Christians in Business." *The Christian Century* (August 12–19): 802–804.

———.1988. *Pastoral Ethics: Professional Responsibilities of Clergy.* Nashville: Abingdon Press.

Sellers, James. 1970. *Public Ethics: American Morals and Manners.* New York: Harper & Row.

Stackhouse, Max L. 1987. *Public Theology and Political Economy.* Grand Rapids: Wm. B. Eerdmans.

Stout, Jeffrey. 1988. *Ethics After Babel.* Boston: Beacon Press.

Toulmin, Stephen. 1958. *The Uses of Argument.* New York: Cambridge University Press.

Selected Additional Works

Douglas, Mary. 1986. *How Institutions Think.* New York: Syracuse University Press.

Hatch, Nathan. 1988. *The Professions in American History.* Notre Dame, Ind.: University of Notre Dame Press.

Jonsen, Albert R. 1968. *Responsibility in Modern Religious Ethics.* Cleveland: Corpus Publications.

Kammen, Michael, ed. 1971. *The Contrapuntal Civilization.* New York: Thomas Y. Crowell Co.

McCann, Dennis, and Charles R. Strain. 1985. *Polity and Praxis: A Program for American Practical Theology.* Chicago: Winston Press.

Reeck, Darrell. 1982. *Ethics for the Professions: A Christian Perspective.* Minneapolis: Augsburg Publishing House.

Spiro, Herbert J. 1969. *Responsibility in Government: Theory and Practice.* New York: D. Van Nostrand.

8

Costing Discipleship:
Clergy Ethics
in a Commercial Civilization

Dennis P. McCann

Is there any valid norm, or indispensable first principle, by
which to set priorities for clergy ethics in contemporary America? If so, how is it to be recognized; and once recognized, how
is it to be asserted persuasively in a secular epoch of modernity? If, as Martin Marty has already suggested in this volume,
ours is a polity that subordinates church and clergy to the civil
concerns of the republic, and if the churches by and large have
adapted their theologies to this situation, the question is
whether there is or ought to be any distinctively and perennially religious imperative at the core of clergy ethics by which
to limit and challenge this process of accommodation. This way
of formulating the normative question precludes straightforwardly traditional answers based on either scripture or any
given community's tradition, for, as Marty's analysis implies,
among the first casualties of this secular epoch is the undisputed authority of "theological-ecclesiastical norms." Alternatively, the way forward may be conceived as an "immanent
criticism" (Troeltsch 1977, 142; McCann and Strain 1985, 77–
80) in which one's ethical reflection is informed by historical
and social scientific study, not only of the phenomena of organized religion, but also of its function within society as a whole.

To seek a normative basis for clergy ethics in contemporary
America, we must probe more deeply into the actual characteristics of this secular epoch and the place of organized religion within it. Furthermore, our perspective on this
development must itself be secular; that is, we must understand the history of religion in America from outside, because

the whole that we are to envision is itself secular and not overtly religious. We must understand the societal context in which Marty's "contractual-entrepreneurial" model of ministry emerges and its consequences for further development. I will therefore outline a perspective drawn from a selection of social scientists concerned with the cultural and political dynamics of contemporary American society. From their observations, the first principle of clergy ethics may be inferred, not straightforwardly from scripture or tradition, but ironically from its striking absence in the culture and politics of secular modernity. Once that first principle appears, I will turn to the work of cultural anthropologists and to the theological reflections of Reinhold Niebuhr to guide this exercise in immanent criticism. The result will be a practical hypothesis about what clergy ethics must be about if American clergy are to discharge the burden of "moral specialization" that Marty, following Tocqueville, discerns at the heart of this secular epoch's continuing need for their ministry.

So much for the methodology. As for substance, I will argue that a capacity for self-sacrifice is and ought to be the indispensable first principle for clergy ethics, regardless of specific denominational traditions, precisely because the role of the clergy in any society is to be the institutional bearers of whatever learning and teaching about sacrifice inevitably goes on in that society. Their distinctive relationship to the social logic of sacrifice does and must continue to differentiate clergy ethics from other forms of professional ethics, including the ethics of business management, on the one hand, and therapeutic counseling, on the other. If this argument is plausible, it will help clergy to understand the distinctive nature of the vocation to which they have responded, and the high moral standards that are imposed upon them, not only by their peers but also, and especially, by the laity they serve.

"Civil Disinterestedness": The Need for Sacrifice in a Commercial Civilization

It is useful to remember that the epoch of secular modernity in America has taken the specific form of a commercial civilization. Thinking of American history in this way, however, not only challenges the theologian's preferred assumption that Christianity has been the decisively active force in shaping American cultural history, a convenient view that allows the clergy to see themselves as significant agents of social change.

It asserts instead the primacy of our struggle to organize a national economy within the emerging global economic system, a view in which the history of America's distinctive set of political and cultural institutions—including organized religion and the role of the clergy within it—is seen as responsive to that struggle and subject to various modifications, subtle and not so subtle, in light of it.

Within such a perspective, the development of the Christian churches in America—as well as our other institutions—can be interpreted in light of two major developments, commonly recognized as decisive in that struggle. It is not my purpose to develop an argument to support this historical interpretation, but merely to suggest its most salient themes: first, the rise of the entrepreneurial ethos characteristic of antebellum America, especially in the states where slavery was prohibited, and its relationship to the distinctive provisions of the U.S. Constitution encouraging commerce; second, its transformation during the period between the Civil War and World War I into the still dominant managerial ethos, marked by the simultaneous emergence of the modern business corporation and the federal regulatory system. The vicissitudes of Marty's "contractual-entrepreneurial" model of ministry are best understood in light of this perspective and, as I hope to show here, so is the normative question about clergy ethics today.

The studies offered by Robert Bellah and associates in *Habits of the Heart: Individualism and Commitment in American Life* (1985) allow us to move from these clues regarding the origins of America's development as a commercial civilization to a more detailed assessment of its cultural consequences. Among the relevant points made by the Bellah group is the assertion that contemporary American culture, having cut loose from its traditional moorings in biblical religion and civil republicanism, finds itself drifting aimlessly in the eddies of "utilitarian individualism" and "expressive individualism." Following the brilliant diagnostic hunches of Alasdair MacIntyre's *After Virtue: A Study in Moral Theory* (1981), the Bellah group seeks to correlate these dominant ideologies with a pair of "representative characters" (Bellah et al. 1985, 39), the "manager" (44–46), and the "therapist" (47–48), who have become the chief agents through which these ideologies are entrenching themselves in various sectors of our society. In particular, it is Bellah's "manager" who, as the embodiment of utilitarian individualism, currently represents the values of a commercial civilization, especially in the world of modern business corporations. To the extent that the process of accommodation that Marty described goes on within the churches, we can expect that clergy ethics will increasingly reflect the values and competences exhibited by the manager and the therapist.

The Bellah group describes the manager's function in the following way:

> The essence of the manager's task is to organize the human and nonhuman resources available to the organization that employs him so as to improve its position in the marketplace. His role is to persuade, inspire, manipulate, cajole, and intimidate those he manages so that his organization measures up to criteria of effectiveness shaped ultimately by the market but specifically by the expectations of those in control of his organization—finally, its owners. The manager's view of things is akin to that of the technician of industrial society par excellence, the engineer, except that the manager must admit of interpersonal responses and personalities, including his own, into the calculation of effectiveness.
>
> (Bellah et al. 1985, 45)

The manager thus is the agent of a process of bureaucratic rationalization that not only transformed enterprises into modern business corporations, but also increasingly reconfigures even the basic cluster of relationships that constitutes the "moral ecology" of our society:

> The most distinctive aspect of twentieth-century American society is the division of life into a number of separate functional sectors: home and workplace, work and leisure, white collar and blue collar, public and private. This division suited the needs of the bureaucratic industrial corporations that provided the model for our preferred means of organizing society by the balancing and linking of sectors as "departments" in a functional whole, as in a great business enterprise. Particularly powerful in molding our contemporary sense of things has been the division between the various "tracks" to achievement laid out in schools, corporation, government, and the professions, on the one hand, and the balancing life-sectors of home, personal ties, and "leisure," on the other.
>
> (Bellah et al. 1985, 43)

Though one may quarrel with the Bellah group's excessively negative evaluation of the ethos of bureaucratic management and their tendency to sentimentalize the moral ecology of preindustrial America, I am persuaded that they are essentially correct in recognizing that the advent of the "Era of Big

Business" nearly a century ago was decisive for shaping the framework of purposes and procedures according to which most contemporary institutions continue to operate.

Robert Jackall's recent work *Moral Mazes: The World of the Corporate Managers* (1988) not only corroborates the Bellah group's suspicion that "a professionalism without content is widespread among those in the higher echelons of American society" (Bellah et al. 1985, 210); it also allows us to examine more closely how many managers regard themselves in the new world of corporate bureaucracy. In the modern business corporation, argues Jackall, the "work ethic" has given way to a "success ethic," according to which managers will do whatever is necessary to get promoted. Jackall's point may be appreciated by considering the moral significance of three work-related terms: *vocation, career,* and *jobs.* Though the entrepreneurs who founded the company may have acted out of a sense of vocation, in the classical Protestant understanding of the term, corporate managers think and act primarily out of their career interests, which are not necessarily convergent with those of the firms that employ them. Those who are managed have "just a job." The pursuit of a career, though often idealized through the rhetoric of professionalism, tends to reinforce the individualisms described by the Bellah group, for it assumes that managerial skills are readily transferable. Therefore a successful manager can be expected to make several career moves within the same firm, if it is large and diverse enough, or from firm to firm within a given industry or "profession."

The ethic of success, as Jackall observes it, however, is based on a subtle and distinctively American adaptation of the Weberian model of bureaucratic organization. Though the essential strategy remains one of rationalization, once in place the bureaucratic structure is compromised by feudal networks of personal loyalties. Jackall coins the phrase "patrimonial bureaucracy" to characterize its divergence from the Weberian ideal type:

> In this world [of the patrimonial bureaucracy], a subordinate owes fealty principally to his immediate boss. This means that a subordinate must not overcommit his boss, lest his boss "get on the hook" for promises that cannot be kept. He must keep his boss from making mistakes, particularly public ones; he must keep his boss informed, lest his boss get "blindsided." . . . A subordinate must also not circumvent his boss nor ever give the appearance of doing so. He must never contradict his boss's

> judgment in public. . . . On a social level, even though an easy,
> breezy, first-name informality is the prevalent style of American
> business, a concession perhaps to our democratic heritage and
> egalitarian rhetoric, the subordinate must extend to the boss a
> certain ritual deference. . . . In short, the subordinate must sym-
> bolically reinforce at every turn his own subordination and his
> willing acceptance of the obligations of fealty.
>
> (Jackall 1988, 19)

Other indications of the patrimonial character of corporate
bureaucracies mentioned by Jackall are the "patron-client relationships" by which subordinates are moved onto "the fast
track" for promotion, and the ideology of "team play" by
which the not surprisingly frequent departures from strictly
meritocratic outcomes are legitimated. The result echoes one's
worst fears that nihilism, after all, may lurk at the heart of the
culture of modernity:

> In short, bureaucracy creates for managers a Calvinist world
> without a Calvinist God, a world marked with the same pro-
> found anxiety that characterized the old Protestant ethic but
> one stripped of that ideology's comforting illusions. Bureaucracy
> poses for managers an intricate set of moral mazes that are
> paradigmatic of the quandaries of public life in our social order.
> Within this framework, the puzzle for many individual manag-
> ers becomes: How does one act in such a world and maintain a
> sense of personal integrity?
>
> (Jackall 1988, 193–194)

Jackall does not look to the clergy for leadership in finding a
way out of this set of moral mazes; nevertheless, it seems clear
that he would regard the clergy as becoming increasingly irrelevant to the extent that they accommodate themselves and
their profession to the values and assumptions of bureaucratic
management.

A similarly bleak picture of the cultural consequences of
utilitarian individualism is evident in Lester Thurow's *The
Zero-Sum Society.* Writing on the eve of the so-called Reagan
revolution, Thurow pictures contemporary America as para-
lyzed by a "political process that is incapable of forcing anyone
to shoulder [the] burden [of large economic losses]" (Thurow
1981, 11). In his view, we as a nation have forgotten how to
make sacrifices, how to accept them voluntarily, how to impose them fairly upon others. Because every organized political constituency is quick to understand the potential economic
benefits and burdens of any shift in public policy, each group

stands poised, in Thurow's view, to veto any policy that will seek to benefit society as a whole by allocating losses to itself. True, in describing this public policy impasse, Thurow does not use the term "sacrifice"; but he does speak of the need to establish a civic "disinterestedness"; that is, "a capacity for disinterested decision-making . . . in a political process in which everyone has a direct self-interest" (16). Civic disinterestedness, in other words, is the missing capacity to envision and act habitually in behalf of the common good.

The argument from the absence of something is never convincing in and of itself, but it may serve as an important sign pointing in a more positive direction. If civic disinterestedness is indeed in short supply, we must ask ourselves, Where does it come from? From what source is the demand for disinterestedness likely to be satisfied? Unfortunately, Thurow hasn't a clue. His book contains several masterly analyses of contemporary social and economic problems, including solutions that will work, if only the losses implicit in them can be allocated freely and fairly. Though he sensibly seeks to avoid policies that would intensify zero-sum thinking by abandoning "either economic progress or economic security" (Thurow 1981, 22), his best advice for coping with the residue of zero-sum problems is to transform our current political parties into disciplined ideological cadres similar to those that operate within the British parliamentary system. This may serve to bring the conflicts over allocation of losses out into the open, but it will hardly satisfy the demand for civic disinterestedness. Intensified ideological partisanship rarely advances us toward the common good. Perhaps the source of civic disinterestedness lies deeper than politics.

Despite Thurow's inattention to the cultural dynamics of the zero-sum society, his point may move us beyond the general diagnosis offered by Bellah and Jackall to a more precise understanding of its implications for clergy ethics. The Bellah group, after all, proposes to overcome the excesses of utilitarian individualism embodied in the cultural hegemony of the managerial style in public life by keeping alive the distinctively American synthesis of biblical religion and civil republicanism. They look hopefully to clergy, like Father Paul Morrison, and religious communities, like the parish he serves, St. Stephen's Episcopal Church in the San Francisco Bay area, to embody this synthesis as participating communions within a "public church" (Bellah et al. 1985, 238–243). But how can our religious communities succeed in transforming American individualism in this way if, as Marty suggests, their own practices are already accommodated to the utilitarianisms that dominate this secular epoch? Organized religion can help make up the deficit in civic disinterestedness depicted by Thurow and can play the role assigned to it by the Bellah group only if there is a renewal of clergy ethics based on a recovery of first principles. For disinterestedness is the routine outcome of the one social practice that historically has been distinctive of the clergy, namely, the social practice of sacrifice. With the increasing atrophy of sacrifice, especially among a thoroughly modernized clergy, we can hardly expect to find within ourselves, and our society as a whole, deep reserves of disinterestedness. Conversely, were the clergy to recover the meaning of sacrifice and embody it ethically, the religious communities they serve seem more likely to fulfill the role that the Bellah group quite properly assigns to them.

Recovering the Meaning of Sacrifice for Clergy Ethics

"Sacrifice," according to the *Encyclopaedia Britannica*, "is a religious rite in which an object is offered to a divinity in order to establish, maintain or restore a right relationship of man [*sic*] to the sacred order" (*Encyclopaedia Britannica* 1974, 16:128). The *Encyclopedia of Religion* adds that the word *sacrifice* "carries the connotation of the religious act in the highest, or fullest sense; it can also be understood as the act of sanctifying or consecrating an object" (Henninger 1987, 12:544). The explanations accompanying these definitions emphasize not only the cultic aspects of sacrifice but also a range of motives, for it is best understood within a paradigm of exchange. As the *Encyclopaedia Britannica* observes:

> In a sense what is always offered in sacrifice, in one form or another, is life itself. Sacrifice is a celebration of life, a recognition of its divine and imperishable nature. In the sacrifice the consecrated life of an offering is liberated as a sacred potency that establishes a bond between the sacrificer and the sacred power. Through sacrifice, life is returned to its divine source, regenerating the power or life of that source; life is fed by life.
> (*Encyclopaedia Britannica* 1974, 16:128)

Such an exchange involving the gift of life is well symbolized by the ancient Latin formula *"Do ut des"* ("I give that you may give.").

Though sacrifice antedates the emergence of either urban societies or patriarchal cultures, evidence of its association with clergy or cultic functionaries seems to begin with agrarian or food-planting civilizations. In archaic high cultures, this cultic function is the disputed possession of both priests and kings. But in Israelite religion and later in Christianity, the link between priesthood and cultic sacrifice is clearly established, the Hebrew cult eventually focusing upon the practices of the Temple priesthood in Jerusalem, and the Christian cult focusing on the ritual of the Lord's Supper, understood as the reenactment or commemoration of the self-sacrifice of Jesus Christ, the High Priest of the New Covenant. Throughout the history of sacrificial practices in virtually all high cultures, but especially characteristic of Western civilization, can be found "tendencies to the spiritualization and ethicization of sacrifice" (cf. Henninger 1987, 12:556). Hence there seems to be unbroken continuity from the ritual offerings of archaic civilizations to the ethical writings of modern American theologians, like Reinhold Niebuhr, who still defend the moral necessity of sacrificial love.

The role of the clergy in the moral ecology of civilizations, of course, must be seen within this pattern of historical continuity:

> The more fully articulated the divisions in a society, the more often there is a class of cultic ministers to whom the offering of sacrifice is reserved. . . . When a special priestly class exists, membership is either hereditary or must be earned through a consecration that is often preceded by lengthy training. . . . The consecrated functionary who is an offerer of sacrifice often must then submit to further special preparation (through purificatory rites, etc.) before exercising his office. A priest may have other cultic or magical functions in addition to that of offering sacrifice; he may, for example, act as oracle, exorcist, healer, or rainmaker, he may be a source of tradition and knowledge, and he may have noncultic functions as well.
>
> (Henninger 1987, 12:545)

The conventional distinction of clergy and laity, in short, has its origins in the social practice of sacrifice. This division of labor relative to the community's relationships with the sacred appears to be the original impetus for the professionalization of the clergy, as well as the laity's routine expectations that the life-style of the clergy be qualitatively different, symbolizing or embodying the degree of holiness appropriate to divine commerce with the sacred. Though other public functions, both religious and communal, have historically become attached to the clergy, these seem to have been secondary and contingent upon the clergy's primary cultic role relative to the social practice of sacrifice.

With this general anthropological perspective in mind, we must consider more carefully the "spiritualization and ethicization of sacrifice," which is a common feature of this social practice, even in archaic civilizations, and not the unique discovery of the Hebrew prophets. Otherwise, the anthropological perspective just sketched may seem relevant only to neo-pagans and pre–Vatican II Catholics, but utterly irrelevant to most Protestant ministers and all Jewish rabbis. A comprehensive interpretation of Jewish and Christian traditions would have to show the continuities between the archaic practices just described and the spiritualized and ethicized forms of sacrifice featured prominently in these traditions. How do the moral teachings of the rabbis emerge from and complement the cultic practices of the Temple priesthood? What is the common ground linking the traditional Catholic interpretation of the "Holy Sacrifice of the Mass" and Protestant understandings of the "Lord's Supper"? Developing an awareness of these historical continuities, of course, would make clear within both Jewish and Christian traditions the historical as well as logical priority of the cultic practices of sacrifice for creating and maintaining the subsequent ministries of preaching, teaching, and pastoral counseling. The social practice of sacrifice, in both Jewish and Christian traditions, may have been spiritualized and ethicized, but it has never been abandoned altogether.

Let us consider briefly the Christian New Testament's Letter to the Hebrews as significant evidence of this pattern of continuity. Whether scholars can sustain the Pauline authorship of this Letter, for our purposes, is irrelevant. The fact remains that it is as normative as any other part of the New Testament for all Christian communities that acknowledge the New Testament as scripture, and that its historic influence on the self-understandings of both Catholic and Protestant traditions can easily be documented. The Letter is notable for articulating a vision of Jesus Christ as High Priest of the New Covenant, and for interpreting Jesus' life, death, and resurrection, but especially his death, as the ultimate sacrifice in expiation for the sin of the world. Remarkably consistent with the social logic of sacrifice articulated by anthropological studies of religion, Jesus is portrayed as the perfect sacrificial offering, freely transferring his own human life to God in order that we might have new life in abundance. Furthermore, the Letter specifically juxtaposes Jesus' priesthood with the Levitical priesthood of the Temple. The argument, among other things, asserts that Jesus' priesthood is more perfect because it hearkens back to Melchizedek, the mysterious "king of Salem" who blessed Abraham. The Letter's perspective is not contemptuous of the Levitical priesthood, but sees it as an imperfect realization of the pattern fully executed in the ministry of Jesus. Indeed, Jesus' death, now understood as the cultic act par excellence, transforms all prior and subsequent sacrifices.

This Christological transformation marks the different trajectories of Catholic and Protestant traditions regarding the cultic practices of the Mass and/or the Lord's Supper and their meaning for diverging styles of Christian clergy ethics. Though the Letter does not specifically define the role of the priest and the churches' expectations regarding his or her lifestyle, subsequent Catholic tradition has borrowed freely from the Letter's imagery to make it clear that the priest must, analogously, embody the characteristics, moral and spiritual, if not also physical, of Christ the High Priest. Distinctively Protestant traditions, however, have tended to challenge what they have taken to be a Catholic pattern of literal imitation and have emphasized, instead, faithful response to the Inimitable One:

> Therefore, my friends, since we have confidence to enter the sanctuary by the blood of Jesus, by the new and living way that he opened for us through the curtain (that is, through his flesh), and since we have a great priest over the house of God, let us approach with a true heart in full assurance of faith, with our hearts sprinkled clean from an evil conscience and our bodies washed with pure water. Let us hold fast to the confession of our hope without wavering, for he who has promised is faithful. And let us consider how to provoke one another to love and good deeds, not neglecting to meet together, as is the habit of some, but encouraging one another, and all the more as you see the Day approaching.
>
> (Hebrews 10:19–25)

The Catholic and Protestant interpretations of the Mass and/ or Lord's Supper seem to diverge over whether to describe the church's cultic activity as a commemoration or a reenactment. The Catholic "Holy Sacrifice of the Mass" is traditionally conceived as a reenactment of the High Priest's sacrifice culminating in Calvary. Protestant understandings of the Lord's Supper, on the other hand, tend to regard it as a commemoration. Catholics fear that commemoration says too little, as if we are not somehow sacramentally included in the High Priest's definitive sacrifice and its benefits; Protestants fear that reenactment says too much, as if Christian ministers might claim a power for themselves independent of the High Priest's sacrifice. In either case, either by way of reenactment or commemoration, a certain degree of spiritualization and ethicization is realized, for the God-man's flesh and blood are no longer torn asunder, but bread and wine are shared in a social practice that extends the High Priest's sacrifice through space and time.

Clergy ethics within Christian communities, therefore, may reflect the distinctive emphases of either tradition's interpretation of this social practice; but just as both interpretations are focused on Jesus Christ's personal example of sacrifice, so the ethics of a clergy who either reenact or commemorate this sacrifice ought to be marked by this example in a preeminent way. There is nothing wrong with a conception of ministry oriented primarily to the "ethics of the Word," so long as the clergy do not forget the referent of this Word. The conversation, in short, is still about sacrifice—the community's faithful participation in the High Priest's definitive sacrifice. The same point even more obviously should govern conceptions of ministry oriented primarily to the "ethics of the Sacrament." In either case, either as facilitators of the community's processes of commemoration or as mediators of a cultic reenactment of the High Priest's sacrifice, the representative nature of the clergy's role ought to be clear. Even under the New Covenant, Christian clergy, like their archaic ancestors, stand in a unique relationship to the community's commerce with the Sacred. It is not surprising, therefore, that the community will expect the clergy to exemplify holiness in ways that resonate with the archaic logic of sacrifice.

A brief review of Reinhold Niebuhr's theological reflections may help to clarify what is at stake in this attempt to recover the meaning of sacrifice for clergy ethics, and not just for clergy ethics, but for the sake of preserving and enhancing the common good achievable within a modern society. Niebuhr's first book, *Does Civilization Need Religion?* (1927), began his lifelong effort to develop "the resources of religion" for this secular epoch (McCann 1981). Niebuhr was seeking to define the same kind of functional understanding of religion relative to the moral ecology of the American civilization that I'm sketching here. As experience led him away from the political radicalism that he had espoused early in his career, he came to recognize that moral disinterestedness was perhaps the most important resource that religion could contribute to the politics of a modern society (Niebuhr 1934). This insight, obviously, anticipates the dilemma of liberal modernity formulated in Thurow's *Zero-Sum Society*. It also formed the basis for Niebuhr's mature understanding of Christian ethics—in particular, his view of sacrificial love as the pinnacle of Christian morality, the uniquely appropriate answer to both the religious paradoxes of human nature and its redemption symbolized by the grace of Jesus Christ (Niebuhr 1935, 1941, 1943; McCann 1981).

Without ever having articulated fully the question of clergy ethics, Niebuhr thus seems to have articulated the first principle that we are seeking to establish. He preached a Christian doctrine of sacrificial love and defended its universal moral relevance, especially for those trying to cope with the vicissitudes of public life in a secular, pluralistic society. Niebuhr, however, rarely attended to the distinctive relationship of the clergy to this doctrine, for only occasionally did he worry himself about the ecclesiological implications of his various insights. His focus is upon the tensions characteristic of life in the public arena. He is at his best in helping professional politicians and Christian social activists to cope with "the nicely calculated less and more" of politics without betraying the uncompromising demands of a Social Gospel.

Nevertheless, precisely because Niebuhr's focus is on America's moral ecology as a whole, his insight into the meaning of sacrificial love is worth considering here. In Niebuhr's view, a just and well-ordered society could never be perfectly realized short of the kingdom of God. Original sin had so warped the human condition that even a society, like our own, in which God's redeeming grace is operative, could only achieve a rough approximation of social justice. Social justice could never be realized apart from love, and love would never be strong and true enough unless it were grounded ultimately in a permanent disposition toward self-sacrifice. This continuum or, if you will, dialectical relationship between social justice and sacrificial love could be observed, Niebuhr believed, in the study of both human moral psychology and social history. The ultimate moral paradox is that altruistic love, which cannot help but be self-interested, inevitably betrays its own aspirations unless it is willing to have them transformed in a permanent disposition toward sacrificial love. What psychological observation suggests, social history so far confirms: civilizations cease to flourish when they are no longer capable of inspiring self-sacrifice.

Not surprisingly, Niebuhr perceived this truth governing both human nature and history as uniquely and definitively manifest in the ministry of Jesus Christ. The Crucifixion, for Niebuhr, is the appropriate religious symbol of the paradox of sacrificial love. As Niebuhr was fond of quoting: "He that findeth his life shall lose it: and he that loseth his life for my sake shall find it" (Matt. 10:39, KJV; see Niebuhr 1935, 33). The fate of Jesus of Nazareth perfectly reflected the meaning of his paradoxical preaching. By freely accepting his own death and by forgiving those who had a hand in it, Jesus became the occasion of new life. In principle, the grace of God triumphs over original sin, but only on the narrow basis of God's own self-sacrifice. Niebuhr's austere and emphatically Calvinist understanding of the mystery of redemption need not detain us here; for our purposes, it is sufficient to note that his theological reflections affirm both the social function, as well as the personal necessity, of sacrificial love, and that this function finds its perfect exemplar in the ministry of Jesus Christ. I infer that whatever else Niebuhr might have said about clergy ethics, he would have seen it first and foremost as an "imitation of Christ," for the whole of Christian ethics must reflect the truth demonstrated in the life, death, and resurrection of Jesus. Could clergy ethics rest content with anything short of that truth, if Christian social ethics as a whole must inevitably be founded upon it?

However compelling Niebuhr's insights, they may be met today with a certain degree of skepticism, especially among the clergy. Niebuhr's so-called Christian realism has been a favorite target for American supporters of virtually all forms of liberation theology. Niebuhr's theological reservations about the possibilities of redemption through politics have been denounced by those sympathetic with Latin American liberation theology as an "ideology of the Establishment"; that is, as a religious justification for piecemeal efforts at social and economic reform, but not for social revolution. More worthy of serious consideration, in my view, have been the criticisms of Niebuhr's doctrine of sacrificial love articulated by a whole generation of Christian and post-Christian feminists. Their skepticism rests upon the undisputed fact that the gospel of self-sacrifice has been heeded mostly by women; that it has had the effect, intended or not, of making it difficult for women to recognize their own oppression at the hands of sexist patriarchal institutions and to work together to overcome it. Given the increasing feminization of the seminaries and other training programs for clergy in America, it is not surprising that the protests of feminist Christians would cast a shadow upon Niebuhr's theology for many in the younger generation of American clergy.

If women have been victimized, as alleged, by male Christian priests and ministers extolling self-sacrifice as the pinnacle

of Christian morality, then our efforts to recover the meaning
of sacrifice as the first principle for clergy ethics will have to
provide good reasons for moving the discussion out from under
this shadow. Unfortunately, those reasons are mostly hypothetical, for it is in the nature of the case that they have yet to be
tested in a society in which the relations between the sexes
exhibit genuine reciprocity. The argument, nevertheless,
would have to go something like this: Sacrifice is a social necessity that transcends the institutions of sexist patriarchy. Were
we ever to overcome sexism definitively, our new society
would still require sacrifice in order to reconcile all its members to their limited share of the benefits and burdens of the
common good. Unless the new society succeeds in overcoming
scarcity itself—in all its material and spiritual forms—the necessity of accepting voluntarily the limits that scarcity imposes
will remain. Thurow's civic disinterestedness, in other words,
will still be necessary in a postpatriarchal society.

But this is only a partial answer to feminist critics. Even if
we can all admit to the social necessity of sacrifice, what is to
prevent the strong and well organized from using this necessity to exploit the weak and the unorganized? What is to prevent the clergy, in other words, from reinventing the
oppression that remains a sinister possibility in even the legitimate demand for sacrifice? My answer is partly traditional and,
for some churches, including my own, partly a deliberate departure from tradition. The traditional safeguard against clerical oppression is for the laity to insist that clergy practice what
they preach. But the forms of oppression are not usually ame-
nable to such maxims, nor are they ever that abstractly ge-
neric. They are manifest, as Christian feminists have
demonstrated, in discriminatory practices that concretely
deny to some persons and groups their very capacity for social
interaction as moral equals. The clergy's commitment to the
sacrificial love that they preach will be publicly verifiable
when women and minorities feel themselves truly welcomed
by their colleagues to participate in the common work of ministry. For in order to achieve such a state of genuine inclusiveness, the clergy in many churches, and not just my own, will
have to learn the ways of self-sacrifice and not just teach them.

There are some indications that clergy in America may be
willing, at least in principle, to practice what they preach. The
recent pastoral letter of the National Conference of Catholic
Bishops, *Economic Justice for All* (1986), is a useful example.
The bishops advocate a variety of economic and social reforms
roughly parallel to those discussed by Thurow. And they go

deeper than Thurow in recognizing that "a renewed public moral vision" will be necessary if this nation is to act politically to implement these reforms (National Conference of Catholic Bishops 1986, par. 27). Their "new American experiment" calls for realigning a whole range of private and public institutions to contribute more effectively to the pursuit of social justice (pars. 295–325). Such restructuring will be costly; yet the bishops do not simply preach the necessity of sacrifice to the targeted institutions. For the first time in an official Roman Catholic document, they examine publicly the morality of the church's own policies as an "economic actor"; that is, the church's accountability not only to its own employees but also to the various stakeholders whom it claims to serve (pars. 347–358).

To raise this issue in a pastoral letter, in effect, is to say: "We know that the struggle for social justice will require sacrifices, relatively small ones from most of us, and in some cases quite large ones from, we hope, only a few; in any case, we are prepared to make an example of ourselves. You will know that we are serious about economic and social reform when you see us making the sacrifices necessary to achieve similar reforms in our own institutions." Would that they were equally responsive to the second, nontraditional part of my test for the authenticity of the clergy's commitment to sacrificial love. If only they could see their way clear to sacrifice a part of tradition itself, so that the Catholic priesthood might become a model of genuine inclusive community. Then the bishops might seem more credible when solemnly assuring us that they will practice what they preach.

Learning and Teaching the Ways of Sacrifice: The Professional Responsibility of the Clergy

Despite the promising example of the American Catholic bishops' pastoral letter, the precise nature of the clergy's responsibility for learning and teaching the social practice of sacrifice, however spiritualized and ethicized, may still need clarification. Even if Reinhold Niebuhr's insight into the social necessity of sacrificial love is perennially valid for Christian social ethics as a whole, what is the relationship between this necessity and the perennial core of clergy ethics? Does not the anthropological perspective outlined here so emphasize the clergy's privileged familiarity with the social practice of sacri-

fice as to obscure their basic moral equality with the laity in all
forms of Christian fellowship, Catholic and Protestant alike?
Though a personal disposition toward self-sacrifice may be relevant to all Christians, whether clergy or laity, what is the
organizational significance for the churches of making the social practice of sacrifice the first principle of clergy ethics?

These questions are not simply a reflection of the suspicion,
already discussed, that an anthropological perspective preju-
dices the discussion of clergy ethics in favor of neo-paganism
and pre–Vatican II Catholicism. For they point not to the problem of diverging traditions, but to the situation common to
Christian clergy in contemporary America—to the challenge
of achieving a plausible professional identity in a commercial
civilization whose chief models of successful professionalism
are shaped by the values of bureaucratic management. Of
what relevance can the anthropologist's reminder of the
clergy's origins in the archaic practices of cultic sacrifice possibly be to Christian communities that must discern where to
draw the line between their own expectations and those characteristic of the secular epoch of modernity?

The most promising way to address this problem may be to
return to the definitions of sacrifice previously presented, all
of which identify it as a form of exchange *("Do ut des")*. Indeed, these definitions suggest that sacrifice is the primordial
form of exchange, the first social form that routinizes the expectation, common to both archaic religion and modern business corporations, that life need not be a zero-sum game. If the
suspicion of magic is applicable to any of our contemporary
social practices, it is surely evident with reference to legitimate business transactions that promise, through market exchanges, that all participants are and will be made winners.
What is it about market exchanges between individual consumers and business corporations that can overcome our normal fears of losing, our fears of being taken in by someone
else's confidence game, to the point where we are willing to
make a deal? Where does this trusting faith in the magic of the
marketplace come from? If we answer that we know these
things by experience, the question becomes one of origins.
Eventually, we get back to a hypothetical situation where the
first dealers had to take the meaning of exchange on faith. Was
theirs a reasonable faith? I think so; for they already participated in and were beneficiaries of a pattern of divine commerce, the social practice of sacrifice, in which all parties
emerged with life-enhancing blessings. The social practice of
sacrifice had already taught them that at least in some circumstances in order to receive anything of value one must first give

up something of value. As it was with the sacred source of life, so it must be in our commercial relations with one another.

This parable suggests that organized religion and organized business activity may have a common source, a hypothesis for which there is considerable evidence both historically and anthropologically. Yet only religious traditions, and those who continue to study them, typically understand the paradox, mediated through this common source, that self-sacrifice is the inescapable key to fulfilling our self-interested aspirations. Apart from this paradox, commercial activities, whether sacred or secular, would be unthinkable. Unthinkable, too, therefore, is any absolute separation between religion and business. Recognizing this common origin may help clergy to reject any formulation of the challenge of professionalism based on too sharp a contrast between clergy ethics and the ethics of bureaucratic management. Ministers and business managers stand on common ground, though at some point their specific responsibilities diverge in significant ways. In a society such as ours, in which both religion and business are separate from the state, the emergence of a "contractual-entrepreneurial" model of ministry thus may count as evidence of this common ground. It need not be seen as a sellout, a zero-sum outcome for both the churches and society, but as offering one possibility for living faithfully within the horizons of modernity.

The implications for clergy ethics are complex but challenging. Clergy most properly fulfill their distinctive professional responsibilities, even within a commercial civilization, when they are most clearly focused on learning and teaching the ways of sacrifice, both ritually and ethically. A commercial civilization, as Thurow's observations suggest, is likely to decline when its participants forget about sacrifice. For to forget about sacrifice is to become confused about the meaning of exchange. An entrepreneurialism completely adrift from its ultimately religious moorings inevitably will fail to meet even its economic goals. Conversely, a proper understanding of the meaning of exchange implies the priority of sacrifice, even within a "contractual-entrepreneurial" model of ministry. Drawing the line, then, on the extent to which the routines of business management ought to shape the professional responsibilities of the clergy, in principle, is fairly straightforward: Clergy can adapt themselves to modern managerial practices in good conscience so long as these do not undermine their primary responsibility as learners and teachers of the ways of sacrifice.

How might this maxim work out in the actual practice of

ministry? The church or congregation that a priest or minister
serves normally is an organization whose continued growth
depends, among other things, upon its leadership's skills in
bureaucratic management. The priest or minister must either
exercise these skills personally or preside over a team that
collectively possesses them. In either case, the priest or minister must understand the social practice of management and
develop some appreciation for the values that are normally
fostered by it. Such understanding is likely to happen when,
following the clues given by writers as diverse as Thurow and
Niebuhr, as well as a host of other observers, the clergy acknowledge the common ground they share with business managers. The anthropological perspective I have sketched here
may make it possible to enter into theological dialogue with
the professional managers in their churches and congregations
as moral equals.

At the same time, however, an awareness of their distinctive
relationship to the social practice of sacrifice will confirm the
message that clergy are likely to hear from lay professionals in
this dialogue. Though the laity may seek to collaborate in the
work of ministry, they also expect the clergy to exhibit personally the social logic of sacrifice in a way that demonstrates
moral leadership. The tokens of this leadership will vary from
one church tradition to another. In the Roman Catholic
Church, clerical celibacy, for example, may continue to be
recognized as an outward sign of the priest's own worthiness
to represent both Christ and the community in its commerce
with the Sacred. But even if it is made optional, and even if
Catholics can look forward to a time when both men and
women, some married and some celibate, will serve as priests,
no doubt the tradition will continue to insist upon some suitable outward sign marking the priest's special relationship to
the social practice of sacrifice. In Protestant traditions, which
have focused on other signs of ministerial leadership, analogous processes of the clergy marking themselves for the sake
of the community as a whole will continue to occur. An overall
simplicity of life-style, coupled with a disposition to challenge
the social and political conventions by which we routinely live,
rather than a narrow emphasis on sexual renunciation, will
remain a significant indicator by which Protestant laity recognize the caliber of the clergy who serve them. In either situation, Protestant or Catholic, the underlying expectation is that
clergy, as a matter of professional responsibility, will exhibit
a degree of self-discipline, based upon personal asceticism and
prayer, that betokens their distinctive relationship to the social

logic of sacrifice. Apart from these signs, and the transformation of consciousness that their habitual recognition entails, there may be nothing to distinguish clergy ethics from the ethics governing other professions.

Admittedly, this expectation may be easier to envision in its personal implications for clergy and their families, than in its significance for collaborative ministry and meaningful moral dialogue among clergy and laity. In typical situations where clergy exercise managerial responsibility over lay employees, as well as in those increasingly frequent exceptions where clergy are supervised by lay congregational managers, there are plenty of opportunities for confusion. Because of the normal dynamics of human association, clergy may tend to become confused about the basis for the difference between them and their lay collaborators in ministry. Clergy may fail to take seriously the otherness built into the basic definition of their distinctive role in the community. As a result, they may either expect too many sacrifices on the part of laity who cannot share in their distinctive life-style, or they may not demand enough of themselves because they no longer see why their commitment should be any different from what they imagine the laity's to be. Conversely, clergy may be overly protective of the otherness built into their distinctive role and either become inordinately reclusive in their relations with the communities they serve or patronizingly lax in their refusal to provide leadership, precisely the moral leadership that they are uniquely poised to exercise.

There is no easy way to respond to these hardly exhaustive comments on the professional responsibilities of the clergy. Based on the perspective outlined here, one could conclude that in the epoch of modernity the role assigned to the clergy is impossible, an attempt to reconcile the irreconcilable, society's ideals of successful professionalism with an archaic morality of self-sacrifice. Alternatively, the perspective outlined here may be rejected as fundamentally wrongheaded, for it assumes a continuity between modern Christian ministry and archaic religion that is theologically false and morally offensive. Because I remain more impressed by the continuities than the discontinuities between Christianity and the history of religions, and because I take seriously the fears expressed by the critics of liberal modernity, I remain convinced that an understanding of the social logic of sacrifice is not only the core of clergy ethics, but also the key to the continued development of our commercial civilization. The role of Christianity within that development, as well as the challenge that it presents to

Christian clergy in particular, may be difficult, but it is not impossible.

The professional responsibility governing the clergy's relations, not only with the laity, but also with other sectors of our society beyond the communities they serve, requires them to take the lead in learning and teaching the ways of sacrifice. Such a demand, if it is a valid one, calls for a renewal of our efforts in education, a renewed appreciation throughout our society of the indispensable cultural contribution of organized religion and, above all, a renewal of the community's demands for integrity and self-discipline in the routine processes of clergy formation. This, finally, is what this chapter's title is meant to suggest. It is not just an oblique reminder of Dietrich Bonhoeffer's classic *The Cost of Discipleship*, though Bonhoeffer's work is clearly relevant for making us aware of the question of vocation latent at the heart of our ambivalence over the professionalization of the clergy. Costing discipleship, however, goes beyond traditional concerns regarding personal faithfulness to highlight the social dimension to the question of vocation. The kind of discipleship for which the clergy volunteer is costly, not only for themselves but for all of us. Hence, for their sake as well as our own, we have an obligation to see that those costs are understood fully and accepted freely.

References

Bellah, Robert N., Richard Madsen, William M. Sullivan, Ann Swidler, and Steven M. Tipton. 1985. *Habits of the Heart: Individualism and Commitment in American Life.* Berkeley: University of California Press.

Encyclopaedia Britannica. 1974. "Sacrifice." 16:128–135. Chicago: Encyclopaedia Britannica.

Henninger, Joseph. 1987. "Sacrifice." In *The Encyclopedia of Religion* 12:544–557. Translated by Matthew J. O'Connell. New York: Macmillan.

Jackall, Robert. 1988. *Moral Mazes: The World of the Corporate Managers.* New York: Oxford University Press.

McCann, Dennis P. 1981. *Christian Realism and Liberation Theology.* Maryknoll, N.Y.: Orbis Books.

McCann, Dennis P., and Charles R. Strain. 1985. *Polity and Praxis: A Program for American Practical Theology.* Chicago: Winston Press.

MacIntyre, Alasdair. 1981. *After Virtue: A Study in Moral Theory.* Notre Dame, Ind.: University of Notre Dame Press.

National Conference of Catholic Bishops. 1986. *Economic Justice for*

All: Catholic Social Teaching and the U.S. Economy. Washington, D.C.: United States Catholic Conference.

Niebuhr, Reinhold. 1927. *Does Civilization Need Religion?* New York: Macmillan.

———. 1934. *Reflections on the End of an Era.* New York: Charles Scribner's Sons.

———. 1935. *An Interpretation of Christian Ethics.* New York: Harper & Brothers.

———. 1941, 1943. *The Nature and Destiny of Man.* Vols. 1 and 2. New York: Charles Scribner's Sons.

Thurow, Lester C. 1981. *The Zero-Sum Society.* New York: Penguin Books.

Troeltsch, Ernst. 1977. "What Does 'Essence of Christianity' Mean?" In *Writings on Theology and Religion,* translated and edited by Robert Morgan and Michael Pye, 124–179. Atlanta: John Knox Press.

Selected Additional Works

Chandler, Alfred D., Jr. 1977. *The Visible Hand: The Managerial Revolution in American Business.* Cambridge: Harvard University Press, Belknap Press.

Cooke, Bernard J. 1967. "Sacrifice IV (In Christian Theology)." In *The New Catholic Encyclopedia* 12:837–840. New York: McGraw-Hill.

Douglas, Mary. 1986. *How Institutions Think.* Syracuse, N.Y.: Syracuse University Press.

Gray, Robert N. 1984. *Managing the Church: Business Administration.* Vol. 1. Austin, Tex.: National Institute on Church Management.

McCann, Dennis P. 1987. *New Experiment in Democracy: The Challenge for American Catholicism.* Kansas City, Mo.: Sheed & Ward.

Marty, Martin E. 1981. *The Public Church: Mainline—Evangelical—Catholic.* New York: Crossroad.

———. 1986. *Modern American Religion.* Vol. 1, *The Irony of It All (1893–1919).* Chicago: University of Chicago Press.

North, Douglas C. 1974. *Growth and Welfare in the American Past: A New Economic History.* 2d ed. Englewood Cliffs, N.J.: Prentice-Hall.

Read, Kay A. 1987. "Human Sacrifice: An Overview." In *The Encyclopedia of Religion* 6:515–518. New York: Macmillan.

Troeltsch, Ernst. 1925. "Ueber einige Eigentuemlichkeiten der angelsaechsichen Zivilisation." In *Deutscher Geist und West Europa,* edited by Hans Baron. Tübingen: J. C. B. Mohr (Paul Siebeck).

9

Pastoral Care
and Clergy Ethics

J. Russell Burck

By this time in the story of modern pastoral care, it is easy to think that the relationship between pastoral care and ethics is straightforward and settled. The moral responsibilities of pastoral care appear to take the form of unambiguous mandates: keep confidences in all the contexts of ministry; maintain the bounds of intimacy in the two-person situation; facilitate the freedom and self-determination of the partner; endure and deepen the personal disciplines that will enable the pastoral partner to learn more about himself or herself; keep promises, such as the promise to visit, and so on. It is possible to claim that, as a form of professional ethics, clergy ethics has achieved its best development in the area of pastoral care, probably because of the affinity of pastoral care to the dyadic or systems-oriented caregiving of other professions, such as medicine, psychotherapy, or family therapy. Against that background, it would appear to be time to turn our attention to some of the less obvious arenas in which questions about the norms of ministerial practice need to be asked. Examples of these would be the pastor's use of his or her power in the congregation, the responsible interpretation of the sources and traditions of the pastor's body of faith, or the pastor's version of the proper relationship between the body of faith and the rest of society or even of the world.

Nevertheless, this paper will attempt to develop some of the benefits of revisiting the territorial boundary between ethics and pastoral care. This paper assumes that moral mandates of pastoral care do not exhaust, settle, or define the relationship between ethics and pastoral care. This essay assumes that this relationship is complex and rich, not straightforward or simple. It cannot be reduced to one or even a few specific concerns. Pastoral ethics is larger than the maxims mentioned above. An adequate understanding of the ethics of pastoral care requires attention to the complexity and richness of this relationship.

The thesis of this chapter is that the relationship between ethics and pastoral care encompasses three areas that should be viewed together: the ethics of caregiving, caregiving as ethics, and the contribution of pastoral care to the shaping of the moral life of the community. These three areas need to be distinguished, on the one hand, and to be viewed as interdependent, on the other.

The Ethics of Caregiving

The ethics of caregiving refers to all the tasks at all levels that shape the norms governing the helping relationship. In their book *Principles of Biomedical Ethics,* Tom L. Beauchamp and James F. Childress identify five levels of ethical or moral endeavor. At the level of (1) action are decisions, judgments, or actions. These may be viewed within the context of (2) rules, which in turn may be viewed within the context of (3) principles. Principles are examined, justified, rejected within the context of (4) moral theories, such as utilitarianism or deontology. Above all these is (5) metaethics, which reflects on the nature and process of ethics, the meaning of central terms such as "good," "right," "permissible," "impermissible," "indifferent," and so on (Beauchamp and Childress 1989, 6–11).

Let's set the stage for considering the ethics of caregiving with two sketches. Before presenting these scenarios, I want to mention several assumptions about work in ethics that are important for me. My experience in clinical ethics at Rush-Presbyterian-St. Luke's Medical Center includes only one or two instances over an eleven-year period in which people came and asked whether they had done the right thing. This same experience includes many instances in which people came to complain about others' ethics. I assume that our first responsibility as pastors is continually to examine our own ethical standards and performance and to be open to hear the observations that others make about our work. With that in mind, I shall write about these encounters in the first person. In addition, I find that students experience moral conflicts related to a profession just as intensely and authentically as

well-established professionals do. Thus, these scenarios will include references to students as moral agents.

The first sketch relates to Janet and confidentiality. Let's
suppose that during my internship Janet told me something
"in confidence," and that I told my supervisor, the parish pastor, that I could not tell him what she said. This situation occurs
often enough in Clinical Pastoral Education, as well as in medical and nursing school. What were my responsibilities, what
were the responsibilities of my supervisor in that situation, and
what would pastoral care have to say about this situation?

In taking up this question, I need to state how my understanding of ethics conditions my approach to this sketch. I
understand ethics as a communal, and thus a dialogical, enterprise. The implication for this sketch is that I need to be able
to look at a range of interpretations of our responsibilities.

To whom was I responsible in the situation? It is equally
possible to say that my responsibility was to the parishioner
and to my supervisor. The parishioner had told me something
in confidence. From a formalist perspective, it would have
been my responsibility simply to keep that confidence, to
honor her wish. From a consequentialist perspective, I would
have been putting confidential communications from her and
other parishioners at risk if I told the pastor, and that may have
put at risk the ministry that they wanted from me.

Despite the prima facie validity of her claim, my supervisor
also had valid interests (Beauchamp and Childress, 63). From
a consequentialist point of view, it is important to note that the
parish was an experiment, bringing together several geo-
graphically remote congregations and employing a considerable amount of money from the judicatory. The pastor was the
one with responsibility for the parish. If Janet needed help
beyond my ability to deliver it, she could be hurt by a rashly
or rigidly honored promise. If trouble were brewing, the pastor would not be as prepared to address it as he would if he
knew about her concern. No matter what, he could minister
to her better if she permitted him to address her distress than
if she thought she could not avoid being estranged from him.

From a formalist point of view, the pastor could have
claimed that my responsibility was to him: he was the supervisor; I was the intern. After I left, he and she would remain in
the parish. I had a responsibility to provide care during my
year's internship, but like all ministers I had a responsibility to
provide for continuity of care at the end of my time of service
in the congregation. The pastor could have helped me go back
to Janet and interpret the price her request was costing herself. He could have added that without him I had no access to

parishioners; my tenure there was time limited and even subject to his continued support.

Now let's add something to the scenario. Let us imagine two different situations that Janet wanted to keep from the pastor. One is a personal need, perhaps one tinged with shame, that she keeps from the pastor because she does not know how to face him if he knows this secret. Down deep, she may want to know what he thinks about her actual situation and how he would react, but she is not up to learning for herself. The other situation is a fight, a conflict with the pastor. She colludes with me, either because she picks up my Oedipal rebellion or because she feels she needs an ally against this person who has now become so powerful in her life that she cannot address the conflict directly.

Suppose that we step outside formalism and consequentialism, these two schools of thought that dominate contemporary applied normative ethics, to ask about responsibilities within the community of faith. Which norm of Christian community would be brought to bear here? For the personal need scenario, it would be important to emphasize the church as a community of renewed sinners, as a community that understands the shame of Jesus' exposure on the cross, and as a people who are continually having to learn about themselves as persons of faith who fall on their face from time to time. For the conflict scenario, it would be possible to identify a mandate for me to go to Janet and to ask for release from my promise, so that she and the pastor could attempt to speak the truth to one another in love.

In either scenario, this superficially ethical requirement of confidence constitutes an interference in the life of the community and even in Janet's own needs.

What would the ethics of caregiving say about the proper solution to the problem? In the modern clinical context, there is a simple convention that could have been employed to resolve this situation. This convention is that confidentiality is "communal." The circle of confidence in the clinical context extends to all those professionals who work in the patient's behalf and who therefore have a need to know some of the private information. Confidences do not include family members (often included, even against the patient's wishes), friends, colleagues at work, employers, insurance companies, and so on. Using this convention, the pastor could have said that as the pastor he needed to know, especially if what she was saying concerned him, so that he could consider how to respond, if at all.

However, the proper application of this convention requires

that parishioners and intern know several things. They have to know that the intern will convey information about them to the pastor, but that the pastor will not needlessly convey information about them to the intern. They need to know that the pastor will use the information that she or he receives from the intern respectfully and with confidentiality. The intern needs to know that when people ask for confidentiality, she or he should tell them that she or he cannot keep significant information from the pastor. Thus there has to be some orientation to confidentiality and some rules or strategies for the intern to interpret it to the parishioners. Without further interpretation and preparation, the convention of communal confidentiality will not work.

Further, the observation that a rigid adherence to confidentiality may harm all the actors in the situation and may damage the church does not justify immediate corrective action to disregard the request for confidentiality. The peace, unity, and purity of the church, which are governing values for my tradition, would require some intermediate steps. Such steps could include something like the following. When the pastor hears about the request for confidentiality, he or she could instruct the intern not to convey the privileged information. The pastor could ask the intern to return to the woman and tell her that he or she felt a need to tell the pastor, but was bound by her request for confidentiality. However, he or she would feel better and would be able to serve her better if she would permit him or her to consult with the pastor about her situation, or even to ask the pastor to visit her about the matter. The intern would review with her the long-term effects of withholding pertinent information from persons who provide some services for us, such as the loss of direct help for the problem, and, of more long-range significance, the encouragement of distrust and distance between pastor and parishioner when there was no experience to justify these responses.

Further, the values of peace, unity, and purity might not permit any remedial action whatsoever.

All of these reflections prompt me to conclude that the relationships within a congregation are too significant and too complex to be reduced to a simple lip-buttoning maxim. As my colleague Laurel A. Burton says, this could merely be "secret keeping" in the very sense that is destructive of human community and personal integrity and development. Some of this information, however sensitive, needs to be shared in reliable circles when the occasion arises.

By speaking to persons who cause offense in the church (see

Matt. 18:15–20), was the mandate to seek reconciliation threatened? Or was the conflict, the potential of conflict, or the threat of a violation of confidence, a threat to the peace of the church?

In terms of the educational task of my pastoral supervisor, this sketch is still quite interesting. The major possibilities for education about ethical interpretation of the situation have already been reviewed. However, education concerning the ethics of caregiving does not stop with ethical interpretation of the situation. It also needs to inquire about me and my relationship with the pastor and to weigh the problem-solving tactics that could have helped resolve the situation. Concerning myself and the pastor, one important question is, What was going on within me or what was happening between us that I chose to tell him I had some information that I could not tell him? Because the salient details of the situation are lost to my memory, I feel free to speculate about it. Was I feeling powerless, and did this event give me some feeling that I had leverage over him? Was this some way of claiming power? Was I transferring or displacing important matters from other significant persons in my life onto him? Another question concerns the effects on the pastor, if I also chose to insist on this confidence.

The easiest problem-solving approach for him would have been to ask me, with proper coaching, to go back to Janet and ask her not to make me have to live with the secret information by myself, where it could not have any constructive effect for herself, and possibly even for the congregation. She could have been asked to speak to the pastor directly herself or to remove the "in confidence" label. Another solution would have been the simple appeal to power: my responsibility was to him as my supervisor. This solution would have permitted several variants. In one variant, the supervisor would not indicate that he knew the confidential information. In another, he would have gone to her and indicated that he had heard that there was some issue; would she be willing to help him understand it? The moral justification of the sheer use of power by the supervisor is difficult to provide, however.

Further educational efforts could have extended to attempts to understand either the parishioner or the pastor. We could have focused on the parishioner's use of the phrase "in confidence." Perhaps she did not mean the phrase with the seriousness with which I took it. Perhaps she may have thought she needed it in order to work out or try out some thoughts, and then when she was done she did not lift the request. Perhaps

·she sensed something in the relationship between the pastor and me that would make indirect communications through me even more unreliable and risky than a direct encounter with the pastor.

This analysis shows that the simple commitment of pastoral care to confidentiality is a complex, nuanced matter.

The second sketch deals with Andy and forgiveness. Andy, a mental patient, asked me to help him receive forgiveness. Another chaplain told me that Andy had made such requests before. When previous chaplains had offered forgiveness, Andy had told them that their ministry had not worked. He had asked for someone to provide more expert help. What were my responsibilities toward Andy?

As complex as the problem with Janet can be, this one is much more so. There is an explicit request for spiritual care, or at least, for some kind of religious ritual. As a chaplain, I have a desire to be of help, and I believe that helping persons to experience forgiveness is a good. It brings all kinds of benefits, not the least of which is freeing their energy for the services that human beings need from one another.

At the same time, I have information that this ministry to Andy has been experienced as a kind of trap. Ministry with him appears to be tainted or contaminated by the wounds that his spiritual anguish, his obsessiveness, or his aggression have inflicted on other chaplains. It may be difficult to avoid letting one's vulnerability shape one's plan of care. That is, some pastors will want to avoid a situation in which they do their best to serve Andy, only to have him turn around and say, "What you did did not help." That is especially the case if his complaint sounds like an accusation of failure, ineffectiveness, or incompetence. His response may evoke feelings of retaliation, and if one is close to those who have had prior experience with Andy, one may be infected by whatever desire they may have had to get back at Andy for putting their work down.

Even more, ministry with Andy is limited by the knowledge and skills we have at the time we work with him. Thus, a chaplain may be able to offer a ritual of forgiveness, but may not yet be able to offer the kind of response that enables Andy to talk about the wrong he recalls doing and the harm he believes he has done; the hurt he bears for it; the impossibility of purging his memory; the excruciating, unforgivable doubt he has about God's power to free him through acts of forgiveness; and the difficulty he has putting his energy into constructive purposes. This situation reminds me of the beginning of Isaiah 40, which commands the prophet to console the people of God and tell them that their punishment has ended, that they have received double from God for all their sins. Andy is one who expects ongoing, continuing estrangement between him and God, and whose experiences of reconciliation do not last. The chaplain may not know any effective way to console Andy and speak to him that his time of service has ended, that he has received more than enough for everything he has done wrong.

Now what does the ethics of caregiving have to say about these two sketches?

The first task of pastoral ethics is like the first responsibility of all "applied normative ethics." This responsibility is to examine the nature of the good(s) that pastoral care is seeking to realize and the harm(s) that it seeks to avoid. It is possible that pastoral ethics can do no better than to make clear statements that the goals of pastoral care are ambiguous and difficult to define. That is, pastoral care could say that we strive to enhance the independence and the authenticity of persons. We seek to enhance their moral decision making and acting by helping them study and identify their values. We seek to strengthen their ability to act morally by helping them sort out what is going on inside themselves, what the influences on their lives are, and so on.

For Janet, under the heading of confidentiality, pastoral care would seek to effect the following goods: that she could speak freely and openly; that she could trust another human being with information and feelings; that she could learn to understand the capacity of the life of faith to include and contain her concerns. The harm that pastoral care would seek to avoid would be unauthorized exposure of her private communications.

At another level it can be seen that mere, unexamined confidentiality can become a source of harm to everyone involved. Thus part of the task of the ethics of caregiving is to seek out ways to honor all the various values that are at risk as far as possible. We have already reviewed some of these values in considering my responsibilities toward her and my supervisor: protection of private communication, avoidance of destructive secrets and power struggles, reconciliation among the faithful, faithfulness and respect toward those who bear accountability for the congregation. For these reasons it is worthwhile for the supervisor and the intern to try to learn what confidentiality meant to Janet. Then it would be important to find ways to get her to lift her request, so that the appropriate communication could occur.

For Andy, the goods that pastoral care would seek to provide and to protect are (1) the sense that there is a larger, loving power to whom distressed persons can turn, including those who are distressed with themselves; (2) respect for Andy's experience of dissatisfaction, for his ongoing sensitivity to himself and his need for further assistance; (3) the hope that Andy can turn loose of enough energy that his guilt has tied up in order to use some of it in the world. The harms that pastoral care would seek to avoid are (1) abandonment and isolation of Andy, (2) retaliation by, or *for,* caregivers whom Andy has wounded, (3) mere repetition of the rituals of forgiveness that have not worked for him.

Within the framework of determining the goods caregiving seeks and the harms that it seeks to avoid, the second task of pastoral ethics is to emphasize competence in professional functioning. The commitment to practical competence is the commitment to be as good as possible, judging by the profession's current self-understanding, at the tasks of pastoral care that are part of one's particular ministry. Not every minister will have to carry out every pastoral task, but every minister should be good at the pastoral tasks that are part of his or her ministry. Usually applied normative ethics does not emphasize this point, but presupposes it. The risk of presupposing competence is that many professionals will not recognize the ethical significance of knowledge or skill.

In the emphasis on competence, pastoral ethics joins with those whose teaching and writing establish the norms of everyday pastoral practice. There are some practical abilities that every pastor should have: the ability to assess the person's need, the ability to determine whether a person needs more than the pastor can provide, and the ability to refer the person. The pastor also needs the ability to maintain the relationship without interfering in the person's new helping relationship and without abandoning or rejecting him or her. In this sense, pastoral ethics is concerned with the knowledge, self-understanding, and skills that pastors need for ordinary day-to-day care of their parishioners and others who will come to them.

With Janet, practical competence would mean the ability to discuss her request for confidentiality until an appropriate decision about it could be made. Perhaps confidentiality would not be required or the pastor could be understood as one who belongs to the circle. Perhaps a referral would be necessary. In that case, however, some communication with the pastor would appear to be unavoidable. Some skill would be required on the part of supervisors to assist their interns in understanding such requests without merely forcing the intern to divulge the information.

With Andy, practical competence would be the ability to ask him what his need was, to inquire what had worked and what had not worked in the past, to learn the meaning of acts of forgiveness "not working," and to express compassionate respect for the distress that he felt when things did not work.

Taken with full seriousness, this task would ask pastoral ethics to participate in, or to encourage, a survey by pastoral experts of the issues for which pastors need to be prepared in their daily pastoral work. This task of pastoral ethics would lead to the development of pastoral care curricula that would cover these areas and would require pastors to pass a minimum skills test for them.

A third responsibility of pastoral ethics is to encourage the quest to improve pastoral functioning. Moral inquiry does not stop with examining present or proposed practices. It is more than a yardstick for present performance. Pastoral ethics also helps practitioners to care for people better, to engage in continual revision of the knowledge and skills required for ordinary pastoral care. One of the interesting problems that faces me as a chaplain is what to do with the principle of respect for persons when I find that some family members or friends of a person who has just died try to keep others from grieving in the way that the others seem to favor. How does the pastor communicate his or her respect for the concern of the "controlling" persons while supporting the grief expressions of the "more active" mourners? The answer to this question involves a careful analysis of the situation of the acutely bereaved, an understanding of the motives of most controlling persons (usually to relieve the hurt of the more active mourners), and the development of a repertoire of responses that usually create a free space for the more active mourners and respect the values of the controlling persons.

An alternative ethic for pastoral care of the acutely bereaved would be simply to acquiesce in the values of the controlling person. After all, the principle of autonomy would support their goals as much as it would support those they are trying to control. Who is to choose between these two types of mourners? Further, resisting these persons can entail having to discover ways to deal with or address their power in the moment, and that could lead to conflict at a time when conflict would be most unwelcome and inappropriate. In fact, it would be possible to say that the controlling persons know the others better and know how to establish the limits that they need. Another possibility would be to say that the controlling persons are weaker, more self-serving, less understanding of the needs and capacities of their other loved ones, and therefore less to be followed than the others. The ethics of caregiving would participate in the research needed to find the best way to meet the needs of both of these groups of grieving persons.

Another problem for research in the ethics of pastoral care has to do with the pastor's communication of his or her own values. For a long time it was thought that the way for pastors to assure the freedom of their parishioners/clients was not to accept a question like, "What would you do, Pastor?" The appropriate response was thought to be some variant of, "What I would do is not important; what I am here for is to help you figure out what you would like to do, what fits you and your values." In many cases, that is still a useful approach, and the principle involved is one that should always prevail: preserve the freedom of the partner to make his or her own decision.

However, there are two good reasons for recognizing some exceptions to the preferred intervention. On the one hand, it is very difficult for most of us to avoid signaling the view that we favor or that we would choose in the situation. As Paul Watzlawick has written, "It is impossible not to communicate" (Watzlawick 1967, 48–51). Very often our preferences come through, even when we try to keep an even hand or to not tip our hand. Therefore, it can be a constructive contribution to state our preferences, if we are asked to give them. There are some very useful ways to mitigate the imposition of our values on others. It is not particularly difficult to protect the clients from our preferences by saying that we may not be seeing the situation as clearly as they are, or that in the actual situation our views could change.

On the other hand, many persons benefit from knowing what others would do and why they would do that. Further, they do not necessarily do what the pastor would prefer. It seems that the Catholic experience with birth control is a good example. The priest's explicit clarity does not always lead to obedience or deference, and the difference of opinion may not even affect the relationship between parishioner and priest.

In each of these situations, the key to the problem is in communicating to the parishioner that the continuation and strength of the relationship do not depend on the parishioner's election of the pastor's preference. If the pastor is unwilling to continue the relationship if the parishioner makes a choice the pastor cannot live with, then the pastor should say that.

In summary, one of the responsibilities of pastoral ethics is to foster and nourish technical improvement of skills and development of attitudes that will lead to desirable, or even more worthy, pastoral goals.

These are three major tasks of the ethics of caregiving, tasks that I have sometimes called "pastoral ethics." First, the ethics of caregiving reflects on the good and identifies the harms. It considers ways in which apparently obvious, algorithmic understandings of pastoral responsibility may require careful scrutiny for the good of all involved. Second, the ethics of caregiving helps the field identify the knowledge and abilities required to provide minimally competent service. Third, the ethics of caregiving seeks to advance the quality of caregiving by seeking to improve pastoral care in its very techniques. But these links between ethics and pastoral care do not exhaust the field.

Caregiving as Ethics

The phrase "caregiving as ethics" refers to ethics as an iterative, an open, and a communal undertaking. Ethics is iterative in that apparently settled matters come under review in the light of new developments, unheeded resistance, or shifts in power relationships. It is open in that there are many ways into consideration of ethical issues. It is communal in that many persons take their place at the table where ethical issues are thrashed out; some spend much time there, some rarely visit the site, all belong and have stakes there. The phrase "caregiving as ethics" also refers to the fact that in the process of caregiving pastors perceive matters that prompt them to do work in ethics. Some of this work is impulsive, off the top of the head, reactive. Nevertheless, even this work deserves careful consideration.

The first area of reflection has to do with the relationship between the ethics of caregiving and the ethics of the ongoing common life. These are not, and should not be, identical. The caregiving relationship has the responsibility to make room for many subjects, themes, and kinds of language and behavior that are not readily acceptable in daily life. The kind of expression of anger that may be essential for the helping relationship taxes ordinary relationships, often burning bridges and destroying constructive possibilities. The expressions of grief that bereaved people need may paralyze caring persons outside the helping context. Before the structures and freedoms of pastoral practice can be applied to life in the daily world, they should be carefully examined. If necessary, they have to be transformed into some less powerful, less intense, form. Thus part of the task of linking pastoral care and ethics is a careful examination of the implications of the structures, freedoms, and learnings of pastoral care for everyday life.

Let us begin with confidentiality. Life in our society, which I shall also call the ongoing common life, the public life, or the life of the people, has a significant stake in confidentiality as an expression of the ethics of caregiving. People need to be able to assume that whatever freedom is being developed in pastoral clients is going to contribute to the life of the community. Confidentiality contributes to the life of the community by assuring everyone that some of their communications will remain privileged and protected from undesired or forced exposure. This commitment of caregiving contributes to the community by providing a shield behind which people can say things in an unguarded manner. There they can try out new thoughts, confess real or imagined wrongs, lament harms they have received without being held accountable. The minimal social contribution of such pastoral care is that it assures others who are not in pastoral care that their thought experiments and unguarded expressions in the protected context will not be divulged without their authorization.

The societal importance of such protections is not diminished by the recognition of some that there are limits to the protection of confidentiality. In the Tarasoff case, a psychologist was held liable for failing to disclose the intent of his patient to kill Tatiana Tarasoff (Tarasoff v. Regents of the University of California 1976). Confidentiality did not protect that kind of privileged conversation.

Although confidentiality serves society, caregiving as ethics leads to the conclusion that pastoral care is not simply a servant of societal ends. Thus pastoral care may not be a major comfort to the society, because the ongoing common life is not entitled to assume that the pastoral caregivers and their clients will avoid raising societally subversive issues. To the extent that bodies of faith are prophetic, they will recognize that subversive events are likely to occur in pastoral care. Further, they will understand that what the society considers subversive may not ultimately be in opposition to its best interests. The society at large cannot even expect that pastors, when providing pastoral care, will refrain from challenging the prevailing moral order.

Further, there are many situations in which privacy about one's intentions is vital to creative production. I am always concerned about athletes who "win in the newspapers," rather than in the arena. Frequently, publicity becomes a substitute for production. Several years ago, I was talking with a woman who was writing a play. As one interested in processes of creativity, I asked her what she was doing and how it was coming along. She said that she could not talk about it, because to talk about it would drain her energy and distract her.

Despite these advantages of privacy, as a people we do not generalize the protection of confidentiality to all dyadic or small-group conversations. Most conversations are legally "discoverable" and are not privileged. That is, we do not, and cannot, conclude that confidentiality in all contexts would benefit the society. Thus the responsibilities of the helping situation can yield such benefits for the society that the society protects the helping context. Yet the society does not adopt the ethical norms of caregiving as the sole ethical framework governing private communications.

Further, the caregiving situation provides ample experiences in which the caregiver recognizes that the client would do just as well, perhaps better, in some ways and for some purposes, if the client had another "layperson" to share his or her story with. When I was teaching pastoral care in the church in Wuerttemberg, Germany, in 1972, a member of the class described the importance of the class to her. She had thought she was all alone, the only one who experienced the difficulties with professional colleagues that were a daily torment to her. Her daily work did not bring her into contact with others who experienced the same problems. Through the class she learned that she was not alone. She probably would not have taken this problem to a pastor. But when she found that others were like her, she received some of the help that she needed.

This even leads to two conclusions relevant for the ongoing common life. First, as important as the protections of confidentiality are, it would also be good if we could find ways to lift them without harming the persons involved. Alcoholics Anonymous is an example. Not all meetings are open, but some meetings are open, and at those meetings AA members give their first name, tell their story, and let themselves be seen. In this way they lift and learn to live with the burden of shame that isolates persons and convinces them that they are alone unacceptable because others do not have the same problems.

Second, the caregiving professions can help educate people through courses, newspaper and journal articles, books, and so on, about the dangers and problems of privacy. We can help educate the society about the commonalities of the human condition, about how frequently persons feel that they are the only ones in a particular situation or that they have brought the situation on themselves or deserved it in some way. Such education should also include some warnings about ways that people can overexpose themselves and how to test the waters before saying too much, and so on.

Thus the process of caregiving prompts some reflections about ways to help. It is even possible to imagine situations in which voluntary suspension of confidentiality would serve the society better and would not substantially damage the person affected. The example of Alcoholics Anonymous can encourage courageous people in the church to be available to persons who are going through what they themselves had experienced in the past. The value of unity and community in the church, even the values of peace and purity, should encourage us to find ways to help people tell the stories of their hurt to one another, even the hurt that they have done to themselves.

Caregiving as ethics is generally a less intentional endeavor than work with the ethics of caregiving. It is more haphazard and reactive. In the course of working with help-seeking persons, pastoral care observes matters that need to be taken back to the public arena. Frequently, caregivers simply assume that the values that are appropriate for the helping situation are appropriate for the ongoing common life. They take their observations back to the public and make recommendations. Certainly, many of these suggestions are appropriate and well-taken. For example, there are those who claim that the professionalization of grief work is not in the best interest of most persons. The recommendation is that grieving persons be left to their present friends and acquaintances, rather than referred to professional caregivers. John McKnight has written an interesting article about this matter. He is concerned that "natural" or "ordinary" caregiving will cease when bereavement services become professionalized (McKnight 1984). Other recommendations are not to move quickly, if possible, after bereavement, and to reduce one's activities.

If we stay with Janet and Andy, what do we see? With Janet, we see that an undifferentiated adherence to confidentiality could isolate persons within the church. If something is true about her that she does not want the pastor to know, then she is left to isolate herself. That should always be her privilege, if she chooses it. However, she should be given the chance to understand what she is doing, if it appears that she does not understand it. Thus some methods need to be developed by which she can examine her need for confidentiality. It is clear that some persons in the church benefit from knowing others who are in the same boat as themselves. Pure confidentiality misses that need.

In summary, through its reflections on the similarities and differences between the helping situation and everyday life, caregiving performs some functions of ethics. These enable us to make the kinds of careful distinctions that help us identify goods and harms in each of these two contexts. Thus we can know more readily when they apply and when they do not. Yet even this link between ethics and pastoral care is not the last one.

The Intrinsic Contributions
of Pastoral Care
to the Shaping of the
Public Moral Universe

The phrase "the intrinsic contributions of pastoral care to the shaping of the public moral universe" implies a claim that pastoral care consists of a set of attitudes and activities that can be directed toward the entire enterprise of ethics today. Instead of seeking to identify these attitudes and activities, I will follow the lead of Don S. Browning, in his book *The Moral Context of Pastoral Care*. Browning distinguishes between "relaxing the demands" of the moral context of pastoral care and helping "shape this moral universe of values and meanings" (Browning 1976, 11). He argues that ministry, including pastoral care, needs to address both functions. There is value in beginning with his perspective, because it is well known, because it has helped bring the field to its present interest in clergy ethics, and because it draws on the work of social scientists who make similar observations about the relationship between helpers and their society. If we apply the term "relaxing values" to the enterprise of ethics, what is the result?

At this point I need to begin to define my understanding of "relaxing values." When I use this term, I mean that the pastor does not immediately draw conclusions or make judgments about a matter. When the pastor does draw them, the pastor does not overtly communicate them until the time is appropriate. Instead, the pastor becomes an observer, a listener, a perceiver. The pastor inquires and seeks to learn. The pastor hears about behavior, speech, attitudes, motivations that concern people, and the pastor waits to express opinions until the pastor has had the opportunity to learn about them. What is their place in the life of the person(s) she or he is with? What is their

history, their function? Even if an act is unacceptable or repre-
hensible—for example, axe murder—are there any adaptive or
coping characteristics that can help others understand how the
person justified or rationalized the act? Certainly, there are
adaptive and coping qualities of human behavior that are far
less one-sided than axe murder.

What would it mean to apply this contribution of pastoral
care to modern ethics? For one thing, it would mean suspending judgment about schools and theories of ethics until one had
explored their history, their social context, the web of meanings with which they resonate, and the areas or purposes in
which they provide some rather good guidance and were particularly contributory. This contribution of pastoral care would
also help identify those contexts in which the recommendations of those same schools or theories raised as many problems
as satisfactions.

For Janet, the relaxing of values would mean suspending
judgment about the place of self-regard and of self-protection
in the life of the church. Does the life of faith recognize self-
regard as a legitimate characteristic of persons of faith? Does
it belong to religious ethics, or is it a forbidden, rationalized
import, a Trojan horse ready to bring down the moral life of
anyone who admits it? Is the person of faith simply to disregard
his or her needs for confidentiality, to place all information
about himself or herself on display for immediate perusal? Is
the person of faith to trust that the community of faith will still
make room, or make the same kind of room, for persons of faith
who have shameful things to disclose about themselves? Is that
a moral mandate that eliminates the need for confidentiality?
To ask the question is either to answer it or to disclose one's
naïveté, but the pastoral approach inquires about these things.
Or is there a valid place for self-regarding claims, such as the
claim of confidentiality, and if so, how far does the valid place
of self-regarding claims extend? Does it extend beyond the
privileged portion of the pastor-parishioner relationship?

Pastoral care is certainly not the only practical field or discipline that can ask these questions. At its best, moral theology
or theological ethics would do this. Yet these questions breathe
the spirit of pastoral care. In fact, pastoral care can push these
questions further. From the point of view of Christianity, is
there anything in the recent history of Christianity that gives
self-regarding actions any legitimacy at all? It would seem to
me that the evangelical appeal has significant elements of
self-regard. Thus it would not be possible for theological ethics
informed by the pastoral enterprise to reject self-regarding

ethics out of hand as sinful, destructive, disrespectful of humanity, and so on. At least such theological ethics would have to admit that some of its roots participate in these self-regarding backgrounds. A critique of self-regarding "ethics" would have to be a self-critique as well.

Further, such a pastoral perspective is particularly well equipped to ask why self-regarding ethics needs to come under judgment, as in Browning's rejection of ethical egoism in his book *Religious Ethics and Pastoral Care* (Browning 1983, 45). In fact, pastoral care, by virtue of its attention to the individual, is in a particularly good position to advocate the importance of self-regarding motivations in the decisions of persons of faith. Pastoral care helps persons explore the directions in which the Spirit of the Universe is drawing them. To some extent, that requires respect for others' expression about one, but it also requires much sensitivity to the inner lures by which persons begin to sense a spiritual direction for their life. Without that, without respect for that, the life of faith could just as easily become one of mere obedience and subjugation to the established judgments of religious elites.

For Andy, relaxing of values could mean suspension of judgment about means-end relationships in religious rituals. If we as persons of faith wish to claim that our religious rituals are effective in removing the kind of self-awareness that brings people like Andy to them, then we are making a mistaken claim. The kind of self-scrutiny, the kind of consciousness of his own fallibility and finitude, the confusion of physical drives with moral violations, all of these are not eliminated by the ritual that Andy seeks. Someone has a responsibility to draw that conclusion and tell him.

I say this, because I assume that part of what drives him back again and again to request these rituals is his intense self-awareness and his desire to rid himself of it. Someone needs to help him appreciate that that kind of self-transcendence is, for some persons, part of the life of the spirit, part of the life of faith. Faithfulness does not eliminate that self-awareness; it may even heighten it. But faithfulness does do something else. It provides something reconciling, something that stabilizes us when negative self-regard would overwhelm us. Further, faithfulness helps us come to terms with those parts of our creatureliness that we have learned or chosen to disown, and to make room for them.

It could also mean a focused consideration of the meaning of hope for persons like him. He hopes in desperation, against desperation, that he will be different. And every time he finds, after a brief while, perhaps a few days, that he is not different.

In the mode that I have called the intrinsic contributions of pastoral care to shaping the public moral universe, pastoral care can join others in the examination and reexamination of the norms of the society.

Another part of the sensitivity, and thus, another part of the task of pastoral care, is to appreciate the spirit of the times. One way to characterize our times is in terms of emotivism. Concerning emotivism, Alasdair MacIntyre writes:

> What I have suggested to be the case by and large about our own culture—that in moral argument the apparent assertion of principles functions as a mask for expressions of personal preference—is what emotivism takes to be universally the case. . . . Emotivism's attempted reduction of morality to personal preference continually recurs in the writings of those who do not think of themselves as emotivists. . . . To a large degree people now think, talk and act *as if* emotivism were true, no matter what their avowed theoretical stand-point may be. Emotivism has become embodied in our culture. . . . The [Enlightenment] project of providing a rational vindication of morality . . . decisively failed; and from henceforward the morality of our predecessor culture—and subsequently of our own—lacked any public, shared rationale or justification.
>
> (MacIntyre 1981, 18–19, 21, 48)

Contemporary pastoral care recognizes that many persons *do* experience themselves as living in a time that has no moral core, no moral center. In that context, moral issues become a matter of personal preference. Some versions of pastoral care may actually favor the preferentialist version of ethics. As a discipline, I believe pastoral care would go too far if it favored emotivism. However, it is part of the discipline of pastoral care to recognize the presence of emotivist themes and subcultures in the society. Further, as a discipline and practice concerned with hearing, it is part of pastoral care to recognize that emotivism will affect the way that people will hear the moral pronouncements of ministers: "That's what *you* believe, Rev., and that's O.K. Just don't expect me to agree." Pastoral care has the ability to make some useful observations about the ways that ministers' moral formulations will come across in the society.

In the same way that pastoral care can explore the dynamic strengths and weaknesses of schools of ethics, it can also examine the absoluteness of the claims that have been made by various schools of morality. Two examples are utilitarianism and deontology. Pastoral care can ask what experience lies behind these absolute claims. Is there an inability to live with ambiguity? Are moral systems covert versions of personal security systems? Pastoral care is in a good position to ask, though not necessarily to answer, whether the contradictions and tensions between such schools are irreducible or whether there are contexts in which each school makes invaluable contributions.

The task of this chapter has been to explore and develop some of the complexity and richness in the relationship between pastoral care and ethics. In order to do that, I have proposed several ways of linking these words together: the ethics of caregiving, caregiving as ethics, and the contribution of pastoral ethics to the shaping of the public moral life. I have sought to demonstrate that the contributions of pastoral care can be profound and constructive. In these ways, pastoral care can help refine and develop the sense of goods and harms that we, as persons and communities of faith, need to understand and address.

References

Beauchamp, Tom L., and James F. Childress. 1989. *Principles of Biomedical Ethics.* 3d ed. New York: Oxford University Press.

Browning, Don S. 1976. *The Moral Context of Pastoral Care.* Philadelphia: Westminster Press.

———. 1983. *Religious Ethics and Pastoral Care.* Philadelphia: Fortress Press.

MacIntyre, Alasdair. 1981. *After Virtue: A Study in Moral Theory.* Notre Dame, Ind.: University of Notre Dame Press.

McKnight, John L. 1984. "John Deere and the Bereavement Counselor." Typescript of fourth annual E. F. Schumacher Lecture, New Haven, Conn., October 27.

Tarasoff v. Regents of the University of California. 1976. California Supreme Court, *17 California Reports,* 3d series, 425, decided July 1.

Watzlawick, Paul, et al. 1967. *Pragmatics of Human Communication.* New York: W. W. Norton.

10

Family Ethics and the Ethics of Ministerial Leadership

Don S. Browning

After several decades of neglect, the mainline American churches are regaining their interest in families. Some of this new interest has been inspired by the family therapy movement. This movement has deepened the realization that for many church members, if not all, the church is like a family. The family therapy movement also has shown the similarities between the way that people relate to their churches and the way they relate to their families.

Edwin Friedman, in his provocative *Generation to Generation: Family Process in Church and Synagogue* (1985) has suggested that the church should make an alliance with the family therapy movement to achieve a stronger ministry to families. The uniqueness of his book is the view that the minister is a leader and potential change agent in three overlapping families: the congregation as family, the families that make up the congregation, and the minister's own family (Friedman 1985, 1). The minister has the power to change any one of these three families. This power rests, however, in the minister's firm self-definition used in a nonanxious way to guide his or her interventions in these family systems.

This raises the question, What is the moral content of this firm self-definition that ministers should use in nonanxious ways in their interventions? What is the meaning of the term *self-definition* or *self-identity?* Charles Taylor, in his recent *Sources of the Self* (1989, 2) argues that self-definitions are developed around understandings of the good. The category of the good is basically a moral category. Therefore, self-definitions, according to this view, are moral at their core. This is a point that is often overlooked in social science understandings of identity. To call a self-definition or identity "firm" does not tell us much. We need to know the moral content of this firmness.

Friedman's point is that a firm identity on the part of the minister helps create a firm and differentiated identity on the part of the members of these three interpenetrating families. But what is the ethical content of Friedman's call for differentiated selves in the individuals making up these three families? What is the family ethic that guides the minister's self-definition? Is it an ethic of autonomy where family members stay together as long as they are supporting each other's self-actualization and growth? Is it an ethic of patriarchal authority where the family obligation rests in obedience to the will of the father? Is it an ethic of sacrificial love in which family members—most generally the mother—are to sacrifice themselves perpetually for the good of the other family members? Or is it an ethic of mutuality in which family members are to take the needs of others as seriously as they take their own, but are permitted within this to indeed take their own needs seriously? Although they would take different forms, firmly defined selves could emerge within each of these understandings of the *good* family. These questions are important for each of the three overlapping families that Friedman discusses: the families in the church, the church as family, and last but not least, the minister's own family. It is not enough to make a formal call for a new family ministry based on a firm self-definition of minister as intervenor. Unless we know the moral content of this firm self-definition, we cannot be certain that the minister's interventions can truly be seen as ministry to any one of these three families.

Continuity Between Public and Private

Formulating the issue in this way points to a continuity between the public and the private in family ethics. If there are psychodynamic analogies between these three families, the way ministers treat their own families will have something important to do with how they will relate to the church as family and the families within the church. Furthermore, solving the question of the ethics of family relations in these three contexts may give the church a new strategy for conducting its ministries in a time of deteriorating growth and vigor. My claim is that there is an important link between the discovery of an appropriate ethic for these three overlapping families and the development of a new revitalizing strategy for the church.

It is now well established in the sociological literature that the denominations that are growing numerically in our society—such as the Mormons, the Assembly of God, and the Southern Baptists—have strong family emphases. In addition, it is commonly perceived that the mainline denominations have retreated from the family field. Whether or not this is actually the case, they are perceived to be more conflicted, less decisive, and more embarrassed by their family ministries than they once were and than are the more conservative manifestations of the church. It is my conviction that the mainline churches should recapture leadership in the family field. They should not so easily permit the family field to be dominated by the more conservative and fundamentalist groups of our society. The complexity of the situation of the modern family requires the commitment to honest biblical, historical, theological, and philosophical inquiry; accurate use of the social sciences; rigorous ideology critique; and appreciation for certain values of feminism that the liberal churches espouse but not always exhibit. Recapturing the family field is not only vital to the survival of these churches; it is vital to the fulfillment of an authentic Christian mission. The development of a viable family ethic is essential to this strategy.

Modernization, the Family, and the Ethics of Autonomy

Understanding more deeply the emerging relation between the church and the family will help us be more concrete and contextual about the ethic needed if ministers are to be effective agents of intervention (to use the jargon of therapy) in these three family systems. Two recent programmatic essays by sociologists have presented powerful descriptions of the interaction of the church and the family within the context of modern societies. Furthermore, they have offered suggestions for a future strategy. In contrast to most sociologists, the authors have used their descriptive and diagnostic work to inform normative proposals of the kind that take them into the realms of ethics and theology.

The essays are by William D'Antonio (1980) and Barbara Hargrove (1983). In his presidential address before the Society for the Scientific Study of Religion titled "The Family and Religion: Exploring a Changing Relationship," D'Antonio demonstrates how both religion and the family have evolved in modern societies toward serving the values of personal autonomy and individual fulfillment. At the time of the publication of Lenski's *The Religious Factor* (1961), there was a clear difference in the United States between Catholicism, Judaism, and mainline Protestantism in the way they respectively influenced the family (D'Antonio 1980, 102). Catholics were less inclined to divorce, had larger families, were more oriented around the extended family, were less socially mobile, and were more conservative in their attitudes toward sexual ethics, contraception, and abortion than were either Protestants or Jews. Protestants and Jews reflected the general social trend typical of modernization that favored personal autonomy and mobility, and saw these values as central for the socialization of their children (94). According to D'Antonio, within the intervening years, almost all of these differences have disappeared, and Catholics have moved toward the values of personal autonomy and individualism typical of the mainline Protestant and liberal Jewish groups (95). In addition, Protestant and Jewish groups have continued in their own drift toward these values.

D'Antonio agrees with recent critiques by Bellah and others that the value of individual autonomy has become significantly disconnected from the restraints that, as Tocqueville noticed so astutely, the Protestant ethic provided during an earlier era. Barbara Hargrove, in her essay "The Church, the Family, and the Modernization Process," extends this analysis and shows how both Western religion, of which liberal Protestantism may be the prototypical illustration, and the family have undergone this persistent drift toward the values of autonomy, individualism, and privatism (Hargrove 1983, 29–31).

At the end of their articles, both authors call for the church to develop a new strategy that provides a reformulated religious ethic of love to guide the documentable widespread hunger among the young for meaningful and enduring relationships with members of the opposite sex (D'Antonio 1980, 102). According to D'Antonio, although autonomy and self-actualization (as Daniel Yankelovich and others have also shown) are central values for the young in the United States, there is also among them a deep-seated hunger for love (Yankelovich 1981). D'Antonio believes that there is a major new mission for the church to address, from a religious perspective, the meaning of love for contemporary couples and families. Hargrove builds on D'Antonio when she writes: "It would appear, then, that what is called for in the present age is a commitment of religious institutions to an ethic of love as strong as the early Protestant commitment to work, giving theological grounding for loving relationships and institutional examples and support for their maintenance" (Hargrove 1983, 45–46). These authors call not only for a new love ethic but for socializing, educational, and ritual procedures to help people grow in its skills and habits.

At first glance, D'Antonio's and Hargrove's proposals sound either bland, trite, or self-evident. But to conclude this would be to miss the sociological context of their suggestions. For the love that they are proposing is one that takes account of the drive for autonomy implicit in most contemporary love relationships—an autonomy that frequently works to the detriment of the very love relation that the autonomous individual attempts to create. The marriages and families that they are envisioning are not based simply on external institutional commands or dry principles of duty. Rather, they propose a love ethic that both takes account of but also redirects the contemporary drive for autonomy and self-actualization. D'Antonio defines love as a "relationship between two or more persons that is concerned with the optimal development of each of them" (D'Antonio 1980, 101). Following her comparison of the liberating potential of the new love ethic with the older Protestant work ethic, Hargrove writes: "As the religious work ethic freed individuals from the externally imposed obligations of the traditional kin group or neighborhood so that they could participate in the economic aspects of modernization, so now a religious love ethic might return them to their families as autonomous persons choosing their own commitments" (Hargrove 1983, 46).

All of this leads to the following questions: What kind of ethic is being proposed by D'Antonio and Hargrove? Is it possible to introduce the elements of autonomy and self-actualization within a Christian understanding of love? What more would this ethic specifically imply for the three families Friedman discusses—the family that is the church, the families within the church, and the minister's own family—and the minister's self-definition?

Autonomy and an Ethics of Equal-Regard

The response of some religious commentators to the emerging ethic of autonomy and self-actualization is to reassert an ethic of duty and self-sacrifice. Such an ethic is frequently behind attempts to defend the hierarchical character of the traditional family; some ethic of self-sacrifice is generally invoked to justify the subservience of the wife. For some, such an ethic is required both by the commands of the Christian faith and the requirements of modern life. This is close to what Robert Bellah and his associates do in their chapter "Love and Marriage" in *Habits of the Heart* (1985), their successful portrait of American life. After detecting in the various languages of love used by their interviewees a widespread utilitarian and expressive individualism, they side with those groups in American society who advocate an evangelical ethic of duty and self-sacrifice. It is a duty and self-sacrifice anchored in a larger covenantal understanding of the couple's common vocation before God (Bellah et al. 1985, 97).

The implicit ethic of love in *Habits* is not unlike the love ethic in much of American neoorthodox theology. For instance, although the great twentieth-century theologian Reinhold Niebuhr could state a role for the energizing power of eros and self-actualization in the Christian doctrine of love as agape, he still believed self-sacrificial love was the meaning of agape and the final norm of the Christian life (Niebuhr 1941, 68). Sociologist Benton Johnson has pointed out that this formulation of love gave mainline Protestantism a moral tone that provided little role for self-affirmation, self-interest, and other values that go into the master value of autonomy (Johnson 1982, 195). According to Johnson, at the same time that Western modernization was pushing American society toward the values of autonomy and self-actualization, the social love ethic promulgated by the church was more and more unable to include these values. When people were searching for a love that included autonomy and self-actualization, they heard from the mainline socially active churches that Niebuhr influenced a screeching ethic of self-sacrificial duty that squeezed out all elements of individual fulfillment and enrichment. Johnson proposes a reformulation of the gospel message based on a more optimistic note, one that affirms a constrained and principled autonomy typical of the older religious liberalism that neoorthodoxy replaced. Although I personally would not want to give up Niebuhr's realistic doctrine of sin, the remainder of this chapter will investigate an ethic of love that incorporates, extends, and balances some of the suggestions put forth by D'Antonio, Hargrove, and Johnson.

Actually, Niebuhr did have a rather positive place in his anthropology for what he called "ordinate" self-concern and self-actualization (Niebuhr 1941, 191). He thought, however, that the universal human inability trustingly to confront finitude and anxiety leads all humans to become "inordinately" concerned with their security, autonomy, and self-actualization. It is this "inordinate" concern, not our ordinate concern, that is our sin. In spite of this, Niebuhr did formulate his love ethic around the concept of self-sacrificial love. In contrast to the extreme position of Anders Nygren, who gave no place in agape at all for eros or self-actualization, Niebuhr believed that agape both builds on yet transforms our natural and ordinate energies (eros) toward self-concern and self-actualization (Niebuhr 1943, 84).

But Niebuhr could never adequately formulate the role of autonomy and self-actualization in a Christian ethic of love. The proof of this can be seen in his continued subordination of love as mutuality to love as self-sacrifice (Niebuhr 1943, 69). An ethic of mutuality was, for Niebuhr, a concession that our finite and sinful human condition requires because of our inability to live steadfastly and constantly the higher call to self-sacrificial living (82). An ethic of mutuality always finds a place for self-regard, just as it finds a place for regard for the other. For Niebuhr, such an ethic of equal-regard for self and other was seen as a concession to the fallenness of history, rather than an essential norm of the Christian life. It is for this very reason that Johnson believed that neoorthodoxy could not and cannot provide a theology of love that builds into it a legitimate place for self-concern. Niebuhr can talk about ordinate self-concern before the fall, but seems unable to find a place for ordinate self-concern in his doctrine of love after the fall.

A better formulation of an ethic of love, both theologically and ethically, can be found in the work of the Belgian Catholic moral theologian Louis Janssens. It also is similar to the ethic of love that is implicit or explicit in several feminist theologians, such as Barbara Andelson (1981), Christine Gudorf (1985), Linell Cady (1987), Judith Plaskow (1980), and Judith Vaughan (1983). Its main virtue is its capacity to include the values of autonomy and self-actualization within a genuinely Christian doctrine of love. It also can contribute to a family ethic for the mainline churches and the three interlocking families that make up much of their life.

Janssens holds that the heart of a Christian ethic of love is found in the formal structure of the love commandment, "You shall love your neighbor as yourself." Variations of this principle are repeated no less than eight times in the New Testament (Matt. 19:19; 22:39; Mark 12:31, 33; Luke 10:27; Rom. 13:8; Gal. 5:14; James 2:8). Janssens believes that the fundamental meaning of the principle of neighbor-love is that "Love of neighbor is impartial. It is fundamentally an equal-regard for every person, because it applies to each neighbor qua human existent" (Janssens 1977, 209). By impartial, Janssens does not mean indifferent, nonaffective, or uninterested. In fact, it is just the reverse. Janssens' ethic of equal-regard means that we are to take the neighbor's needs and interests with seriousness equal to our own. But the reverse is also true. The principle of neighbor-love tells us to take our own needs and interests as seriously, but no more seriously, than those of the neighbor. Gene Outka, the American theological ethicist, writes that "valuing the self as well as others remains a manifest obligation" (Outka 1972, 290). The reasons one is obligated to value the other also constitute the reasons one should value oneself.

In Janssens' formulation of a love ethic, there is room for autonomy, ordinate self-concern, and self-actualization; they can be, however, no more important than the autonomy, self-concern, and self-actualization of the other. Furthermore, a healthy concern for oneself can be a positive guide to empathizing with the needs of the other and promoting the other's growth and enrichment; as we come to know and accept our own needs, we are more able to recognize and accept the needs of the other. This is a formulation that coincides with the proposals for an ethic of love put forth by D'Antonio and Hargrove—one that combines a concern for autonomy and self-actualization with a dedication to the autonomy and self-actualization of the other.

Yet, if this love ethic is to be Christian, there must be within it a place for sacrificial love and the way of the cross. But Janssens' formulation reverses the logic of Christian love proposed by Niebuhr. Rather than self-sacrificial love being the norm of the Christian life, as it is for Niebuhr, mutuality in the sense of equal-regard is the normative meaning of Christian love for Janssens. And rather than mutuality being a concession to fallenness, for Janssens it is self-sacrifice that fallenness requires in order to restore the mutuality that is itself the goal of the Christian life. Janssens writes, "In short, self-sacrifice is not the quintessence of love. . . . Self-sacrifice is justified derivatively from other-regard" (Janssens 1977, 228). For Janssens, other-regard is itself part of the structure of equal-regard and mutuality. Self-sacrificial love is required as a transitional ethic designed to restore unequal and unmutual situations to the true goal of mutuality. Self-sacrifice serves mutuality and equal-regard; it is not an end in itself.

A love ethic built around mutuality and equal-regard is more consistent with certain famous New Testament passages than might seem possible at first glance. This is especially true of the famous Ephesians passage that contains the infamous words "Wives, be subject to your husbands as you are to the Lord" (Eph. 5:22). But a consideration of the full contextuality of this passage and its general direction strongly limits any simple unmitigated patriarchal call for the subjugation of women to the arbitrary will of their husbands. As we read on, we learn that the husband, in this passage, is to be like Christ and be a servant to the family as Christ was a servant to the church. And at the end of the passage, we learn that the husband is to treat his wife as his own body and to "love his wife as himself" (Eph. 5:33). Against the background of the traditions and laws of the Greek metropolis, which formed the social context of the early church, this was a radical statement indeed. For in this tradition, only men were free citizens with agency and autonomy, and women, children, and slaves were all the subjects of men. To say that a husband must treat his wife with the same regard and mutuality as he treats himself and his own body would be a statement regarded in that context as both radical and seditious. The direction of this passage and others like it is toward the rule of neighbor-love applied to the domain of intimate relations.

The Family and the Ethic of Equal-Regard

Such an ethic may seem attractive at first glance, but also may appear rather abstract and vague upon deeper inspection. This is the case with any attempt to formulate general ethical principles, even the principles governing an ethic of love. General ethical principles never stand alone. In real life, they are surrounded with several other ethically relevant dimensions that give these principles life and concreteness. In my other recent writings, I have argued that ethical thinking is in reality quite thick; by this I mean it consists of several different interpenetrating and mutually qualifying dimensions. General principles such as the ethic of neighbor-love are always surrounded by metaphors and narratives (what I sometimes call the "visional" level of ethical thinking) that define the origins and purposes of the moral life. For instance, in Christianity the story of the life, death, and resurrection of Jesus Christ tells us both about the purposes of life and provides a model of sacrifice that empowers our need to work hard—indeed go the second mile—to restore our relationships to mutuality. The theological concepts of grace and forgiveness help us overcome our inordinate self-concern by releasing us from the guilt of past failures and empowering us to renewed efforts to mutuality, even at some sacrifice to ourselves.

In addition to this visional or narrative level of our morality, principles such as neighbor-love are also informed, at another level, by concepts cataloging our fundamental human desires, needs, and tendencies. These catalogs (generally quite implicit) of our fundamental wants and needs are theories of what Louis Janssens calls the "premoral good," or the *ordo bonorum*. The premoral good refers to all the ways we use the word *good* in the nonmoral, in contrast to the moral, sense of the word (Janssens 1977, 228). Premoral goods are realities inside and outside of us that we have a positive response to and believe are worthy of promoting and bringing into heightened realization. Premoral goods are such goods as food, water, pleasure, affection, physical and mental health, joy, friendship, and such cultural values as science, art, technology, and education. Love as equal-regard is a very formal principle and can only have living significance when it is informed by a sense for the premoral goods that love deems it worthy to promote in the self and the other. Paul Ricoeur says it well in commenting on the meaning of the golden rule. Ricoeur says that "to do unto others as you would have them do unto you" means "to do *good*" to others as you would have them "do *good* to you" (Ricoeur 1987). In the formal terms of moral philosophy, the golden rule gives priority to the deontological principle of equal-regard, which, in turn, is used to mediate between necessary but sometimes conflicting teleological concepts of the premoral good. Janssens' and Ricoeur's formulation of neighbor-love holds that love is moral insofar as it is guided by the principle of equal-regard. But in contrast to more strictly Kantian formulations, love is only *fully* moral (in contrast to *formally* moral) when equal-regard includes, guides, and mediates between the rich range of both compatible and conflicting premoral goods that life seems to set before us. Other positions similar to Janssens' and Ricoeur's can be found in the work of William Frankena, Ronald Green, and my own writings (Frankena 1973, 43–52; Green 1978, 132; Browning 1983, 63–70).

Within the context of a family guided by the love ethic developed here, our task becomes not only to exhibit with our loved ones the formal principle of mutuality and equal-regard; it is to inform this equal-regard with a sensibility about the relevant and timely premoral goods that the various members of the family want and truly need. This, of course, becomes the real challenge for an ethic of love for families. Different members of the family need different premoral goods. We do not always know which premoral goods are relevant at any particular time, either for ourselves or for others. And sometimes, even if we know which premoral goods are relevant, there may be a scarcity of such goods and a conflict between goods relevant to more than one member of the family. In addition, there also may be a conflict between the goods relevant to the family and its various members and the goods needed by others outside the family. To give expression to the ethic of equal-regard and to demonstrate how it includes but also guides various premoral goods is not to provide an ethic of the family that is beyond ambiguity. In fact, it is precisely because there always is ambiguity and, indeed, moral failure that a Christian ethic of equal-regard also requires grace. This grace, in turn, empowers us to exert self-sacrificial love in an effort to restore mutuality to our broken and disrupted family relations. But this view of the love ethic at least has the virtue of stating explicitly the way in which one's own autonomy, differentiation, and self-actualization are included within an equal-regard for the autonomy, differentiation, and self-actualization of the other.

Spheres of Equal-Regard and the Life Cycle

When the ethic of mutuality and equal-regard is supplemented with considerations of the premoral good, equal-regard looks somewhat different depending upon the spheres of the premoral good to which it is being applied. In fact, one can speak of spheres of equal-regard paralleling the title of Michael Walzer's book *Spheres of Justice* (Walzer 1983, 6–10). Equal-regard, of course, is another name for distributive justice but is stated in such a way as to be more applicable to the field of intimate human relationships. Although I differ with Walzer on a variety of points, his main point is well taken: equal-regard takes on different meanings depending upon which sphere of premoral good it is trying to order justly. Equal-regard functions differently in the corporate workplace, at the public school, at the dinner table at home, and in the marital bed. This is because one is pursuing in these different spheres of life slightly different premoral goods, and therefore one distributes tasks, recognitions, and rewards differently. In fact, we tend to get quite upset, and with reason, when some goods of the family, such as sexual favors, get projected into the goods of the school or office. We also become disturbed when the goods of the office or factory (such as technical rationality or the pursuit of wealth) get projected into the family and dominate its purposes and goals.

Within the context of the family, there are different pre-moral goods provided for the children and the parents. This means mutuality or equal-regard look different depending on whether it is being expressed between the parents, between parents and children, between children, or between children and their parents. Without moving into all of the complexities of the ways equal-regard can work out from these different angles, let me illustrate my point by concentrating on the way they shift in meaning throughout the life cycle of the family.

When parents are dealing with infants and very young children, equal-regard and mutuality are both actual and promissory. If one takes seriously the work of Erikson, Winnicott, Kegan, and others on the first years of life, mutuality between parent and infant primarily comes at the level of glance, eye contact, and the nonanxious affirmation of the budding self of the infant (Erikson 1963, 247–251). The infant reciprocates with delight, satisfaction, and fleeting moments of I-Thou recognition. In fact, a fundamental mutuality of recognition can be present even at this level of interaction. Of course, in other ways, the parent-child relation is decidedly unmutual. The child is tremendously dependent upon the parent and only gradually develops the skills to be an equal contributor to the family. Hence, equal-regard means in the parent-child relation primarily the parent's willingness and encouragement for the relation to evolve toward the eventual reality of an adult interaction that is marked by these characteristics.

Although mutuality is both partially realized but also promissory in the parent-child relationship, it can become more fully actualized in the adult relationship between parents and grown sons and daughters. Here adult children join the mutuality that should characterize the relation between the parents. Parents and adult offspring, then, can create a community of mutual respect and mutual helpfulness.

Equal-regard can mean something else again as parents move toward old age. Now parents develop a greater dependency upon their children not unlike the dependency their sons and daughters once had upon them. Equal-regard can still take the form of mutual respect, but in other areas of premoral good such as health, living arrangements, or even finances, children may take the initiative and the greater responsibility. Yet the memory of the fuller mutuality that was earlier achieved can still permeate their relationship even amidst the emergence of new patterns of dependency and initiative.

Family Ethics and Feminism

This ethic of equal-regard and mutuality has much in common with certain expressions of feminist ethics. In addition to the authors mentioned above, the relational ethic of Carol Gilligan and her followers has strong similarities to the ethic of mutuality outlined in the above paragraphs (Gilligan 1982). Although there is an emerging ethic of mutuality in certain quarters of the feminist movement, most feminists have not brought it into the area of family ethics. Therefore, as the sociologists Brigitte and Peter Berger and political theorist Jean Bethke Elshtain have observed (and with some sadness), the general public perceives the feminist movement as celebrating the values of autonomy unmitigated by equal-regard. Furthermore, the public perceives feminism to be, on the whole, antifamily (Berger and Berger 1984, 24–25). Few feminists use the ethic of mutuality not only to advance the position of women but to advance and strengthen the family as well. Hence, needless resistances have developed against feminism among people who believe that they must choose between their dedication to the family and the attractions of the feminist movement. My proposals deal not only with making a rearticulated family policy central to the mainline churches; I recommend as well that this family policy be closely associated with those aspects of feminism that are stating a positive ethic of self-actualization that is, at the same time, restrained and guided by an ethic of equal-regard. This brand of feminism has both much to give to a revitalized family strategy as well as much to gain from a closer identification with the interests of families. The mainline churches should be interested in both feminism and the family, and in crafting a creative relation between them within an ethic of mutuality.

Family Ethics and the Plurality
of Family Forms

One should not conclude consideration of a new family ethic for the mainline churches and clergy without assessing this proposal from the perspective of the plurality of family forms that now occupy the sociological scene in Western societies. There are many typologies of family forms to choose from. One economic typology distinguishes between seven types of families: living together, DINKS (dual income with no children), single parent, two career (with children), traditionals (working husband with wife at home caring for children), blended (parents and children from previous marriages), and sandwich (middle-aged parents caring for both their own children and their parents) (Schurenberg 1989, 56–57). Although the mainline churches may never explicitly sanction couples living together, all of the last six types in this list can be the consequence of legitimate marriages functioning more or less within the values of heterosexual covenanted marriage and some variation of the nuclear family.

The ethic of love proposed here can be relevant to all of them. It is also true, however, that the different family types must order slightly different premoral goods; and for that reason, mutuality and equal-regard will do their ordering and actualizing tasks somewhat differently for the various family patterns. For example, mutuality means something different for the divorced single parent than, for instance, for the DINK. The single parent has no one within the nuclear family unit with whom to work out his or her adult needs for mutuality. For this reason, the single parent may need to arrange patterns of adult friendship and support to compensate for certain kinds of mutuality that the family unit itself cannot provide. Even though the single parent has to meet the physical and psychological dependencies of growing children, he or she should do this within an ethic of equal-regard for the emerging selfhood of the children. DINKs, on the other hand, may have the financial resources to support a wide range of mutual exchanges and enrichments not only between themselves but with the outside world. On the other hand, they may be tempted to use these resources to develop more or less autonomous and parallel lives. The ethic of mutuality is relevant to and will make a difference in how two-career and childless couples actually live out their lives together. Obviously, the most complicated and demanding issues pertaining to mutuality would come with the so-called blended family, where highly complicated and separate family histories of affection and tension are brought together into a new synthesis. With all of these types, the principles of mutuality and equal-regard cannot be applied statically; they must be seen as goals that families grow toward as they go through their family life cycles and as they try to relate responsibly to the outside world. Rather than static images of mutuality, it is better to think of families in terms of evolving histories or pilgrimages of mutuality. The family, as Herbert Anderson and Eric Fuchs have suggested, is an open-ended *project* in mutuality (Fuchs 1983, 176–206; Anderson 1984, 30–40).

Family Ethics and Public Issues

In contrast to the impression that developed in the 1960s and 1970s, a family strategy on the part of the church does not need to preempt its involvement in the wider public world. To the contrary, starting from a family angle of vision, many issues that would seem remote and irrelevant suddenly take on new meaning and can call forth our deepest energies. There are now available new historical and sociological insights showing how the family, in contrast to standard Marxist perspectives, is not always a passive entity molded and sometimes battered by whatever social and material forces are in ascendancy (Engels 1985). The writings of Theodor Adorno, Mark Poster, the Bergers, and Emmanuel Todd are just a few examples of scholars that show how the family can shape society as well as be shaped by society (Poster 1978, xvii; Todd 1985, 1–7). Mutuality and equal-regard, as an ethic for the family, can be a guide for the family as it attempts to shape wider social issues in the areas of work, education, taxation, the environment, and even foreign policy.

Work patterns provide the most immediate examples for how this can function. Patterns of work in the public realm must be so structured as to support the mutuality and equal-regard of families. Without getting into the technical details of specific proposals, this might mean, for example, more flexible work hours, childbirth leaves for both wives and husbands, more adequate child care, various tax breaks for children, and so forth. These are provisions in which many European countries, and probably the United Kingdom, are more advanced than is the United States. It would be possible to give illustrations of a similar kind for other sectors of the public world as well.

Finally, the principles of mutuality and equal-regard, although relevant to the ordering of the internal life of the family, are also pertinent to the family's moral action in the world. Families can only make demands on the public world and on other individuals and families that they, in turn, are willing to have made on them. Hence, families must be willing to live by the reversibility implicit within the principle of neighbor-love as equal-regard. Or, to state it more aggressively, the considerations that families demand for themselves they must, in principle, be willing to work hard to realize for other families with similar needs. This is the meaning of equal-regard as applied to relations between families; it entails the willingness to take the needs of other families as seriously as one takes the needs of one's own family. And within a distinctively Christian context, it would entail the willingness to take meaningful sacrificial action as a family in order to restore disadvantaged families to a situation of more genuine equality.

The impetus from the family therapy movement to make families more central to the ministry of the church is both right and healthy. It first of all has implications for the families of ministers. Ministers more than other people have difficulties balancing equal-regard and self-sacrifice, both in their families and in their professional ministries. The subtle shift in the priorities of love recommended here has implications for the ministers' personal lives in families, but it also has implications for their ministry with other families and the family that is the church.

References

Andelson, Barbara Hilkert. 1981. "Agape in Feminist Ethics." *Journal of Religious Ethics* 9 (Spring): 69–80.

Anderson, Herbert. 1984. *The Family and Pastoral Care.* Philadelphia: Fortress Press.

Bellah, Robert N., Richard Madsen, William M. Sullivan, Ann Swidler, and Steven M. Tipton. 1985. *Habits of the Heart: Individualism and Commitment in American Life.* Berkeley: University of California Press.

Berger, Brigitte, and Peter Berger. 1984. *The War over the Family.* New York: Doubleday & Co.

Browning, Don S. 1983. *Religious Ethics and Pastoral Care.* Philadelphia: Fortress Press.

Cady, Linell. 1987. "Relational Love: A Feminist Christian Vision." In *Embodied Love,* edited by Paula Cooey, Sharon Farmer, and Ellen Ross. San Francisco: Harper & Row.

D'Antonio, William. 1980. "The Family and Religion: Exploring a Changing Relationship." *Journal for the Scientific Study of Religion* 19 (2): 89–104.

Engels, Frederick. 1985. *The Origin of the Family, Private Property, and the State.* New York: International Publishers.

Erikson, Erik. 1963. *Childhood and Society.* New York: W. W. Norton.

Frankena, William. 1973. *Ethics.* Englewood Cliffs, N.J.: Prentice-Hall.

Friedman, Edwin. 1985. *Generation to Generation: Family Process in Church and Synagogue.* New York: Guilford Press.

Fuchs, Eric. 1983. *Sexual Desire and Love.* New York: Seabury Press.

Gilligan, Carol. 1982. *In a Different Voice.* Cambridge: Harvard University Press.

Green, Ronald. 1978. *Religious Reason.* New York: Oxford University Press.

Gudorf, Christine. 1985. "Parenting, Mutual Love, and Sacrifice." In *Women's Consciousness, Women's Conscience,* edited by Barbara Andelson, Christine Gudorf, and Mary Pellauer. New York: Winston Press.

Hargrove, Barbara. 1983. "The Church, the Family, and the Modernization Process." In *Families and Religions,* edited by William D'Antonio and Joan Aldous. Beverly Hills: Sage Publications.

Janssens, Louis. 1977. "Norms and Priorities of a Love Ethic." *Louvain Studies* 6 (Spring): 207–238.

Johnson, Benton. 1982. "Taking Stock: Reflections on the End of Another Era." *Journal for the Scientific Study of Religion* 21 (3): 188–199.

Lenski, Gerhard. 1961. *The Religious Factor.* Garden City, N.Y.: Doubleday & Co.

Niebuhr, Reinhold. 1941, 1943. *The Nature and Destiny of Man.* Vols. 1 and 2. New York: Charles Scribner's Sons.

Outka, Gene. 1972. *Agape: An Ethical Analysis.* New Haven: Yale University Press.

Plaskow, Judith. 1980. *Sex, Sin and Grace: Women's Experience and the Theologies of Reinhold Niebuhr and Paul Tillich.* Lanham, Md.: University Press of America.

Poster, Mark. 1978. *Critical Theory of the Family.* New York: Seabury Press.

Ricoeur, Paul. 1987. "The Teleological and Deontological Structures of Action: Aristotle or Kant?" Lecture given at the Divinity School, University of Chicago, June.

Schurenberg, Eric. 1989. "The New Gospel of Financial Planning." *Money* (March).

Taylor, Charles. 1989. *Sources of the Self: The Making of Modern Identity.* Cambridge: Harvard University Press.

Todd, Emmanuel. 1985. *Explanation of Ideology: Family Structures and Social Systems.* Oxford: Basil Blackwell.

Vaughan, Judith. 1983. *Ethics and Social Change: A Critical Appraisal of Reinhold Niebuhr's Ethics in the Light of Rosemary Radford Ruether's Works.* New York: University Press of America.

Walzer, Michael. 1983. *Spheres of Justice.* New York: Basic Books.

Yankelovich, Daniel. 1981. *New Rules.* New York: Random House.

11

Women
in the Roman Catholic Ministry:
New Vision, New Ethics

Ann O'Hara Graff

There is nothing short of a revolution going on in the Roman Catholic Church. Nowhere is this more visible than in the rapid way that ministry is changing, with or without Vatican approval. Theologians and social scientists are calling this period, especially in North America, a crisis (Coleman 1982, 155–166). Perhaps it would be more apt to use Tillich's term *kairos*. I suggest the latter because the present fluid, often confusing, situation presents opportunities that may carry the church into the twenty-first century with great élan, or the church may become increasingly narrow and sectarian. This chapter is a reflection on this *kairos* from the vantage of my own experience and thinking about these dramatic changes, especially as I have participated in them among Catholic women ministers in Chicago. I do not claim that the direction in which I find these women moving is either universally characteristic of them or exclusive to them, but it is powerful among them. It is a direction shared by much of the moderate to liberal wing of the American Catholic church as is widely evident in its publications, organizations, and conferences.[1] Their concerns are also shared by women in the Protestant ministry who seek to build up the church in similar ways (Rhodes 1987). Thus, although this paper will focus on the Catholic situation and its theology, much of what Catholic women seek is of a piece with

---

[1] See any issue of the *National Catholic Reporter* or *Commonweal;* note the Women's Ordination Conference, the National Association of Women Religious, or the Institute for Pastoral Life in Kansas City.

a wider Christian feminist, even womanist, vision. I will briefly indicate the situation, and as I take up its theological and ethical dimensions, I will continue to reflect on the vision of the women involved.

The Situation in Chicago

The Roman Catholic Church in Chicago is experiencing a change in ministry that is typical of the other local Roman Catholic churches in the United States. We have about 450 parishes, all of which were staffed by priests, a pastor and his associate pastors, prior to Vatican II. Whereas most, not all, of the parishes today still have a priest pastor, there are about three hundred women "pastoral associates" now working in the role of the former associate pastors. A few women pastoral associates do have a pastor's administrative and pastoral responsibility for parishes, though they remain without ordained empowerment to celebrate the sacraments formally for the parish community. This change has occurred largely within the last ten years. In the majority of the parishes, there are also women serving as directors of religious education (DREs), a highly responsible pastoral ministry that has been growing steadily since the early 1970s. Both pastoral associates and DREs are usually members of religious communities, although some are lay people. The net picture is that the much discussed shortage of priests is a phenomenon concurrently present with a tremendous recent growth of alternate forms of largely female ministerial presence. Other ministries are burgeoning as well. Lay and religious women are widely involved in work for social justice in a variety of ways. I am attending to the parish situation because that is where the issue of clergy particularly arises.

With these additions and changes, something else has also appeared—team ministry. Although the priest shortage threatens, and in some cases does leave parishes with only one lone priest or one who travels among several parishes on Sundays, the arrival of pastoral associates, DREs, and often also permanent deacons, financial managers, youth ministers, ministers of care, and even music ministers *inter alia* has generated the practice of ministering within a parish as a team. The school principal is usually included in this team. This new practice of a collaborative ministry at the level of the parish staff is a major innovation in a church in which the norm was that the pastor ran the parish, and under him, a sister principal ran the school. We are experiencing critical changes in who

ministers and how those ministries are exercised that have
far-reaching administrative and pastoral effects.

The purpose of this chapter is to ask how this new situation,
particularly as it is shaped by women, affects clergy ethics,
especially in the Roman Catholic Church. I understand ethics
to be principles that guide just action rooted in a vision of the
good that is their source and end. Our theological visions are
profoundly moral. Therefore, the subsequent sections of this
chapter will describe three interlocking theological visions
that arise from and speak to the situation I have described—
visions of the church, of human beings, and of ministry. I am
particularly interested in theology promoted by the institution
itself, because the entailed critical demand for just practice
can be put directly to those who espouse the vision. This is
important for the issue of clergy ethics in this denomination,
because the first concerns are for justice in the work of ministry itself.

An Emerging Vision of Church

Although the situation that I described above is the result of
multiple causes, the struggles that belong to its theological
visions of church, persons, and ministry are rooted in the documents of the Second Vatican Council, especially *The Dogmatic
Constitution on the Church, Lumen Gentium,* and *The Pastoral Constitution on the Church in the Modern World,
Gaudium et Spes* (Abbott 1966, 14–101 and 199–308). In particular, *Lumen Gentium* affords a dual vision of church (Graff
1986, 46–124). On the one hand, it supports and continues to
empower the church as a "perfect society," hierarchical in
nature, under the rubric of its theology of the church as the
mystical body of Christ. The different tasks of the body neatly
allow for traditional divisions of roles and power. On the other
hand, the document forwards a vision of the church as the
people of God, and so calls for multiple forms of collaborative
structures but does not empower these structures as decision-
making actors. Rather, the former theology immediately inter-
venes to ensure that the new institutions be only advisory to
whichever hierarch is appropriate. Thus, synods advise the
pope, pastoral councils advise a bishop, parish councils advise
a pastor, and so on. *Gaudium et Spes* pushes even further
toward a dialogical, collaborative church, especially in its mission of evangelization; but again, no institutional empowerment is forthcoming.

This heritage is not far from the average Catholic in the

United States. It is experienced everyday in the relationships between clergy and laity, nowhere more acutely than among the pastoral staff. Perhaps the most painful rub is that the latter, collaborative vision, bears a felt authority consonant with our American democratic experience, while the pastor remains in full control. The conciliar vision of a participatory church coincided with the economic and political coming of age of U.S. Catholics marked by the Kennedy presidency. Thus, it corresponds with the felt needs of many who now see themselves as adult Catholics and competent citizens, no longer uprooted immigrants in need of a pastor. This is our cultural share in an exciting and painful worldwide awakening to a coresponsible church.

Today the women pastoral associates and DREs, among others, have taken up the vision of collegiality articulated at Vatican II, and have considerably expanded it. For them, a collaborative church does not simply name a style of advisory conversation to benefit church governors, but is a way of being church together. It also names a vision of a new kind of church governing, a new experience of power as empowerment of people and not domination over them, and a new understanding of authority as people authorizing what we undertake and who undertakes it. In short, they call for a new Catholic self-understanding as persons who together constitute and are constituted by the church.[2] This is a kind of liberation of the church itself from older, now oppressive structures that severely limited lay, especially female, involvement, and toward a household that is both more free and more responsible for itself and to the gospel. Women are calling the church to Jesus' inclusive vision of God's kingdom and God's heavenly banquet, where all do the work of justice and love and all sit down to the same feast.

As staff members, women are working for a church that is a household of mutuality and reciprocity. They look toward a community in which people sustain one another, forgive and help one another, nourish and celebrate each other's gifts. Coresponsibility is the key. Ministry is exercised from within the community to facilitate and empower the members, to enhance the well-being of each, and to work for the welfare of the whole. This community of equals is rooted and nourished in Christ, and the vision of the kingdom guides its action. This

---

[2]See James and Evelyn Whitehead (1986) for a clear articulation of some of these values. This also reflects Chopp's recognition, in her chapter in this volume, of a shift from a church in service to modernity toward a church in service of human liberation.

vision includes a recognition of human sin as it mars the church and the society. The cross often appears in women's reflections. Their hope is to meet needs and transform unjust situations as they are named locally, and to work to live with and for each other as a community of adult Christians who are responsible together for the quality of their lives ecclesially and socially through their outreach to others in Christian love and justice.

This vision grows out of the council's symbol of the church as the people of God. The council's failure formally to empower the structures it urged in using this symbol did not mitigate its imaginative and generative power. The critical factor is the symbol's dimension that reveals a community or communion of equals in faith, hope, and love, before God. It is a church in which the full humanity of each person, together with others, can find nourishment, challenge, and acceptance. The wider church is thus a community of communities or a communion of communions. The people of God evokes a vision of an adult church that coincides with and incorporates some of the dimensions of other ecclesial symbols, such as the multiply gifted body of Christ whose members' diverse charisms build up the whole (but do not segregate it), and the provocative, utopic vision of the kingdom of God where justice for all is realized.

This is the positive climate that gives rise to the roles of women pastoral associates and DREs. There would be no institutional place for them without this alternative symbolic vision. At the same time, they, and others like them, are the very people now enlarging the council's vision and shaping the church of the future. I want to emphasize that the impact of the changing symbol system as critical to the identification of the church cannot be underestimated. It creates a new way of being church.

Clearly, new wine has been poured into old wineskins, and the old ones are bursting. We are looking at new kinds of institutions to support this vision both in the parish and at the wider geographical levels of the church. I will leave the latter issue aside here. In the parish, the multiple efforts of women staff to enact, support, and empower cooperation and collaboration both on the staff and among the parishioners is creative of new ways of enacting church. This happens in the administration as the emergence of team ministry indicates. It also occurs in the coordination of parish undertakings, in the management of meetings, and in prayer and liturgy. Consonant with their aim, women staff are as concerned about factions among parishioners and their moves to dominate parish activities as they are about overcoming the staff's own inclination to manage by itself without parish process. Yet these are only the first incremental steps toward the practical realization of a truly inclusive church. That still is before us, beckoning in the symbols.[3]

These women's practical efforts are further supported by their commitment to Vatican II's vision of the human person, a vision enhanced by American and feminist sensibilities. They also challenge traditional priestly ministry to transformation. These are the next issues to which we turn.

The Dignity of the Human Person

Gaudium et Spes sets out a theological anthropology and its ethical implications that are fundamental to contemporary Roman Catholic thought. This position belongs to the tradition of social justice encyclicals that begin with Leo XIII's *Rerum Novarum* in 1891, and continues through *Gaudium et Spes* and in the work of John Paul II. It informs and is expanded in the major pastoral letters issued by the American bishops: *The Challenge of Peace* (1983), *Economic Justice for All* (1986), and the first draft on the concerns of women, *Partners in the Mystery of Redemption* (1988). Perhaps its most elegant exponent in moral theology is Bernard Häring, who had a hand in shaping *Gaudium et Spes,* and who is a major Catholic thinker in this area (Häring 1978, 1979, 1981). This theology is important precisely because it is the anthropology consistently promoted by the institution. Thus, although there are more nuanced and critical positions elsewhere, this one is politically the most powerful in this church.

In briefest form, this theology begins with an assertion of the dignity of every human being that is grounded in scripture's claim that we are made, male and female, in the image and likeness of God. Created together, human beings are not solitary, but are bound up with one another in community. Despite the divisions and diminishment of our sinfulness, we are yet given new freedom and strength in Christ, individually

---

[3]A more fully developed ecclesiology would have to include careful attention to the problems of leadership and community, both in the Catholic tradition and in relation to the Protestant experience of congregational churches. The vanguard in the experiment of creating new styles of truly communal church life in this denomination are the orders of women religious who are trying to transform their leadership on inclusive models using common discernment.

and communally. Gifted with dignity and freedom as well as with the abilities to love and to pursue truth, wisdom, and joy in common with each other, we shape the possibility and extent of our realization of these gifts. Social, economic, and political institutions enhance or limit the dignity and satisfactoriness of our lives very concretely. As an adult people, called by God to wholeness and holiness, we are responsible together to shape our social, political, and economic arrangements to allow for the greatest number of people to participate in them and to benefit from them in accord with our human dignity.

These themes echo in the church today, and the women involved with parish ministry espouse them in practice. For them, to name the church as the people of God is to name it a community of adults, responsible together for their institutions and their faith. Thus, the theological anthropology undergirds the ecclesiology of the people of God outlined above. In this context, the ethical implications for the church are quite clear. Precisely because of our God-given dignity, institutions that provide for collaboration and process must shape the church and its ministry. The church persistently urges such institutions in the political realm on this anthropological basis (*Gaudium et Spes*, par. 75). That the church should not be an exception to this no doubt appears self-evident, especially to American Catholics, given our allegiance to the correlation between human rights and appropriate democratic forms of government. Certainly, many American Protestant churches reflect this correlation, as did John Carroll's early Roman Catholic Church in this country. Again, because the church does except itself from participatory leadership, we find that the Catholic institution has not yet realized the practical insights of its own theology, indeed even of the Enlightenment, although it is now already challenged by new movements for liberation around the globe.

Moreover, as this dignity accrues to both men and women, if women are truly members of the community of adults, then patriarchal institutions of domination and subordination or exclusion are no longer acceptable or just. Again, the principle appears self-evident. Catholic practice, as I have indicated, differs dramatically between what is happening in parishes and what the hierarchy is willing to countenance. A real sign of hope here was the first draft of the American bishops' new pastoral letter, *Partners in the Mystery of Redemption* (1988), which condemned systems of male dominance and sexism in the church, and urges expanded ecclesial roles for women. The second draft, *One in Christ Jesus* (1990), is clearly a retrench-

ment. It acknowledges systemic sexism, but clearly indicates
that there will be no change in church structures. Although
women are in fact full members of the church and in fact
acting as if they were ordained in many cases, the hierarchy refuses to acknowledge women as equals, and so refuses
to practice the justice they promote. Thus, we arrive at
the threshold of the third theological issue—hierarchy and
ministry.

From Sacred Priesthood to New Ministries

With the critical shifts in the identity of the church itself and
the espousal of the theological anthropology that grounds the
contemporary social justice tradition, there is an accompanying crisis, or *kairos,* in the area of church ministry. The shortage of priests and the rise of new ministries are only due in part
to the shift in theological sensibilities I have described above.
There are historical, sociological, and cultural factors as well.
There are also further issues in the changing theological landscape, and it is to these I turn here. We are moving from a
sacred priesthood to multiple new forms of ministry.

First, let us recall how the priest has appeared among Catholics in the recent past up to the Vatican council. Catholics have
recognized a holy man in the priest. He is ordained by the
bishop and empowered to celebrate the holy sacrifice of the
Mass and to forgive sins. The priest also shares in the power of
the bishop, and under him, the priest is to teach and to govern
in his own parish church. Edward Schillebeeckx offers a detailed account of the development from presbyters to sacrificial priests (Schillebeeckx 1981, 5–74; 1985, 13–208). What
appears is a convergence of sacred powers tied both to cult and
to hierarchy. The cultic power is further reinforced by being
bound to ritual purity in the form of celibacy. The priest, as a
cultic figure who stands in the place of Christ, belongs to another realm. The convergence of priesthood with the ascetic
tradition sets this person in the sphere of the holy.

Vatican II shifted the church liturgically away from cultic
sacrifice toward community Eucharist. It also shifted us toward
collaborative institutions for teaching and governing, even
though it did not empower them. Clearly, both of these shifts
had an impact on a Catholic notion of priesthood. Moreover,
the progressive valuation of women as full human beings has
brought with it a new valuing of sexuality and of marriage.
Whereas this has happened to a greater extent outside than

inside the church, one of its major effects within the tradition has been to put the values of ascetic life in question. This is particularly true in regard to the denial of sexual life for ordinary secular (diocesan) priests. One illustration of this collision of values is the recent literature on how to be a sexual celibate. Another is the new mainstream designation of celibacy as living for the kingdom without reserve. Certainly, the most dramatic illustration of the loss of credibility in the conjunction of asceticism and the secular priesthood has been the exodus of men from priestly life and their failure to seek it now in any numbers. It is interesting to note that the male religious orders face the opposite challenge. They are asking whether their life is not the place for a contemporary asceticism, joined with prophetic and servant roles, but not priesthood.

I suggest that not only is the role of the priest changing in this instance, but also the Catholic conception of a holy life and its circumstances. Religious orders are consciously calling themselves communities. As one such community of religious women clarifies their stance, they look for vocations to community life and its possibilities for service to peace and justice, rather than a vocation to a single life or to marriage. However, secular priests live as single people, without the support of their own family or a religious community. Because they were once set above the rest of the church as living a higher, holier life, they had a special respect and status. That has largely eroded because of the value now placed on life in relationship, especially to intimate others. Married life is respected as both normal and holy for mature people. The values of contemporary psychology have wedded and energized those present in the theological anthropology described above.

In sum, the cult has changed, the vision of holiness has changed, and the church's identity has been redefined, especially referent to its administration. Who is the priest today? A variety of responses are being made that differ from the traditional view. One response understands the priest to be the ritual maker of the community. This continues to tie the priest to a cultic, but not an administrative, role. Note that it does not have to keep the priest linked to a sacrificial cult, however. Nor does this role have to involve rules for ritual purity, or a lifetime commitment, or maleness. With these cautions in mind, however, cultic mediation of the holy remains central to the life of the church. Put simply, we need the church as a focus for our ongoing experience of God. Therefore, we also need people who can lead or facilitate our religious rituals. Moreover, it seems typically Catholic that the community have members whose lives symbolize holiness in some particular way, whether ascetic or in another form.

Another possible response is to expand the role rather than reduce it. It can be argued that cultic priesthood itself is a reduction of a broader embodiment of the ministry of Jesus, especially as *diakonia*. William Burrows argues that sacerdotal office needs to be remodeled as pastoral office, a concept he derives from the practice of the pre-Constantinian church and in which he finds a broader way to meet the needs of today's church, as well as to be faithful to the gospel (Burrows 1980, 66–112). He sketches two "families of ministry" essential to the church. The first is within the church. It involves men and women able to help others understand and grow in the faith, to foster natural, healthy communal life, and to help the community reflect on the meaning and challenge of the gospel. The second family reaches beyond the church itself. People involved in these ministries live self-consciously out of Christian symbols and bring this focus to bear on challenges that face us in the public social sphere. This model of two families of ministry, oriented internally and externally, gives shape to his, and others', sense that priesthood should be revised in the direction of a *diakonia* with broad pastoral dimensions.

If I add the ritual-making function implicit in Burrows' internal family of ministries, then I take his model to be particularly helpful in identifying ministry. The interesting aspect of his model is that these multiple ministerial functions are now being carried out by many different people, often women, in the form of the burgeoning of ministries I have indicated. This description also could serve to tighten the use of the term *ministry* in the Catholic church today. It is being employed quite loosely to denote many different activities that serve the church in any way.

Note that both the changes on the side of cult and Catholic experience of the holy, and the changes that involve a burgeoning of pastoral, outreach, and administrative ministries are directly related not only to the dearth of priests, but also to the identity crisis many priests face. There continue to be pre- and postconciliar models for priestly identity both that priests choose to enact and that are expected of them by different members of their congregations. Also, some priests feel caught between the role the diocese/institution asks of them and the one they may find more pastorally appropriate. No doubt that is a problem shared by many persons in ministry, one that poses difficult questions about discernment of the gospel.

A third stress on contemporary priests is administrative. Although some want to resist the presence of women and lay people in ministry, others solicit it. In either case, the pastor may remain overburdened. Minimally, for those who are working to share decision making and ministry, new styles of decentralized organization and facilitation need to be explored. This is another part of the skills that we need to create new ways of being an inclusive church. Team ministry is one such effort that has simply happened without planning. As one alternative, it too needs to be reflected upon and developed. Again, whether we view the Roman Catholic situation in this country through the eyes of the women who are laboring toward the future or the priests who are struggling with the past, what is visible is a disintegration and a new integration of church, both symbols and structures.

Let us move from the problem of priesthood itself as the locus of ministry and explore the new forms further. Typical of the dual impetus of Vatican II, ministry is being renewed and expanded in two different directions. On the one hand, the council reestablished the permanent diaconate. Although this was a new effort to meet the needs of the church, it is of a piece with the vision and practice of the hierarchical church. The deacon is ordained into the hierarchy at one step below the priest. Further, the deacon must be a male, over thirty-five, and if married, should he lose his wife, he may not remarry. Thus the deacon is also affected by the strictures surrounding the "sacred power" of the priest. In keeping with the male-dominated hierarchy, the diaconate training program in Chicago only admits candidates who have the support of their wives, and whose wives attend all the classes with them for three years. Thus the patriarchal hierarchy reinforces itself with some severity. The diaconate is steadily attracting substantial numbers of candidates. It is the occasion of much good work, as well as significant criticism regarding its clericalism.

On the other hand, the council's vision has made possible numerous ad hoc ministerial developments, notably those of pastoral associates and directors of religious education, but also lay ministers, youth ministers, ministers of care, family life ministers, coordinators of liturgy, of music, of social service, and of evangelization. Here we find the mushrooming of Burrow's "families of ministries." People involved in these ministries are engaged in training of all sorts; workshops, classes, and assorted certificate programs are blooming in every diocese in official and unofficial forms. There is great pressure to formalize standards for at least some of the more critical ministries at a professional level. In Chicago, ministers recently spent a year developing such standards, and the Archdiocese has now published them.[4]

Some of this pressure is because of the reservation of ordination as a credential for only those who meet the older standard of being male, who have an ascetic commitment, and who then can participate in diocesan training. Professional public standards and training provide an alternative and powerful credential for exercising ministry in the church today. Yet this may be appropriate only in a limited way. Protestant experience teaches us that professionalization can serve simply to create another kind of elite. Although we need to consider what we may gain from professionalization, this would not yet render a truly inclusive church with shared forms of internal and external ministries that women envisage.

It is also important to recognize that many of the women who are doing pastoral work that warrants ordination do not want to be ordained at present if it means buying into hierarchical power and authority as that is and has been practiced in the church. They want ordained ministry in a renewed and transformed body of ministers that works in a collaborative way with and among people, not over them. They want to surface needs and hopes—to coordinate talents, not direct them. People are not understood as the objects of ministry, but subjects—persons—who share in ministry in the community. The women I know want a church of mutual ministries in which care for one another and support of outreach to work for love and justice are based on common discernment of the gospel in our local situations. Thus ministry is constitutive of the life of the community, never separate from it.

In sum, I think it is clear that, until now, ministry has been understood in the Roman Catholic Church as pastoral and cultic activities engaged in by the community's holy man, the priest. The term *ministry* has not been used, nor has the life been considered a profession, as would that of a doctor or lawyer. The fact that so many lay people and religious women are becoming professional ministers has caused the priesthood to begin to define itself in those terms as well. This is evidenced by the profiles of the pastor and associate pastor in the new archdiocesan publication. Thus we may be moving from a sacred priesthood to a professional ministry, but more, we are creating new families of ministry.

---

[4]See the booklet *Coordinating Parish Ministries,* Archdiocese of Chicago (1987). This contains profiles on most of the ministries that could be found in a parish, on selecting candidates for those jobs, and on coordinating ministries.

Shifting Ministry and Shifting Ethics

Regarding the ethical issues involved in these changes, let us first consider professionalization. Through training, professionals meet publicly agreed-upon standards for competence and are accountable to their superiors and to their clientele for upholding them. They are subject to grievance processes if they do not. They are also paid appropriately. The public vision and code of the standards provide a base for public judgments about professional ethics.

As holy men, priests are not held to a standard of public accountability. When difficulties arise, they are supposed to be matters for private confession or perhaps consultation with the bishop. Grievances often result simply in such a conference and the removal of a man to another parish. This becomes a serious public problem when a troubled priest molests altar boys or rapes women. Because the official church does not deal with these issues in a public professional way, lay people are bringing legal suits against the offenders, but have no recourse within the church itself. Nor is there due process for lesser ills, such as simple incompetence or the destructive behavior of little tyrants. Diocesan personnel boards are a first step toward professional review and parish arbitration, but only a small step. The move toward professionalization is a move toward public standards, accountability, and due process that is only in a beginning stage.

It is also a move toward adequate payment for services. The older rubric of service to the church being rendered in a spirit of humility, charity, and poverty is not just. The bishops themselves recognized this in their pastoral on the economy (National Conference of Catholic Bishops 1986, par. 351).

Further, professionalism requires something perhaps more subtle, but nonetheless important. Ministers must be able to relate comfortably and respectfully with other adults. Here the style of ascetic training some priests have had has done them and the other members of the church a grave disservice. Some priests have been taught to avoid friendships and to fear women. Because of this they often fail as pastors, and the welfare of both the priest and the community suffers.

However, professional ministry may come with some liabilities. If ministry is not simply going to shift to another core of elite persons, again separate from the community, we need to keep in mind the women's vision of a truly inclusive church of multiple kinds of ministry. Perhaps we need to ask what kinds of ministry require training, and at what level. For example, teaching and counseling seem to require some public qualification, whereas visiting the sick or organizing a justice walk may not.

There is a second kind of ethical issue related to the ordained priesthood today, and that has to do with the welfare of church communities in relation to the celebration and protection of the meaning and truth of our sacraments, especially the Eucharist. The shortage of ordained priests, together with the appearance of alternative ministers, has created the difficulty. The community who has a minister, not a priest, cannot celebrate Eucharist fully because the minister is not institutionally authorized to consecrate. That church has to bring in either a priest or consecrated bread. These options endanger our understanding of the Eucharist and tend to qualify the blessing of the bread as a quasi-magical act. This problem argues for a more inclusive ordained ministry in the interest of the spiritual welfare of the church.

Another obvious argument against the limitation of ordination flows from the theological anthropology. I have already indicated that the systemic exclusion of women because they are women is unjust. Here the welfare of the community also plays a part, both in how our symbols function to teach people who they are, and in terms of meeting the needs of church communities.

In a sense, all the issues I have dealt with here look backward. They revolve around solving problems in institutional functions and roles that obstruct the good. The final portion of this chapter must look forward. A coresponsible church of adults requires ministers who collaborate with them. Along the lines that Burrows suggests, the minister needs to ask how he or she fosters the common life, aids in the deepening of faith, and witnesses to the challenge of the gospel in the church and society. As the theological anthropology suggests, this is a ministry directed toward enabling people, individually and together, to become more fully human.

Perhaps no term has become more readily used to advance this concept today than *empowerment*. Catholic ministers, especially pastoral associates and DREs, want to empower people to own and build their own church communities, and to become free and responsible Christian actors in the public world. They envision an enabling ministry that has both a private, personal dimension, and a public, systemic one. Ministers enable people personally through trust, acceptance, affirmation, as well as forgiveness and challenge. They enable people vis-à-vis social systems when they work with them to name their experience within these systems, to recognize the power of institutional symbols and language, and to provide alternative angles of vision, illumined by the gospel, together with the possibility of acting in constructive or challenging ways. This kind of creativity should provide a positive measure of the just activity of our ministers.

As I indicated at the beginning of this chapter, the vision of the Catholic women I have referred to here is shared with women within Protestant denominations. Lynn Rhodes (1987) talks about Protestant women ministers sharing a vision of a church of friendship and solidarity, one that rests on relationships of mutuality, love, and the work of justice. This feminist vision is broader than denominational boundaries, and it poses its set of critical questions to all Christian churches.

Jesus worked where he was to heal, to love, to challenge in accord with his vision of the kingdom. This ministry of enabling people to grow in wholeness and faithfulness to the gospel is a contemporary form of discipleship. The visions of the church, of persons, and of ministry, insofar as they are concerned for human welfare, personal and social, participate in the work of Jesus. The upheavals in the contemporary Roman Catholic Church, especially in ministry, present us with the challenge to seek the good, and to recognize in them the *kairos* of the kingdom.

References

Abbott, Walter M. 1966. *The Documents of Vatican II.* New York: America Press.

Burrows, William R. 1980. *New Ministries: The Global Context.* Maryknoll, N.Y.: Orbis Books.

Coleman, John A. 1982. *An American Strategic Theology.* New York: Paulist Press.

Coordinating Parish Ministries. 1987. Chicago: Archdiocese of Chicago.

Graff, Ann O'Hara. 1986. "Vision and Reality: Discernment and Decision-Making in Contemporary Roman Catholic Ecclesiology." Ph.D. diss., University of Chicago.

Häring, Bernard. 1978, 1979, 1981. *Free and Faithful in Christ: Moral Theology for Clergy and Laity.* 3 vols. New York: Seabury Press; Crossroad.

National Conference of Catholic Bishops. 1983. *The Challenge of Peace: God's Promise and Our Response.* Washington, D.C.: United States Catholic Conference.

———. 1986. *Economic Justice for All: Catholic Social Teaching and the U.S. Economy.* Washington, D.C.: United States Catholic Conference.

————. 1987. *Partners in the Mystery of Redemption: A Pastoral Response to Women's Concerns for the Church and Society.* Washington, D.C.: United States Catholic Conference.

————. 1990. *One in Christ Jesus: A Pastoral Response to the Concerns of Women for Church and Society.* Washington, D.C.: United States Catholic Conference.

Rhodes, Lynn N. 1987. *Co-Creating: A Feminist Vision of Ministry.* Philadelphia: Westminster Press.

Schillebeeckx, Edward. 1981. *Ministry: Leadership in the Community of Jesus Christ.* New York: Crossroad.

————. 1985. *The Church with a Human Face: A New and Expanded Theology of Ministry.* New York: Crossroad.

Whitehead, James, and Evelyn Whitehead. 1986. *The Emerging Laity: Returning Leadership to the Community of Faith.* Garden City, N.Y.: Doubleday & Co.

12

A Sociology
of Ministerial Preparation

Eleanor Scott Meyers

In a time of dramatic social change within organized religion in the United States, what is the appropriate form of ministerial education? The need for an educated clergy within religious organization is unquestioned in this chapter. Rather, the institutional structure and focus for ministerial preparation is the issue addressed here. If this education is to be based on ethical commitments, these must arise out of an assessment of the social, political, and economic setting of seminary education as it relates to organized religion.

The issue of ministerial preparation must be discussed in relation to the context of modern society and the situation of organized religion. Some aspects of the current model of professional education continue to serve parts of the church, yet many aspects of the model no longer pertain today. These issues are part of the larger question concerning the redefinition of ministry itself as new forms of family and community life develop.

The shape of our teaching environments within all professional education today, including the structure of knowledge itself, can be viewed as part of the problem of the establishment and maintenance of ethically based professional leadership. Curtis Berger of the Columbia University Law School, speaking at a convocation for the opening of the school year, said: "I do not assert that legal education makes our graduates evil, but I do believe that [it makes them] less feeling, less caring, less sensitive to the needs of others . . . even less alarmed about the injustices of our society than they were when they entered law school" (Barr 1990, 626).

Educational processes for ministerial preparation participate heavily in shaping the self-perceptions of future ministerial leaders. Professionalized educational models that prepare organizational leaders for credentials, a career ladder, upward mobility, organizational and cultural power—all under the aegis of self-determination—continue to suggest to ministerial students personal and collective ethical responsibilities based in commitments of the dominant class, race, and gender within society. The important question of professional ethics, in theology as in all areas, relates to the ethics and goals of professional education itself.

Professionalization in the church involves both the establishment of an educational course of preparation and its parallel development of bureaucratic organizational processes that surround the work of ministry. An increase in the professionalization of clerical leaders heightens the tension between the needs of local churches for leadership and those bureaucratic and educational forces molding professionalization processes. Many aspects of these processes have operated at considerable social distance from congregations that are characterized today by declining resources—both human and financial.

In this chapter I will present aspects of a case study of the rise and decline of bureaucratic processes within one mainline Protestant denomination, the Christian Church (Disciples of Christ), also identified here as the Christian Church or Disciples. This case study raises issues about the professionalization of the ministry within the "free church" tradition of which this denomination is a part. One goal is to develop a discussion of the present dilemma facing this denomination and others like it—the decline of organizational strength. The basic themes of this case study are found within all organized religion today. Some broad generalizations can be made between the Christian Church and other old-line Protestant denominations. However, those churches most closely associated with the traditional belief in local autonomy will more nearly reflect the organizational characteristics reported here. Discussion of these issues is of critical importance to theological education.

There are two opposing social forces within organized Protestantism today. Since the close of the nineteenth century, we have been in an era during which structural changes in authority and power relations in church organizations (forces for centralization) have been in the ascendancy. Yet there have been since the early 1960s broad societal changes within the environment of religious institutions (forces for decentralization) as organized religion within the traditionally white Protestant mainline has declined in relation to population growth and economic privilege in the United States. Even though institutions of theological education hold differing relationships to denominational structures in the United States, the strength of the former still depends in large part on the strength of the latter. What is occurring across the old mainline denominations today is more than an issue about organizational strength; it is about a change in organizational ethos.

The Decline of Local Autonomy in the Free Church Tradition: Forces for Centralization (1890 to 1960)

A basic organizational contradiction exists within this traditionally "free church" because of the formal establishment of a division of labor and other organizational characteristics of a central bureaucracy. A change in organizational power has occurred due to a shift in resources. Local church leadership, traditionally held by the laity in the Christian Church (Disciples of Christ), has shifted to the clergy; and the organizational decision-making power, traditionally held within local congregations, has shifted to the regional and national church personnel and programs. As these changes took place, major accommodations were made to the structures of Disciple belief itself.

Max Weber (1964; 1968), the classical student of bureaucracy, believed that leadership, and the legitimation and succession processes that surround it, was of great importance in the rationalization process involved in the rise of bureaucratic forms of organization. Weber tied different forms of authoritative leadership to different forms of organizations. Bureaucracy, as he defined it, is the centralized administrative form of rational-legal authority structures. This is a type of authority or power relationship established and legitimized through the rules that legally constitute and guide a bureaucracy. According to Weber, under the forces of expanding rationality, the contemporary society makes it necessary for organizations to hire people qualified to apply rules. We frequently refer to these persons as "professionals." Weber asserts that the very first professional was the [male] priest (Bendix 1977, 318). Professionals can be identified by their position in a clear division of labor; a hierarchy of authority; a system of standards, rules and procedures for their application; and the establishment of expertise so that their employment is based on technical qualifications.

One primary problem that Weber identified with these processes is the organizational strain that arises under expanding rationalization—one that often lets organizational "means" displace the organizational mission or "end." Once the priest becomes the professional, his allegiance often turns from the original mission to maintenance of the organization and his position and status in it.

The unintentional displacement of institutional goals poses a contradictory situation for organizations that benefit from bureaucratic developments, including professional leadership. My study of a traditionally nonbureaucratized church through historical and survey analysis reports on this process and attempts to draw implications from it for theological education today.

A Division of Labor Between Clergy and Laity

Anticlericalism ran deep in all early forms of the "free church" tradition that followed the western movement of the frontier. Since the early 1800s, members of these autonomous Disciple congregations debated the role of clergy. Some said clergy should be educated and "hired," whereas many claimed no interest in "paid exhorters." Yet today in the Christian Church (Disciples of Christ), as in many churches from this free church tradition, a division of labor between laity and clergy has developed.

Sentiments against a formal clergy grew out of the traditional belief in the priesthood of all believers and local autonomy. Members of congregations had always identified their talented members, called them to the ministry of the local church, and ordained them to preach to them, to teach their children, and to be a pastor to their marriages, births, baptisms, and deaths. Sometimes, if funds were available, these local leaders pursued seminary education, but it was not expected and never required.

In the Christian Church, the major organizational processes that led to the development of a division of labor were orchestrated by Willard Wickizer, a key national leader in the 1930s. With the ending of geographical expansion of the frontier—and therefore the church—the Reverend Wickizer lobbied for a new goal of program development in the work of home missions. He identified the new mission work as the strengthening of local organizations. This task, as defined by Wickizer from his national church position on the Board of Home Missions, became the focus of national church planning. Wickizer's new church strategy began to systematize the work of church leaders (Wickizer 1937). From that time, certain ministerial tasks such as preaching began to be assumed by the ordained members, and the call for an educated clergy grew.

These developments initiated the first step toward the functional organization of the churches at the local, regional, and national levels (Blakemore 1962). In this way, the education and authorization (ordination) of professional leadership increasingly was viewed as a denominational instead of a local church issue. Strong opposition occurred throughout this process, but such voices were increasingly marginalized amid the poorer congregations because the denomination as a whole was increasingly made up of people who were moving into land and home ownership and had access to education. Those without economic and educational privileges were unable to organize institutional power against those with expanding social power and began to lose the national assembly debates on church structure.

Organizational Rules and Procedures for Their Application

A further division of labor developed regarding the training and selecting of the ordained leaders, including a licensing process carried out by newly established regional commissions. In the establishment of functional organizations, some well-organized regional (or state) societies set up a committee on the ministry. Being unfamiliar with the historical traditions of Disciple church structures, at first these committees appeared unclear of their task and lacked a sense of authority.[1] Local churches continued their practice of independent ordination, but eventually the unfolding process altered the tradition of both local autonomy and lay initiation. The result is that whereas once the task of ministry was the diffuse responsibility of the congregation, with little distinction between ordained and nonordained, ministry became a set of tasks carefully assigned to various levels and positions of a complex bureaucracy.

In 1962 the rise of positional authority within the growing hierarchy of Disciple ministerial leadership was made evident

---

[1]Personal conversation with Disciple historian Lester McAllister, March 1981.

with the passing of a resolution at the national convention. Resolution 40 declared that duly ordained and licensed individuals were the only persons who could be listed in the official *Yearbook* of the national church. At the same convention, an authority of "expertise" was institutionalized with the passage of Resolution 51. This resolution set down standards for ordination and made the regional Commissions on the Ministry the official overseers of the application of denominational ordination standards. The new rules required the Bachelor of Divinity—today's Master of Divinity—seminary degree (or its equivalent) and a process of application and interview with the Commission on the Ministry. The specific processes were to be defined by the regional commissions as they selected and credentialed leaders for the denomination.

Analysis of the historical documents of the denomination shows clearly the important role in these developments played by ordained clergy. That in a denomination with its roots solidly in free church beliefs, the power for institutional definition was largely in the hands of educated ministerial leaders is a self-contradictory but true statement. From the perspective of organizational analysis, this outcome is not self-contradictory; one goal of professional education is the development of organizational leaders who hold particular knowledge that enables organizational planning, action, and survival.

The Role of Theological Education in Bureaucratic Development

Theological education as a primary organizational strategy was an important factor in the rise of denominationalism and the professionalization of the clergy in the Christian Church. The movement of certain constituencies within Discipledom into the middle and upper-middle strata in the economically fluid period at the end of the nineteenth century helped to shape this organizational outcome (Ahlstrom 1972). Seminary-trained Disciple ministers, through their access to expanding financial and educational resources, created the institutional base from which the denomination continued to develop.

Seminary education across the United States was ready for these new organizational developments that were occurring in all the growing Protestant denominations that had been established amid the flux of frontier life. A professional model of theological education, one borrowed from other established professions, had been adopted in the seminaries early in the twentieth century.

Within the Disciples, the professionalization of the clergy took about 125 years. The present institutional outcome was fully rationalized in the late 1960s in the denominationally organized "Restructure" program. This process formalized the collection of independent Christian Churches as a legal-rational bureaucracy in an official denomination. Segments of the church had acted in increasingly centralized processes for decades, but under restructure it became official. Other broad social forces were in motion that signaled major changes within religious institutions of the old mainline churches. One might consider the possibility that the final push—on the part of professional ministers who had become denominational leaders—to complete institutionalized bureaucratic procedures was part of the first dramatic moves by centralized authoritative leadership to develop organizational responses to a growing sense of impending deep trouble.

Disestablishment of Religion: Forces for Decentralization

The present era of disestablishment of religious organizations in the white Protestant mainline is a matter of record (Roof and McKinney 1987). A major part of the broader social forces for the de-legitimation of religion and religiously moral leaders is found in the expansion of a secularized life and ethic. Robert Bellah and his associates in their book *Habits of the Heart* point to the existence of a primary "dual tradition" within North American society of "rugged individualism" and "commitment to community." Bellah writes: "The language of the self-reliant individual is the first language of American moral life" (Bellah et al. 1985, 154). Descriptions of moral leadership no longer occur in direct relationship to the traditional vocations identified as the professions. Professionalization today is the aim of all economic labor, despite its connection or lack of connection to the traditional idea of vocation or "call." The term *professional* has been emptied of its original meaning; it has been secularized and individualized. A Weberian reading suggests that the *means* themselves have become the only goal, and employees seek "professionalization" even when it bears no particular social value, economically or organizationally.

Aspects of these developments can be documented concerning the Christian Church (Disciples of Christ). Under the pressure of economic retrenchment, a national task force evaluated the financial procedures of the denomination. Their report reads:

We see our members, congregations, regions and general mani-
festation constantly giving and receiving from one another, as
we help one another to fulfill our common mission. We have
grown increasingly aware that in this church, if one member
suffers, all suffer together; if one member is honored, all rejoice
together.

(Church Finance Council 1989, 1)

Such language is of greater importance in relationship to the
changing political and economic characteristics within middle
America, where the major populations of this denomination
have traditionally centered. The report cites the following
development:

The slowdown in the growth of the American economy, our
declining position in international trade, and the decreasing
value of the dollar have altered the expectations and capacities
of many [of our] members and churches. This generation of
young people is the first in the US that can expect to have less
real buying power than their parents. In two-thirds of the
congregations in one of our major regions (Mid-America) total
annual receipts amount to less than the minimal compensation
package recommended for a minister just graduating from
seminary.

(Church Finance Council 1989, 4)

Numbers from the last twenty years show the shape of institutional pressure: membership has declined 43 percent;
church school enrollments, 41 percent. Increasing numbers of
congregations cannot afford a seminary graduate in the pulpit.

It is important to assess the potential impact of religious
disestablishment on professional education of the clergy in the
coming decades. There will continue to be a need for educated
leadership in the church, but who will redefine the professionalization process?

Political economy theory, based on the work of Max Weber,
suggests that as a bureaucracy emerges, dominant coalitions of
organizational leaders form where resources are available
(Zald 1970; Karpik 1978). Following the shift in denominational processes concerning ordination, the Commissions on
the Ministry were constituted to act with authority in the centralized professionalization process surrounding ordination. Is
there empirical evidence that these commissions have been
legitimated? Do they really control access to and definition of
ordination and ministerial leadership?

The Role of the Commission on the Ministry

I conducted a survey of those who had been ordained by the 34 regionally based commissions of the Christian Church (Disciples of Christ) across the first nine years following their official establishment (1970–1979). The data show 909 interviews held during this time by the 34 Commissions on the Ministry. Only two rejections were identified. One person was interviewed and not recommended by the commission but was ordained by the local church without commission approval. Another individual was interviewed and not recommended and, though there was an approval from a local congregation, was not ordained. Because only one out of approximately 500 persons interviewed was rejected as a candidate, we may conclude that there is no variation in the "decisions" reached by the commissions.

In the period of only one decade, almost 100 percent of the proposed ordinations were authorized by these structures. Though obviously legitimated in the eyes of Disciples, the commissions may just as quickly have become a rubber-stamp mechanism of formal co-optation. If the decisions for ordination are not being handed down by the regional commissions, where does the actual power lie?

One possibility emerges. Decision-making power might lie with the regional minister, the top administrator at the regional level. Regional ministers often sit *ex officio* on the commission and so can cause trouble for a candidate, but they do not have actual power to deny access to ordination because a candidate is free to go to other regional commissions.

An alternate explanation emerges from the historical analysis that suggests that the real key to access to the Commission on the Ministry and its credentialing process is a seminary degree. A common factor of all of those seeking ordination through the commissions is a seminary degree: completing seminary is their prime criterion for ordination. In this way, the process of seminary education plays a major role in the definition of ministry and the church through the training of organizational experts.

The Role of Professional Ministers

Among the various types of power and authority professional ministerial leaders have in their congregations, a major one relates to their impact on organizational decisions made by the membership. In particular, pastors hold significant power over budgetary decisions. In my study of about four hundred Disciple congregations, I found that those with seminary-trained, denominationally credentialed clerical leaders are more likely to give a higher percentage of their total annual financial resources to the denomination—monies over which the membership relinquishes control. This is one major way in which professional preparation for ministry reinforces the development and maintenance of the church structures beyond the local level.

Decentralization has always been part of Disciple organizational reality. Ordained clergy are not present in all Disciple congregations. Almost 30 percent of Disciple congregations in 1982 did not have ordained clerical leadership. Although some congregations reporting a lack of ordained leadership are between personnel changes, over half of these congregations have for various reasons shunned the centralized procedures of the broader church. Such congregations, ones that depend on lay leadership, tend to be poorer, with older members, and their lay ministers frequently serve in that capacity for many years. These local churches contribute essentially no financial support to the centralized bureaucracy, and their church leaders do not have positions in the professional career ladders of the broader regional and national church structures.

It is the presence of educated ministerial leadership that has a significant effect on the creation of a denominational structure. Churches with professionally trained ministerial leadership give a higher percentage of their annual financial resources to the bureaucracies of the church. It is through their support of broader institutional processes that local church ministers do—or do not—develop access to careers within the denomination.

Congregations that have professional ministers and tend to give more support to the denomination also share other characteristics. They are generally the larger, white, urban congregations that show at least some growth in membership. They tend to have established relationships with the broader organizational and programmatic structures of the denomination. These congregations are more likely to have seminary-educated ministers ordained through the regional Commission on the Ministry. About 55 percent of Disciple congregations reflected this model of professionalized ministerial leadership during the 1980s.

Local churches that are less likely to have trained leadership generally have the characteristics opposite to the more professionalized: they are smaller, rural, not growing, and live somewhat independently from the broader denominational structures. The small number of black Disciple congregations fall into this category. Though the clergy in many of these congregations are ordained, many of them ignore denominational reporting and commission procedures and ordain their members. Just under 16 percent of local churches are typical of this less-centralized clerical leadership. Since the establishment of the Commissions on the Ministry, many of these church leaders do not carry "official" denominational standing—another example of their lack of organizational ties to the national and regional church and the professional cadres of organizational leadership. There is little in the way of organization to help maintain the ties of these congregations to the national structures of the denomination.

The data on Disciple congregations suggest that effective bureaucratic processes are absent in a significant percentage of Disciple congregations. Only a slight majority of Disciple congregations employ the type of professionalized ministerial leaders who can be identified as having a significant impact on the decisions to support national and regional church programs. Under the present decline of membership and churches, this margin of support is at risk.

The underlying social forces for destabilization are readily identifiable. If professionally trained and denominationally credentialed clergy represent the primary support of the bureaucracy, then the broader structures of the denomination may be facing harder financial times ahead under the spread of disestablishment across the white Protestant mainline, of which the Christian Church is clearly a member.

At the beginning of this chapter, I stated that an increase in professionalization of ministerial leadership usually heightens the tensions present within the competing forces for centralization and decentralization within institutionalized religion. The forces for professionalization continue to develop amid the bureaucratic structures but under a seriously declining resource base. This suggests that organizational tensions are likely to expand.

Most educational processes for preparation of the leadership for the churches continue to produce students prepared by programs developed under the turn of the century idea of the professions. Such educational preparation may have served the development of denominationalism and the strength of the mission of the national church; but in the present disestablishment, the political and economic organizational strain favors the development of local communities of faith—in effect, new forms of the church. Theological education today is generally not prepared to give professional support to this new organizational task.

Seminary Education: Caught in Contradictory Social Forces

Evidence of the strain caused by decentralizing forces is found in the problems within theological education. The traditional model of professional theological education has during recent decades become increasingly rationalized and turned more "professionalist" (Sweet n.d.). Signs of problems with this careerist model are numerous in the literature addressed to theological educators (Farley 1983; Heyward 1985; Hough and Cobb 1985; Stackhouse 1988; and Hough and Wheeler 1988).

A major issue is the decline of student enrollments, a decline that runs parallel to the decline in church and church school membership. In particular, there is a decline in the traditional student pool of postbaccalaureate males. Today, young men, even those raised in the traditions of a family church background, are selecting educational and career strategies that suggest a better income and more "promising" life-style than does the ministry. One result of this change is the altering of the age and gender distribution within theological education.

This professional model has always been a white male structure aimed primarily at the development of the typical white male professional whose goal was to become a senior minister in a multiple-staffed congregation—with a good salary. Today, most local churches available for ministerial leadership assignments are in small and economically fragile rural congregations. Most congregations—whether rural, urban, or suburban—are small, and most have declining resources. Such churches are unable to fulfill the expectations defined by the contemporary understanding of what it has meant to be a minister—a professional person with the privileges traditionally attributed to other professions under the favorable economics of religious establishment. Half of the seminary students today are women, primarily white women who have access to the economic support needed to sustain their efforts to match the male model. Yet women face the well-known male bias within educational and professional structures in both the seminary and the local church.

Organizational pressures on seminary education are immense today because of its particular position in relationship to these processes of decline and bureaucratic struggle for survival. Bureaucratic leaders demand that new pastors be schooled in the tactics of "church growth"; for many, "evangelization" has become the code word for what they want to guide theological education and then the practice of ministry. Some regional leaders and local church members chide seminary administrators because they do not produce "good" preachers. The implication is that if they did, churches would be growing instead of declining. Many seminary professors continue to work away within their isolated disciplines, teaching Bible or church history the only way they know how to do it. Students, who are often financially desperate and trying to study while holding down two or three jobs in the midst of stress-filled lives, demand lighter loads in classes.

These are reductionist strategies for the preparation of ministerial leadership, born out of various perspectives of impending crisis. Under the economic pressures at all levels of church organization, demands made of theological education today often parade as a false front to the desperate search for survival strategies. Affluent churches attempt to maintain themselves under increasingly depressed and overextended professionally trained leaders, while "hard working, hard living, local people" (Sample 1990) continue to need access to faith communities of support to enable their survival as a group. Yet they can't pay the preacher.

In communities bereft of educated leadership, the loss of dialogical, self-critical methods engendered by a broader, ecumenically based educational process adds to the problem. Leaders developed outside a quality professional model often cannot help members of the community struggle with dilemmas posed by the pluralism of the modern social world. Roof and McKinney (1987) point to changes on the landscape of religious life and describe the development of new social cleavages based on differing moral and life-style lines. These sociopolitical cleavages across organized religion today are experienced by many, but are not well understood.

Under the organizational strain of disestablishment and denominational decline, the goals of seminary education fall prey to displacement themselves. While we are educating professional leaders who can use their educational knowledge to support the wider church structures and mission, we can lose sight of the educational needs of the changing local communities and families in which they must labor. Hough and Wheeler (1988, ix) suggest that the problem with the professionalist model of theological education is that it has the wrong goal. The underlying curricular purpose of the professional model is individualistic, aimed only at the formation of individual clergy character and skill. They suggest that the focus should be on congregations. I suggest that the focus of theological education should be on the "field" of emerging communities.

Educational Models for Ethically Based
Ministerial Leadership

New tasks for ministry and the church require new forms of educational preparation. Those interested in the development of ethical leadership for religious institutions must acknowledge that the political economy within church organizations is shifting from central to local units. Part of this necessarily involves the reemergence of the minister as general practitioner and one whose commitments are less bureaucratic—at both the local and wider levels. Educational strategies aimed at the individual—professionalized and specialized—will no longer be valid. Educational programs required for the churches at the beginning of the twenty-first century will develop out of assessments of the social context of the emerging church—especially the political and socioeconomic structures of community life as it is taking new forms in suburban, rural, and urban areas.

If the work of sociology is to have application vis-à-vis this actual development within changing social life, then an important application should be the wide diffusion of knowledge about the nature of social relationships in a given society. This is an important educational strategy aimed at the "increase [of persons'] conscious self-regulation" of their needs (Bottomore 1976). A key to enabling this type of social process is to look for places where certain constituencies and certain "ordained" thought patterns and intellectual commitments exclude people with differences. As Harrison suggests: "Each of us must learn to extend a critical analysis of the contradictions affecting our lives in an ever-widening circle until it inclusively incorporates those whose situations differ from our own" (Harrison 1985, 236). Educational strategies rooted in present structures of dominant social power based on race, class, or gender must be addressed and changed. This is a difficult challenge, because the defining institutional power within the churches and within education is in the hands of the socially dominant players (West 1988).

A seminary curriculum based on the traditional structure of the classical disciplines does not address theoretical and practical gaps in the education for ethical leadership for today's changing religious communities. We cannot afford a professionalized seminary education that prepares individual leaders only for a few affluent congregations and ignores the collection of ministerial issues found in the practices of diverse types of ministerial settings. The aim of theological education today must be the awakening—among all social constituencies—of the conceptual energy to develop diverse ministerial models. This will require a diversity of teaching models as well.

Far too much of the education that goes on in North America today, including theological education, lives under the "near dictatorship of a narrow tier of society" (Sweet n.d., 2). Economists warn us that class lines in America are hardening society into two tiers: one with high incomes and middle-class values and privilege, the other encased in poverty; one primarily white, the other primarily people of color and whites ghettoized in rural or urban pockets of poverty with lack of access to resources, including education. These two tiers are economically and culturally uncoupled, and the upper tier controls the economic and cultural social order. Sweet asserts that "seminaries are offering an "upper-tier" education, and theological educators are *declassing* students from where they came from and are unfitting them for ministry to where they are going" (p. x).

How can the church prepare persons for ethical ministerial leadership, given the underlying power struggle within society and therefore within the church? The main argument I hope to have developed is that preparation for ministry must be conceived from a sociological base, one rooted in realities of class, race, and gender-structured social relations, including ethical leadership commitments. This is the model of seminary education that must stand over and against individualistic professionalistic or management-oriented models. A socially responsible educational strategy affirms the development of professional ethical leadership instead of a careerist clergy for whom means have become ends and education is primarily a privilege aimed at the extension of personal positional and economic power.

Today, models of socially conscious education are developing within, but primarily around, theological education (Burks 1989; Gray 1989). We must develop within seminaries learning strategies based on deeply held ethical and faithful commitments of the church.

Such a mode of study would be immersed in what I call "field" education, an educational strategy that relies on the integration between the theory of ministry and an assessment of the social settings for ministry. Field-based theological education must be located in proximity to the diverse locations of ministry but be "loosely coupled" (Weick 1981)[2] to those settings and also to the highly bureaucratized church and the academy.

Locally based field education, uncoupled from the traditional structure of the seminary placement office, can guide the preparation of leaders for new forms of the church. As long as internships and field education are based on the need for seminary student financial support, education for ministry will take place primarily in relationship to the more affluent settings for ministry, a process that skews student ethical self-perceptions regarding professional ministerial leadership.

Education for ministry located in the fields of local ministry will depend on the disciplined study of anthropology, the arts, Bible—including biblical languages—communication theory, education, ethics, history, psychology, sociology, theology, and world religions. A primary emphasis in the total educational program will be the development and practice of a critical hermeneutic (including a self-critical one) as students are engaged by diverse communities and constituencies in the various settings for ministry. The focus will be on the preparation of ritual leadership for organizational and community development among constituencies that are not today part of the old white mainline.

Such an educational program conceived and carried out in relation to emerging "fields" of ministry requires a carefully integrated educational strategy. There are four major components for a field-based model of education.[3] First, teaching and learning best take place in interdisciplinary settings. Team teaching is highly useful though not always necessary to develop interdisciplinary work. Interdisciplinary settings do not merely pair different disciplines, but spark creative engagement between the disciplines. All the disciplines named above must participate fully and equally in this dialogue.

Second, an integrative curriculum is best described as committed to what one author identifies as "andragological"

---

[2]Loose coupling intends to convey the "image that coupled events are responsive, but that each event also preserves its own identity and some evidence of this physical or logical separateness" (p. 219).

[3]Comments in the concluding paragraphs regarding the components of an educational program reflect the work of the faculty and administration of Saint Paul School of Theology in Kansas City, Missouri. Across the 1988–1989 year, under the leadership of the Curriculum Committee led by Assistant Professor of Theology Kristine Culp, a new curriculum was developed following these guidelines.

(Knowles, quoted in Sweet n.d.). Andragological, or adult-centered learning, instead of pedagogical, or child-centered, learning, is based on integrative curricular designs, deals with contexts and content, and thus treats students and communities as subjects, not objects. Such a strategy prepares persons holistically to be reflective practitioners of ministry.

The third component of this educational strategy teaches a pattern of critical reflection on the practice of ministry in relation to a set of understandings and important contextual issues facing the churches today. As the membership in the churches continues to age and as traditional religious communities change, new issues must be addressed. The study for ministry today must address the new loci for community development, the growing numbers of isolated elderly who are poor in urban and rural areas, single women with dependent children, children without families, people with AIDS, the newly arrived poor in rural areas (mostly young people who have given up on urban living, which they cannot afford, but who are unchurched and are outsiders to the traditions of the rural countryside), gay and lesbian communities in the city, and the baby boomers everywhere who are now in the overextended life-style of dual careers and parenting, but who have no established ties to the churches.

Finally, educational strategies for the preparation of ministerial leaders today must affirm the importance of religious diversity, understand the methods of interfaith dialogue, and be committed to a global perspective. These are today the components of the ecumenical vision within theological education that lie at the center of ethical and educational commitments of theological education.

My aim here has not been to outline a proposal for specific curricular revision; my interest is in what the tools of social science suggest to us about the contradictory location of seminary education today within a new religious political economy.

The issues before traditional white mainline religious organizations are immense and complex. The generation of leaders that defined the contours of the present church and its mission—including theological education—constructed their plans and vision in a world that no longer exists. Thus much of the church has been socialized into and still operates out of what is now an outdated vision. A suggestion that it is now time to reform the conceptual energy of theological education to focus on the task of redefinition of the church and its ministry in the "fields" of emerging communities could place the present institutional players in defensive postures.

For instance, the suggested strategy does not promise the immediate development of professional clergy or local congregations that will lend basic support to the structures of the denomination; it does not promise to develop growth strategies to save existing but declining local churches; it does not promise to leave seminary professors alone to set their agendas and teach merely what (and how) they were taught themselves; it does not promise seminary administrators a student pool that can afford education and help them maintain their institutional budgets; and it does not promise potential students that their financial and status returns from a professional education will place them within socially privileged society.

It does suggest (1) the continuing need for denominational structures, including the important support of theological education, (2) the integrity of disciplines whose conceptual energy will be required, (3) the support for ethically based choices of committed Christians to become students to the new ministries and faith communities, and (4) the organizational transformation of many committed congregations and their present leadership to the development of a new form of the mission of the church. This final point is key: the more affluent members of the present churches must agree to pay for a new form of ministry and its educational preparation, one that does not serve them directly.

Together, these strategies form the structure and content for ministerial preparation in the development of religious discernment and ethical action among professionally trained clergy. The "discipline" of clergy ethics is the curriculum of a locally organized but globally conscious andragological educational formation for organizational and community development, a curriculum that places the considered practice of making ethical judgments at the heart of religiously committed life, for faculty, for ministers, for members of communities—new and old.

References

Ahlstrom, Sidney E. 1972. *A Religious History of the American People.* New Haven: Yale University Press.

Barr, Browne. 1990. "Ministry as Midwifery." *The Christian Century* 107, no. 20 (June 27/July 4): 625–626.

Bellah, Robert N., Richard Madsen, William M. Sullivan, Ann Swidler, and Steven M. Tipton. 1985. *Habits of the Heart: Individualism and Commitment in American Life.* Berkeley: University of California Press.

Bendix, Reinhard. 1977. *Max Weber: an Intellectual Portrait.* Berkeley: University of California Press.

Blakemore, W. B. 1962. "A Theological Paper on Disciple Polity." *Mid-Stream,* 2, no. 2 (December): 64–80.

Bottomore, T. B. 1976. *Sociology as Social Criticism.* New York: William Morrow.

Burks, Janet. 1989. "Seminary in the Streets." *Christianity and Crisis* (vol. 49, April 3/17): 117–118, 121.

Church Finance Council. 1989. Final Report of the Panel to Evaluate the Financial Procedures of the Christian Church (Disciples of Christ), Indianapolis, Ind., March 22.

Farley, Edward. 1983. *Theologia.* Philadelphia: Fortress Press.

Gray, Joan S. 1989. "New Life on a Traditional Campus." *Christianity and Crisis* (vol. 49, April 3/17): 113–116.

Harrison, Beverly Wildung. 1985. *Making the Connections.* Boston: Beacon Press.

Heyward, Carter, ed. 1985. *God's Fierce Whimsy: Christian Feminism and Theological Education.* New York: Pilgrim Press.

Hough, Joseph C., and John B. Cobb, Jr. 1985. *Christian Identity and Theological Education.* Chico, Calif.: Scholars Press.

Hough, Joseph C., and Barbara Wheeler. 1988. *Beyond Clericalism: The Congregation as a Focus for Theological Education.* Atlanta: Scholars Press.

Karpik, Lucien, ed. 1978. *Organizations and Environment.* Beverly Hills: Sage Publications.

Meyers, Eleanor Scott. 1985. "Professionalization and Centralization in the Free Church Tradition." Ph. D. diss., University of Wisconsin.

Roof, Wade Clark, and William McKinney. 1987. *American Mainline Religion.* New Brunswick, N.J.: Rutgers University Press.

Sample, Tex. 1990. *U.S. Lifestyles and Mainline Churches.* Louisville: Westminster/John Knox Press.

Stackhouse, Max L. 1988. *Apologia.* Grand Rapids: Wm. B. Eerdmans.

Sweet, Leonard I. n.d. "The Ladder or the Cross: The Plover Report." Nashville: United Methodist Church.

Weber, Max. 1964. *The Sociology of Religion.* Boston: Beacon Press.

———. 1968. *Economy and Society.* Berkeley: University of California Press.

Weick, Karl E. 1981. "Educational Organizations as Loosely Coupled Systems." In *Complex Organizations: Critical Perspectives,* by Mary Zey-Ferrell and Michael Aiken, 217–226. Glenview, Ill.: Scott, Foresman.

West, Cornel. 1988. "The Crisis in Theological Education." *Prophetic Fragments.* Grand Rapids: Wm. B. Eerdmans.

Wickizer, Willard. 1937. "Home Missions Today and Tomorrow."

International Convention. St. Louis: Christian Board of Publication.

Zald, Mayer N. 1970. *Organizational Change: The Political Economy of the YWCA.* Chicago: University of Chicago Press.

13

An Ethics
for the Interpretation
of the Contemporary
Jewish Experience

Joseph A. Edelheit

This chapter argues for an ethics of interpretation. It attempts to explain and illuminate the rabbi's relationship with people, both Jews and Gentiles, as being analogous to the relationship between a reader and a text, and hence, presents the rabbi as the interpreter of contemporary Jewish experience. Insofar as one accepts the premise that a rabbi is an interpreter of Jewish religious experience, an ethics of interpretation used by rabbis becomes rabbinic ethics, a very specific, subjective aspect of clergy ethics from which a more general, universal position can be derived. I will apply this ethics of interpretation to rabbinic involvement in two areas of critical, contemporary concern within the Jewish religious experience: interfaith marriage and AIDS.

The Rabbi As Interpreter

We can derive the notion of the rabbi as the interpreter of the contemporary Jewish religious experience from the Babylonian Talmud, tractate *Hagigah,* 14b:

> Our rabbis taught, four men entered the *Pardes* (the garden), namely Ben Azzai and Ben Zoma, *Acher* (Elisha ben Abuyah), and Rabbi Akiva. Rabbi Akiva said to them, "When you arrive at the stones of pure marble, say not 'water, water' for it is said that he who speaks falsehood shall be established before my eyes" (Psalm 101:7). Ben Azzai cast a look and died. Of him, scripture says, "Precious in the sight of the Eternal is that of

God's saints" (Psalm 116:15). Ben Zoma looked and became de-
mented. Of him, scripture says, "Hast thou found honey so much
as is sufficient for you, lest you be filled therewith and vomit it"
(Proverbs 25:16). *Acher,* namely Elisha ben Abuyah, "mutilated
the shoots" (apostatized). Rabbi Akiva departed unhurt.
                    (Babylonian Talmud, tractate *Hagigah,* 14b, p. 89)

This rabbinic fable is usually understood as a statement
about theosophic speculation, but I will argue for a different
reading that plays on the word *Pardes. Pardes,* in this passage,
means "garden." In later medieval times we find a homonymic
acronym, *PaRDeS. PaRDeS* is a mnemonic that stands for the
four modes of rabbinic textual interpretation: P—*'Peshat'* (the
simple or literal meaning); R—*'Remez'* (the hint); De—*'Drash,'*
(the exegetical); and S—*'Sod'* (the secret or mystical). By reading *Pardes* homonymically as *PaRDeS,* the mnemonic of four
modes of interpretation, one can re-read this rabbinic tale as
a statement about the awesome power of rabbinic interpretation. Rabbi Akiva, one of the founders of the accepted school
of rabbinic hermeneutics, is not therefore, coincidentally, the
only one who survives. We learn that those who know how to
interpret the text correctly will not be blinded, go mad, or be
drawn into another religion; rather, they will become leaders
who interpret for others.

Rabbi Peter Knobel, in the anthology *Rabbinic Authority,*
shows that the contemporary rabbi's role as an interpreter of
Torah comes through his or her own scholarship and role mod-
eling of Torah. Contemporary rabbis are interpreters of the
contemporary religious Jewish experience when they interpret the classic texts of scripture, liturgy, Jewish law, Jewish
philosophy, and Jewish history in relation to people. Added to
the classic texts are the life experiences through which the
interpretation of Judaism is refracted. The rabbi, through his
or her own personal knowledge, interpretation, and explanation, offers guidelines, paths, and direction for Jews. "The rabbi
is the one who helps to shape the form and substance of Jewish
living" (Knobel 1982, 52). Contemporary as well as traditional
interpretations of Torah are made real within Jewish lives and
institutions. "The rabbi must be the one who, understanding
the process and the modes of thought which created the Torah
in the past now creates Torah anew" (48). "Creating Torah
anew" means promulgating Jewish values, whether personal
or institutional.

Any theory of interpretation requires an awareness of the
limits between the reader and the text (Ricoeur 1976). Thus,

when interpretation is used in a broader scope to illuminate the role and purpose of rabbis, we must also assume an awareness of the limits of persons as they relate to life, and a knowledge and an understanding of the situation in which they find themselves. David Tracy expands this specifically with regard to those who think and interpret religiously:

> Every theology lives in its own situation. The creative and liberating resources of the tradition provide a horizon of questions which theologians bring to bear upon their interpretations of the situation. In this move, theologians are no different from other cultural critics who bring their own orientations, questions, and possible, probable or certain modes of analysis and response to the situation encompassing all. Sometimes as we have seen, theologians tend to speak of this aspect of the theological task as the role of the "world" in theology, or as an attempt to "discern the signs of the times."
>
> (Tracy 1981, 339)

David Tracy's analysis of the theologian's work is also valid for all clergy who must always bring to bear their understanding of "the situation" and their discernment of "the signs of the times" as refracted through the tradition of the faith community that they serve. It is the clergy's awareness of "the situation" and their involvement in the lives and circumstances of those to whom they respond, as clergy, that analogically suggest that people and life experiences are "the texts" that a rabbi interprets. The rabbi is an interpreter of the classic texts and traditions of the Jewish religious experience; and equally as important, he or she interprets "the situation" within which there are lives that make up the human boundaries of the contemporary Jewish religious experience.

My re-reading of the story from the Talmud emphasizes that three of the rabbis' interpretation and speculation led them astray or harmed them. It was only Akiva, who knew how to interpret the situation (the text) and who was committed to hermeneutics as an ethical structure within which God's word could be interpreted, was able to walk out of the *Pardes/ PaRDeS* unscathed. Analogically, I would argue that contemporary rabbis who are unaware of their place within "the situation" and are not engaged in an attempt to understand "the situation" will harm themselves and those about them by their inadequate interpretation and transmittal of Jewish tradition. Thus the rabbi, the interpreter of classic texts and lives, requires an ethics of interpretation.

The rabbinate is unlike the biblical roles of priest and

prophet, which are both divinely ordained. The biblical priest was set aside through the lineage of a specific family; the tasks, as well, were specifically commanded by God. The prophet responded specifically to God's call and then uttered, on behalf of God, statements of both judgment and hope to motivate the people. The rabbinate is, however, a completely human institution. Whereas the priest and prophet are commanded and ordained by God historically, the rabbi derives his or her legitimacy, authority, and role definition only through the interpretation of the Divine Word within the human context. The contemporary rabbi must also ground his or her self-understanding within the limits of the process of interpretation of texts, people, and the "situation" and relationships with people and events. Such a process and, therefore, rabbinic self-understanding, requires an ethical foundation. The continual interpretation of the Jewish religious experience is necessarily limited by the personal subjectivity from within which the rabbi understands "the situation" and the relationships with people and events.

The rabbi is historically and essentially a reader of texts, and is therefore always an interpreter of the Torah and the traditional rabbinic texts that follow. Since the first century C.E., rabbis have required hermeneutics, a structure of interpretive rules by which the textual interpretations have remained authoritative and legitimate. Contemporary hermeneutics teaches us that all understanding is interpretation and all interpretation is understanding. This allows for and celebrates the subjectivity of the interpretations and the interpreter, rather than disclaims it as an inherent flaw, a lack of objectivity. I am arguing analogically that the contemporary rabbinate, specifically the congregational rabbinate, necessarily relates to human beings, human events, and human dilemmas as if they were the texts that rabbis have always been required to interpret (Capps 1984, 37–60; Mikvah 1990, 23–34). Further, it is within these various human contexts that the classic texts and the contemporary interpretation of these texts must be provided in order for Judaism to grow and be relevant as a human value system. An ethics of interpretation morally directs the rabbi to acknowledge the limits of his or her subjectivity as the boundaries beyond which authentic interpretation cannot go. Within these subjective limits, it is the rabbi's distinct role to maintain "the to-and-fro" of interpretation as a means of illuminating, teaching, counseling, and living Torah—"creating Torah anew."

The rabbi must acknowledge that the task of adhering to an

ethics of interpretation requires a response to the very first question asked in the Torah, "Where are you?" This is the question God asked Adam, the first human being. It is not a spatial but a relational question. Where are you in relation to Me, asks God? This question has yet to be finally or completely answered, and it is *the* foundational question of a covenantal religion. In the Torah's second question, God asks Cain, "Where is your brother?" We understand that this question is also relational. "Where are we in relation to our fellow human beings?" These two questions are cornerstones of interpretational ethics, because they help the rabbi locate the focus of his or her rabbinate. Is the rabbi a scholar/teacher, serving in a college/Hillel community; a chaplain at an institution; an institutional administrator; or a congregational pulpit rabbi? These are not merely different job descriptions in relation to an ethics of interpretation. The difference of these rabbinic roles permits each rabbi a unique means of articulating God's presence and interpreting the contemporary Jewish experience.

As the author/rabbi who is arguing for this ethics of interpretation, I must acknowledge the subjectivity from within which my interpretation begins. I am a pulpit rabbi of a large urban Reform synagogue. This statement defines the focus of my "calling" ideologically, theologically, and socioeconomically. Further, it indicates that my primary task is one of working with and relating to a specific multigenerational community of eight hundred families. Another essential limiting factor that illuminates my subjectivity is the intellectual and religious presumption of my commitment to and involvement in dialogical theology, specifically Jewish-Christian dialogue. Furthermore, my dialogical theology is formulated on the basis of a post-Auschwitz reality in which Auschwitz represents a caesura after which theology cannot be done in the same way. Finally, and of most importance, I respond to those theological claims on my conscience that enhance a radical pluralism of inclusivity. This means that I begin from a position in which any comparison of Judaism to Christianity or any other religion, for that matter, raises only the specter of difference and never superiority. All of these issues define the subjective vantage point from which I begin my interpretation. It is important that rabbis acknowledge such limits as the subjectivity from within which their interpretation of the contemporary Jewish religious experience is justified.

In order to further limit the focus and expectations of this discussion, let me note what this chapter will *not* raise but must acknowledge as pertinent to an ethics for interpretation.

This is not a presentation of rabbinic ethics that pertains to issues of authority and legitimacy within the rabbinate per se. Thus, this is not how Orthodox rabbis, as compared with Reform rabbis, ethically establish legal and religious parameters—*halakah*. This is also not an ethics of interpretation that illuminates the issues of intra-Jewish communal pluralism, ergo, the legitimacy of Reform Judaism as compared with traditional Judaism. This is not a theory of rabbinic ethics as applied to an interpretation of the relationship between the State of Israel and the Diaspora, though this certainly involves the interpretation of classic texts, history, and the extraordinary experience of the rebirth of the Jewish state after Auschwitz. This is not an ethics for the interpretation of the Jewish communal infrastructure, which is to say, the issue of the legitimacy of the synagogue as an institution as compared with the Jewish Federation, or either structure in relation to the vast majority of Jews who are unaffiliated. This is also not a theory of rabbinic ethics as applied to the interpretation of the rabbi and his or her relationship with other rabbis, other Jewish professionals, or lay people as such. This is not an ethics that deals with the professionalization of the rabbi as an interpreter and how that has changed the interpretation of the Jewish religious experience. Finally, this is not an ethics for the interpretation of such problematic sociological issues as anti-Semitism or Jewish-Christian relations.

Although these and even other issues not listed are pertinent to the question of rabbinic ethics, most specifically, to the question of the rabbi as an interpreter and therefore an ethics for interpretation, this discussion will look only at an ethics for interpretation as applied to a congregational rabbi, which assumes a rabbi's relationship with people as teacher, preacher, pastor, and exemplar of Torah.

An Ethics for Interpretation

The following constitutes the ethics for an interpretation of the contemporary Jewish religious experience, specifically for the congregational rabbinate.

1. Congregational rabbis must both know and understand the primary focus of their rabbinate.
2. Congregational rabbis must both know and understand the significant indices of "the situation" in which their rabbinate exists.
3. Congregational rabbis must both know and understand

the Jewish tradition, its classic texts, and the interpretive process within which, as rabbis, they must respond to people in any situation.

4. Congregational rabbis must both know and understand the transcendent goals of Judaism and Jewish tradition toward which they are hoping to lead the congregation.

Such an ethics for the interpretation of the contemporary Jewish religious experience is reflected, but not definitively articulated, in the observations of Murray Polner, in his work *The Rabbi and the American Experience.* Polner points toward some of the essential qualities of the American rabbinate:

> A synagogue's selection committee insisted upon, above all, the rabbi's scholarship. The rabbi had to be at ease with the Torah texts, so that he [she] might guide his [her] congregants in the light of Jewish tradition. "What we want," said the member of the congregation, "is a rabbi who knows something about the Torah without slighting the prophetic tradition or his [her] pastoral obligations."
>
> (Polner 1977, 211)

In the final passage of Polner's book, he quotes Philip Bernstein, a Reform rabbi and past president of the Central Conference of American Rabbis: "We must bring to bear a certain basic and essentially religious attitude on the crucial problems of our times—the long view of history, the faith in the ultimate triumph of justice, the rejection of defeatism, the assertion of hope" (Polner 1977, 213). What Polner and those whom he quotes presumed even twenty years ago was that the American congregational rabbi had to respond to a set of ethical imperatives regarding his, and now her, relationship with the Jewish community as interpreters of the contemporary Jewish religious experience. These ethical standards ground the rabbis'/interpreters' understanding of their legitimacy as well as provide an imperative for their responsibility as interpreters of the contemporary Jewish religious experience.

In each of the four ethical statements, I have used the words "know and understand" in order to suggest the essential dynamic of to-and-fro within the process of interpretation. The word "know" suggests cognitive knowledge derived from the facts of an "objective" interpretation of the reality and from which a logical argument can be deduced. "Knowing" is always held in creative tension with "understanding," which I use to mean the willingness and willfulness of being open to the always changing, emerging possibilities within life. In

Abraham Joshua Heschel's terms, to understand means to be open to "radical amazement, awe, and surprise." Tracy challenges us: "If one demands certainty, one is assured of failure. Patrons of certainty and control in the interpretation of religion are boring, and whatever else religion is, it is not boring. It is other, different, disturbing. It is not more of the same" (Tracy 1987, 22). In other words, to understand is to be open to differentness, which is in tension to knowing, which always conveys control and certainty. It is within this tension that the to-and-fro of a conversation and, thus, interpretation, takes place; it is within this tension that the rabbi/interpreter is a role model within the community.

The first ethical statement underscores the importance of the rabbi's awareness of the irreducible tension of the to-and-fro, "know and understand," within a specific constituency with whom he or she is working. It is equally important that the rabbi be keenly sensitive to the history of the community/congregation. Any good interpreter of a text takes seriously the author of the text, his or her history and style, as a significant component of reading the text. An ethics for interpretation demands this no less of the rabbi/interpreter than the reader/theologian of a classic religious text (Tracy 1981).

The second ethical standard refers to "the situation"; the history, in part, of the outside reality and context within which both the constituency and congregation define themselves. One cannot, for instance, separate oneself from the worldly reality of an urban setting in which the homeless and the hungry are a living, significant statement within the immediate environs of a congregation. Likewise, the affluence of large suburban areas and their value systems cannot be ignored as key components of the situation of a given Jewish community. Issues such as abortion, AIDS, feminism, and racism are among the "ideas" that forge the boundaries of our contemporary "situation" and cannot be ignored by the rabbi/interpreter.

The third ethical standard underscores the primacy of textual authority that illuminates Jewish tradition. A rabbi who does not know the classic texts cannot understand the interpretive process that illuminates the always emerging tradition, and therefore has less of a claim on the title rabbi/interpreter of the Jewish religious experience. It is particularly significant that the contemporary Jewish community is disproportionately well educated in secular areas but not in Jewish texts and traditions. Therefore, rabbis must bring legitimacy to their specialized intellectual and theological credentials; otherwise, they undermine their own authority as interpreters of the contemporary Jewish religious experience.

The fourth ethical standard highlights the question, To whom and how does my rabbinate represent a response to a "call"? (My use of the idiom "call" does not mean that a divine sensibility, which both motivates and sustains a rabbinate, should be equated to the divine ordination or call of biblical priests and prophets.) The Ultimate Reality toward which I strive to lead the Jewish community must, in my own mind, represent the melding of both the knowledge and understanding of transcendent goals. The rabbi as interpreter must be the exemplar of passion and prophetic concern—a person of convictions whose life is a response to a call. This permits the rabbi to both lead and urge others toward a higher life.

The Issue of Interfaith Marriage

The ethical standards to which the rabbi/interpreter must respond as leader, teacher, and healer are represented by two specific and very different contemporary issues within the Jewish religious experience. The first issue, mixed marriage and intermarriage, is very pervasive and, more than any other issue in the last twenty-five years, has radically and permanently molded the American Jewish community into a significantly different reality. A mixed marriage is a marriage between a Jew and someone who is not Jewish. An intermarriage is a marriage between a Jew and someone who, though not born a Jew, becomes a Jew. Since 1971, the Jewish community has been forced to integrate increased rates of mixed marriages and intermarriages that exceed 30 percent. Since the late 1980s, in large urban areas the rate has fluctuated between 40 percent and 60 percent.

The scope of this problem involves every single congregational rabbi, regardless of his or her ideological movement and congregational affiliation. The issue is as much a problem in the Conservative and left-wing Orthodox movement as it is presumed to be in the Reform and Reconstructionist movements. It is difficult to delineate fully which movement has seemingly fostered "the most number of interfaith marriages." The largest number may, in fact, be in none of the religious movements per se, but rather may be among the unaffiliated or so-called secular Jews. None of this after-the-fact demographic labeling is relevant, however, to how the issue challenges congregational rabbis in their response to the human context.

In my seventeen years as a rabbi, no issue has been as consistently painful, frustrating, and also as hopeful as the challenge of interfaith marriage. My own work in this area represents more than merely congregational experience in both a large urban setting and a small-town single congregational setting. For four years, I was the chairperson of the Central Conference of American Rabbis committee on matters of *gerut* (conversion), during which I edited the Reform rabbinate's guidelines on *gerut.* I was also one of the primary authors of the patrilineal descent resolution, the rabbinic resolution that defines the child of any mixed marriage as Jewish, insofar as either parent is a Jew and both parents publicly declare the child to be raised as a Jew. I later served on the initial task force of the Union of American Hebrew Congregations/Central Conference of American Rabbis on Outreach. I have also been the author and dean of the Joint Introduction to Judaism Class taught jointly in Chicago by the Reform and Conservative rabbinate. My involvement in education, policy, and administrative issues regarding mixed marriage only illuminates what I have found to be true in my own congregational experience. No contemporary Jewish community is freed from the issue of young people, middle-aged people, as well as senior citizens marrying others who are not Jewish. Unlike the neo-romantic self-serving circumstances represented in such television sitcoms as "Bridget Loves Bernie," or the period piece on Broadway, "Abie's Irish Rose," or the unfortunate Hollywood version of "Fiddler on the Roof," the issue of interfaith marriage involves a great deal of real human pain.

All of these human situations raise questions and ultimately require rabbinic interpretation, for which a rabbi can afford little equivocation. The questions begin with wedding officiation, premarital counseling, how the children will be raised, and how there can be an extended family in which Jews and Christians coexist. The rabbi must help the couple understand how to achieve a careful and sensitive integration into the Jewish community, especially if one person chooses to remain not Jewish or actively Christian. There are many questions involving the process of *gerut,* choosing Judaism, as well as helping Jews find the strength to be supportive of those spouses who choose to remain non-Jewish and how to deal with the impact that such a decision has on the Jewish spouse's parents. There are problems often raised that deal with the anger, fear, and often bigotry, specifically anti-Christian prejudice, that interfaith marriages will often provoke within the Jewish parents. Likewise, there are problems with helping Christians deal with unexpected anti-Semitism as evoked by the integration of a Jew into the family or the decision of the non-Jew to become a Jew. The rabbi must teach others how to blunt their Jewish chauvinism, which is often stimulated by the

Christian's choice to become a Jew. Finally, the large percentage of interfaith marriages within the contemporary Jewish religious experience has made us aware of a balance between what is "Jewish" and what is "Judaism," the ethnocentric in creative tension with the religious faith. With each of these issues the rabbi must interpret tradition and "the situation" in meaningful, inclusive statements.

The scope of the challenge is reflected in a 1983 document of the Archdiocese of Newark on guidelines for Jewish-Catholic marriages. This document states unequivocally that "for the required dispensation from the impediment of disparity of worship, the Catholic partner must promise to preserve his or her own faith and to do all in his or her own power to share this faith with the children of the marriage" (Kroner 1985, 102–108). This requirement, on behalf of the Catholic church and the written or oral commitment of the Catholic partner, presents one of the most serious problems that any rabbi can face with regard to a specific couple and the Jewish partner's relationship with his or her own family. A section dealing with the wedding ceremony states unequivocally that in any ceremony officiated at by a priest, the rabbi "may not share in the marriage ritual as such, and is not an official witness to the ceremony." The same is true of a Catholic-Jewish couple for whom a rabbi is presumed to officiate. The priest, according to this Catholic document, is not to share in the marriage as such. The document goes on to say that the priest should be aware that Orthodox and Conservative rabbis are forbidden to officiate, whereas some members of the Reform rabbinate will officiate; but only a very small group will officiate together with a Christian clergyperson. The fact that in 1983 a large urban archdiocese saw fit to put out such a document illuminates the depth of the problem, in that the Catholic clergy has an obligation both to know and understand the issue in their role as interpreters of the contemporary Catholic religious experience. Further, it shows how interfaith marriage has had an impact on the relationship between the Catholic church and the Jewish community.

James F. Moore, another Christian thinker, notes in his work *Sexuality in Marriage: The Christian Foundation for Making Responsible Choices:* "We would even suggest that the rabbi or pastor ought not officiate at such a wedding [that is, an interfaith marriage]" (Moore 1988, 141). Moore notes that "a pastor and/or rabbi can witness to their faith and aid in the process of conversion, if a non-Christian (or non-Jew) is sincere in the desire to convert. This is quite apart from the proposed marriage. Nevertheless, a pastor and a rabbi cannot give counsel for conversion as a part of premarital counseling and thus cannot honestly expect mutuality in the marriage covenant" (141). Further, Moore states that both the rabbi and pastor would misrepresent their communities in the actual circumstances if they acted officially to consecrate the marriage. And finally: "The integrity of the two faiths would be diminished if somehow marriage were accepted as a mixed marriage with direct clergy officiation. Rabbis and pastors cannot be a part of that which serves to weaken rather than strengthen the matters of faith" (142). Both of these Christian statements underscore the dynamic of interfaith marriage as a critical challenge that a Christian clergyperson, who as an interpreter of the contemporary Christian religious experience, must now also begin to know and understand.

Interfaith marriage is one of the primary examples of why every congregational rabbi must be consistent in the use of an ethics of interpretation, because every human situation, especially as illuminated in the challenge of mixed marriage and intermarriage, is different. Each couple or family brings its own horizon of meaning, as would any text, but the rabbi represents the consistent standard by which all different situations can then be interpreted. My own view regarding rabbinic officiation at mixed marriages is negative. Rabbis are ordained solely as representatives of a parochial Jewish tradition that allows the rabbi to officiate at only those life-cycle events and rituals that are Jewish by definition. The definition of a Jewish wedding ceremony requires that two Jews be the focus of the wedding. Therefore, any couple not included in this definition is also necessarily beyond the limits of Jewish tradition within which I am ordained and at which I may officiate. There are rabbis who argue otherwise, but their choice has nothing to do with my ethical responsibilities as an interpreter of the contemporary Jewish religious experience.

The issue of mixed marriage and intermarriage has created a permanent change within the Jewish community; therefore, insofar as the ethical standards of interpretation require that we know and understand the focus of our rabbinate and "the situation," interfaith marriage and the Jewish extended families are a critical factor. Consider the simple definition of a traditional Jewish family, which no longer represents more than 15 percent of the Jewish community. Many extended Jewish families now include Christians who are the parents, siblings, and other family of those who become Jewish or those who remain not Jewish. When one adds the factors of divorce and remarriage, the exponential possibilities of extended Jewish families are mind-boggling. You can literally have two Christians raising Jewish children from an earlier mixed marriage. Conversely, there are Christian children raised in a blended family in which a Christian converts in a second Jewish marriage and later has a Jewish child who is being raised alongside the Christian children of the first marriage. The rabbi must be able to relate to these and other specific pastoral needs; for example, the Jewish person mourning a Christian family member through the appropriate Jewish ritual. Thus it is no longer curious that the memorial list for *yahrzeit/kaddish* read at the end of a service often includes names of persons who are not Jewish, but who are the parents and grandparents of people who have become Jewish.

The complexities of interfaith marriages and a newly constituted Jewish extended family were further exacerbated or enhanced (depending on your point of view) by the decision of the Reform and Reconstructionist rabbinates in the early 1980s regarding the identity of children born of mixed marriage. These resolutions radically changed the standard definition of the *halakah* (Jewish law), which defines a Jew as someone born of a Jewish mother or legally adopted or converted into the Jewish community. The patrilineal or nonlineal resolution defines the child born of a mixed marriage as Jewish insofar as one Jewish parent, either mother or father, actualizes the identity through appropriate public commitment. This would mean that the child born of a mixed marriage who is not actively raised or identified as a Jew, even if his or her mother is a Jew, would not be regarded as a Jew in the Reform community, yet would, in fact, be regarded as a Jew within the Orthodox community. This major shift in the definition of identity has also caused an additional friction within the Jewish communal infrastructure.

Interfaith marriage also represents a major challenge for Jewish education and requires complex reinterpretations of Jewish tradition. How does one educate people about the issue of interfaith marriage without presenting the reality as the ideal and simultaneously not condemning the reality as a failure? This is particularly pointed in the case of someone who like myself does not officiate at mixed marriages but has a very active outreach program in which children born of mixed marriages are educated in the religious school and the congregation goes out of its way to be inclusive of the families of mixed marriages. The refusal of the rabbi to officiate suggests to some that there will be a simultaneous denial of all other connections, which in fact, need not be true. Another complex and extremely important irony is preventative education. When talking to teenagers about interfaith dating, one must realize that a significant minority, or in some cases majority, of these young adults come from homes in which one parent became a Jew or one parent is not a Jew. Thus any traditional statement to teens regarding making only Jewish choices for mates is now radically different because of the choices made by many of their own parents.

Finally, the problem of interfaith marriage represents a new challenge in Jewish-Christian dialogue. Very often, relations between a Jewish and a Christian clergyperson can be deeply strained over the rabbi's somewhat surprising refusal to co-officiate or share in what otherwise is perceived to be a liberal and humane way of dealing with a Jewish-Christian couple. If so much can be shared on so many social issues, pulpit exchanges, and just basic collegial levels, why would a rabbi refuse to be inclusive in a mixed marriage? Much more work has to be done in order to incorporate an ethics for interpretation with which Christian and Jewish clergypersons can understand the radically pluralistic differences within each community that stimulate the different approaches each must take. The ethics for interpretation suggested earlier relates very specifically to how a congregational rabbi must prepare him or herself for the persons and events that the complex questions and dealings of interfaith marriage represent in the Jewish community.

The Issue of AIDS

The AIDS pandemic (though relatively "new") is another issue within the Jewish community that represents a challenge for an ethics of interpretation. AIDS is clearly a Jewish issue, as it is an issue in other communities, insofar as Jews are infected with the HIV virus or sick with AIDS (Acquired Immune Deficiency Syndrome). There are Jews in various family relations to those Jews with HIV/AIDS, and, of course, there are countless Jews dealing with HIV/AIDS as health care workers, lawyers, funeral directors, social workers, researchers, journalists, and so forth. AIDS is a pervasive social issue; however, it cannot be seen as merely a "universal" issue, for each community—ethnic, religious, racial—brings to bear its own value response to the crisis. It is of particular concern for the discussion at hand, because AIDS requires each rabbi to interpret the social crisis within Jewish traditional contexts, even though there is no referent of any kind. A rabbi who tries to explain or understand AIDS within a specifically traditional Jewish context as a biblical plague or as some divine punishment for sins will find such a traditional theological interpretation as hurtful as the virus.

The AIDS crisis has drawn rabbis into pastoral realms with which they have little, if any, experience or, sometimes, basic literacy. Rabbis have been thrust into counseling persons, conducting funerals, making hospital visits, and answering questions. All of these realms, in addition to his or her own personal reflections on AIDS, force each rabbi to confront the traditional sources. Here an ethics of interpretation is most instructive, for it provides guidelines within which the rabbi's limits of knowledge, experience, sensitivity, and even prejudice are all formative issues within each interpretation.

My own work in the area has become far more extensive than I ever imagined it would. I have become an AIDS activist cochairing national and regional Jewish AIDS committees. My reflections on the issue are meant to be instructive and not judgmental of others who, though responsive, choose not to be activists. My initial involvement and continued perseverance is, however, directly linked with the callous and cruel rabbinic and Jewish institutional failure to respond fully to those in need. The first Person-With-AIDS I met, Richard, had been told by his "rabbi" that there was no place in Judaism for him! I learned a great deal from Richard during the many months we visited until he died. His was the first AIDS funeral for which I did a eulogy in "euphemisms." I struggled with a private but not public recognition of his gay friends and confronted the terror of his mother, a school nurse, who was afraid she would be fired because her son died of AIDS.

The circumstances transformed me and spurred me to reinterpret some Jewish tradition through the life and events of Richard and AIDS. I decided to preach/teach about it to my congregation. On the evening of Rosh Hashanah in 1987, I described to the congregation how I felt the first time Richard extended his hand to me:

> I got up to leave, and he extended his hand to thank me for my visit. I froze—for an agonizing instant that will remain caught in my mind for eternity—it seemed as if I was staring at his extended hand, which was lovingly inviting me to touch him as an act of physical connection. I remember my brain screaming to my heart, "you're embarrassing him—you cannot just stand here." Richard never flinched—his patient loving eyes never

blinked. He never embarrassed *me;* rather, his outstretched arm just came closer; his eyes more appealing, as if to say, "It's all right. I have AIDS, and you can shake my hand and live." I'm sure it was no more than an instant, but my own horror at how I had frozen with fear was put in perspective by Richard's confidence in himself.

(Edelheit 1987, 1–2)

I shared this self-reflection with my congregation to raise their consciousness about an issue that was then still spoken of in whispers. I argued that old theological interpretations were flawed in fully dealing with the lives of people. Reflecting on the agonies of the Black Death of the fourteenth century, I asserted that the fear and contagion of fear were as dangerous as the disease. Ignorance, not God, was the cause of the behaviors by which HIV was spread. In order to be true to the spiritual context of the evening, and hoping to offer a theological interpretation that would take the sting out of peoples' judgment, I reinterpreted a traditional medieval liturgical poem of Rosh Hashanah, *Unetaneh Tokef:*

On Rosh Hashanah it is written
On Yom Kippur it is sealed
Who shall live and who shall die.

Who shall die of a disease because of ignorance,
And who shall live because of knowledge.

Who shall live in fear of the past,
And who shall struggle to find hope in the future.

Who shall not take the test because of arrogance,
And who shall twist fitfully in limbo waiting for the results.

Who shall seek redemption in the test,
And who shall find themselves condemned by the results.

Who shall be isolated more by the fear of others than the disease,
And who shall be embraced more by love than knowledge.

Who shall live afraid of the sting of discrimination,
And who shall fight for their rights, even while dying.

Who shall have to explain their hidden life,
And who shall continue to hide unable to explain why.

Who shall lose the dignity and security of their profession or
    professional calling,
And who shall be protected as a co-worker by others who speak
    out to save their own integrity.

Who shall rise up self-righteously to judge and to condemn others,
And who shall find compassion for even that which they cannot
    understand.

Who shall innocently be infected never knowing why,
And who knowing why they became infected will hide in the
    solitude of innocence.

Who among the children and the very young shall die too soon,
And who among the parents and the grandparents shall mourn
    bitterly confused.

Who shall die of AIDS alone and afraid,
And who shall die of AIDS embraced and serene.

We can no longer expect the traditional repentance, prayer, and
    charity to temper these severe decrees. However, we can and
    must
Repent for the sins we commit against others when fear and
    ignorance cripple our judgment, when prejudice distorts our
    reason, and selfishness uproots our compassion.

We can and must
Pray for new insights into a world forever changed by disease, for
    the blessings of serenity to be granted to the patients and their
    families, for the researchers who seek vaccines and cures, and
    for a human community that will not be ruptured morally and
    spiritually.

And we can and must
Be more charitable to those who are forced to turn to their
    families, friends, co-workers, and society to support them as
    they die, and we must make Tzedakah our guide in responding
    to the urgent needs of those who are made so vulnerable by
    the disease.

Let us proclaim the sacred power of this day—
It is awesome and full of dread.

Let us understand that our lives are changed forever and reflect
    somberly on our desperate need for God and one another.

Amen.

(Edelheit 1987, 8–9)

The response was mixed, with some very strong negative
reactions, including the resignation of some members. The
sermon proved, once again, that an ethics for interpretation

does not always guide the prophetic spirit within a political reality called a congregation. There continues to be a silent "pride" with most people supporting one's "right" to speak out!

My involvement and need to continue to reinterpret my rabbinic role increased when the State of Illinois passed a law requiring a premarital antibodies blood test. My work with an AIDS interfaith network drew me into clergy education. The law went into effect without any consideration for the illiteracy of most clergy in handling this very sensitive counseling issue. Rabbis, like most clergy, are not prepared for the reactions that merely taking the HIV antibodies test often provokes. (See Edelheit 1989b.) In what classic religious text or seminary course is the rabbi prepared for asking a couple if they are concerned about any high risk sexual behavior of the past ten years? What does the clergy do when a "false positive" test result transforms all aspects of trust and intimacy, possibly shattering a marriage even before the wedding? I wrote an article based on my experiences as a clergy educator, hoping to offer reinterpretations of premarital rabbinic counseling techniques in order to save rabbis and couples from hurtful errors of misjudgment.

Though the law requiring the HIV premarital test has now been repealed, I have reconsidered my own rabbinic position regarding the test as it regards the conception of a child. Just as medical information regarding Tay-Sachs motivated rabbis to reinterpret what couples should know about "the sanctity of life," so too our increased knowledge about HIV/AIDS and the early use of drugs such as AZT suggest, at least, rabbinic encouragement of the antibodies test. How one raises this question requires a whole body of information and self-reflection; thus rabbinic literacy *outside* of the classic religious texts is mandatory during this social crisis. A willingness to guide others within the precarious realm of religion and sexuality assumes that the rabbi has prepared for the unexpected. A state-mandated HIV antibodies test has proven that politicians can legislate how premarital counseling is done. The still increasing transmission of HIV/AIDS has added terror to each person's intimate past. Now the rabbi must learn and reflect in order to serve those who are touched by the power of the state or the terror of the transmission of disease.

My work on a national Jewish commission on AIDS stimulated an essay, "The Rabbi and the Abyss of AIDS," which was published in *Tikkun*. The paper was written to illuminate questions about AIDS and the lack of rabbinic involvement.

The article argues that rabbis, as interpreters of Jewish tradition, must confront the transformative nature of AIDS in order to serve their communities honestly. Monroe E. Price, dean of the Cordoza School of Law, Yeshiva University, speaks to the need of this confrontation and the search for a new paradigm in an age of AIDS:

> We are forced in the presence of AIDS to acknowledge a thin veneer of civility that orders our relations with one another and perhaps to treasure those connections all the more. Instructed by AIDS in the fragility of civilization, we are moved to its articulate defense even as we are thrown back on ourselves. ... An abiding legacy of the AIDS epidemic in America will be its effect upon the individual and the community. No similar period of intense, widespread introspection and reexamination of how private life should be conducted has occurred since the 1960's. Now in the context of fear, the haunting reminders of the tenuousness of survival, our ties with the past and with each other, are restored.
>
> (Price 1989, 118–119)

Susan Sontag establishes AIDS as a source of new metaphors, whereas Larry Kramer speaks of it as the analogy of the Holocaust in a gay analysis of Hannah Arendt's thinking. These are only two of the first attempts to think about how we are thinking about AIDS. We are only at the starting point of translating this extraordinary socioeconomic, ecological caesura into moral, religious terms. The transformative nature of AIDS is very much a challenge to any ethics for the interpretation of a contemporary religious experience. To that end, the piece "The Rabbi and the Abyss of AIDS" attempts to establish new limits and boundaries for establishing a change in how one actualizes and lives with these ethics for interpretation as a rabbi in an age of AIDS:

> How do rabbis teach other rabbis about AIDS? We rarely talk together about sexuality and IV drug use, and certainly not in graphic terms. Is there an issue of *tzeni'ut* (immodesty) which impedes rabbis from addressing these worldly matters? When one is trying to achieve communal rabbinic support for an AIDS education program, should ideological differences compromise rabbinic integrity? Is it possible to have an AIDS program that does *not* emphasize the use of condoms, since premarital sexual activity is not permitted by the traditional rabbinate? Should the organized Jewish community support AIDS education programs that, in order to achieve Orthodox support, ignore homosexual

behavior? Was it appropriate for me to be compelled to accept the title "doctor" in lieu of "rabbi" in order to teach a group of Orthodox rabbis about AIDS and premarital counseling? . . .

Rabbis, Jewish educators, and Jewish lay leaders are like everyone else. We weren't more ready than anyone else for AIDS, and many of us may feel that AIDS is bigger than we can handle politically, morally, emotionally, and psychologically. Still, the changes that the AIDS epidemic has wrought cannot be reversed. We cannot stop asking questions about AIDS merely because they don't lie explicitly within Jewish tradition. We cannot simply say that homosexuality is an "abomination." And we cannot, as Jews, be responsive to AIDS and deny the transformative nature even of the questions themselves that are provoked by the epidemic.

(Edelheit 1989a, 69)

AIDS, more than any other contemporary event in society, demands that we respond most critically to the fourth ethical imperative of interpretation—knowing the transcendent goals for which we are attempting to lead our congregation. This involves interfaith dialogue, intracommunal networking, and reviewing with a critical apparatus, an awareness of the challenges that an epidemic like AIDS represents. Mark H. Ellis, in *Toward a Jewish Theology of Liberation,* concludes his thesis by pointing to what it will take in the Jewish community for a transformative theology to emerge. He asserts:

First, a contemporary Jewish theology feels a tension between particularity and universality as a self-critical voice that comes from the depths of the Jewish tradition. It seeks to serve the world. It must be distinctly Jewish in category and speech, yet generous towards other religious and humanist communities.

Second, Jewish theology needs to acknowledge that genuine affirmation comes only through critical discourse and responsible activity in light of historical events. It must seek to be present in history rather than pretending to isolation or transcendence.

Third, Jewish theology has to emphasize inclusivity (e.g., religious and secular Jews, women and men), a search for renewal of community life in the midst of the Holocaust and empowerment in the refusal to be silent despite pressure from the political and religious neo-conservatives for a moratorium on a critique of the Jewish community.

Fourth, Jewish theology has no choice but to balance the survival of the Jewish people with the preservation of its message of community. It is compelled to assert that survival and preservation of its essential message were ultimately one and the same thing. There is no survival in any meaningful sense without a deepening of the values its witness offers to the world.

Fifth, Jewish theology requires the recovery of Jewish witness against idolatry as testimony to life in its private and public dimension as the essential bond of Jews everywhere and as the fundamental link to religious and humanist communities of good will and around the globe.

Finally, Jewish theology, in its essence, must be a quality to *Tzeni'ut,* a commitment to solidarity in all of the pain and possibilities as well as a critical understanding of the history we are creating and the courage it takes to change the course of that history. Within an emerging Jewish theology of liberation, the revival of the prophetic and the pursuit of liberation is critical.

(Ellis 1988, 112)

Ellis's provocative challenge need not be only or perfectly delineated as it relates to AIDS. Each rabbi will have to unravel the challenge of an Ellis liberation theology as he or she understands AIDS in his or her own life. It is clear, however, that among the many challenges that rabbis must interpret—such as Israel and the Palestinian question, the continued issue of feminization, Black-Jewish relations, homosexuality, to name but a few—AIDS is a challenge that demands knowing the goals toward which we are striving. If those goals are appropriately framed within a liberation theology, one must be, as a rabbi, an interpreter of classic texts, "the situation," and the resources from within which any new reading is offered. But of most importance, rabbis, as interpreters of the contemporary Jewish religious experience, must be role models through their own commitment to and enthusiasm for the goals toward which we are striving through the pain and transformative experience of AIDS.

Conclusion

The rabbi was originally only a reader and interpreter of texts. It was historically the rabbi who brought God's word, not through a divine command of animal sacrifice or a prophetic utterance, but rather through the more provocative and powerful ongoing illumination of the texts that bore the divine interpretive imprimatur of the priest and prophet. The contemporary rabbi is not the same as those four who went into the *Pardes/PaRDeS,* and yet surely the contemporary rabbi brings his or her hermeneutic and interpretative skills with no less challenge than the four who entered the *Pardes/PaRDeS.*

An ethics for interpretation is therefore foundational to any understanding of rabbinic ethics and, therefore, the moral boundaries within which a rabbi can serve others.

References

Capps, Donald. 1984. *Pastoral Care and Hermeneutics.* Philadelphia: Fortress Press.

Edelheit, Joseph A. 1987. "Who Will Die of AIDS Alone and Afraid? A Sermon for the Eve of *Rosh Hashanah.*" An unpublished manuscript.

————. 1989a. "The Rabbi and the Abyss of AIDS." *Tikkun: A Bimonthly Jewish Critique of Politics, Culture, and Society* 4, no. 4 (July/August): 67–69.

————. 1989b. "The Rabbi and the Mandatory Premarital HIV Antibodies Test." *Journal of Reform Judaism* 36, no. 3 (Summer): 1–9.

Ellis, Mark H. 1988. *Toward a Jewish Theology of Liberation.* Maryknoll, N.Y.: Orbis Books.

Epstein, Isidore, ed. and trans. 1935. *The Babylonian Talmud, Tractate* Hagigah. London: The Soncino Press.

Knobel, Peter. 1982. "The Rabbi, an Interpreter of Religious Experience." In *Rabbinic Authority,* edited by Elliot L. Stevens. New York: Central Conference of American Rabbis.

Kroner, Helga, ed. 1985. *More Steppingstones to Jewish-Christian Relations: An Unabridged Collection of Christian Documents, 1975–1983.* New York: Paulist Press (A Stimulus Book).

Mikvah, Rachel. 1990. "Text and the Human Document: Toward a Model for Rabbinical Counseling." *Journal of Reform Judaism* 37, no. 3 (Summer): 23–33.

Moore, James F. 1988. *Sexuality in Marriage: A Christian Foundation for Making Responsible Choices.* Minneapolis: Augsburg Publishing House.

Polner, Murray. 1977. *The Rabbi and the American Experience.* New York: Holt, Rinehart & Winston.

Price, Monroe E. 1989. *Shattered Mirrors: Our Search for Identity and Community in the AIDS Era.* Cambridge: Harvard University Press.

Ricoeur, Paul. 1976. *Interpretation Theory: Discourse and the Surplus of Meaning.* Fort Worth: Texas Christian University Press.

Tracy, David. 1981. *The Analogical Imagination: Christian Theology and the Culture of Pluralism.* New York: Crossroad.

————. 1987. *Plurality and Ambiguity: Hermeneutics, Religion, and Hope.* San Francisco: Harper & Row.

14

Clergy and Politics:
The Black Experience

Robert Michael Franklin

This hour in history needs a dedicated circle of transformed nonconformists. . . . The saving of our world from pending doom will come, not through the complacent adjustment of the conforming majority, but through the creative maladjustment of a nonconforming minority.

Martin Luther King Jr.

Politics is a matter of boring down strongly and slowly through hard boards with passion and judgment together. It is perfectly true, and confirmed by all historical experience, that the possible cannot be achieved without continually reaching out towards that which is impossible in this world.

Max Weber

In light of the recent political victories of the Reverends Walter Fauntroy, William Gray, Andrew Young, and Floyd Flake made possible by the vigorous political activism of black churches, we have sufficient reason to pause and consider the impact upon American public life being made by African American clergy. That impact is not altogether a recent phenomenon. Of the twenty-two blacks elected to Congress between 1870 and 1900, three were ordained ministers: Hiram Revels, Richard Harvey Cain, and Jeremiah Haralson (Wills 1989, 21). As political theorist Manning Marable has correctly observed, "Almost every Black minister was something of a politician, and . . . every aspiring Black politician had to be something of a minister. With the rise of Jim Crow and the electoral disenfranchisement of most Blacks after 1900, one of the few remaining roles in which articulate and militant young Black men could exercise political influence was as a preacher" (Marable 1983, 197).

Given this history, we are behooved to ask why black clergy are permitted, indeed encouraged, to engage in politics more enthusiastically than are their white counterparts? What are the benefits and burdens of this more explicit and intensified manner of political participation? What can we all learn from the experience of these clergypersons and communities?

In this chapter I interpret the phenomenon of black clergy in the political arena. The presentation is divided into three sections, beginning with an account of black clergy in politics, continuing with a typology that suggests a fascinating variety of political styles and options open to clergy in the changing political environment, and concluding with normative reflections on the vocation of political clergy. What broader ethical implications for political involvement are there for clergy of other racial or ethnic traditions?

The Tradition of Political Preachers

How and why have black clergy been attracted disproportionately to explicit and direct (vs. implicit, indirect) political activism? This sociological question invites a biblical answer. In general, the black community is a biblical community whose collective inner life has been reshaped by the symbols and poetry of Hebrew spirituality. Listen to any accomplished black blues artist or rap singer and you can hear the sorrow, celebration, and protest typical of biblical poetry.

Most persons are aware of the historical affinity blacks have felt with the biblical narrative of Israel's experience of enslavement, suffering, exodus, liberation, nationhood, and exile. In both communities of suffering, the word (sacred words) held intact both the community and individual selfhood. Hence, imaginative and communicative competence in black understandings of ministry have taken on extraordinary importance. The minister is first and foremost a preacher. And ministry, in the final analysis, is the process of liberating persons for Christian discipleship through the dynamic proclamation of the gospel and through direct public action in pursuit of justice. Ministers are understood to be charismatic persons (not simply professionals) who tell the liberating story of human fallenness and redemption, thereby empowering persons to struggle for justice and reconciliation in the public realm.

Black pastors have found in Moses a potent paradigm for strong, directive, liberating leadership. In contrast to white clergy in mainline churches, who have developed understandings of ministry that cohere around the image of servanthood, black male clergy have developed, and have had projected upon them, the benefits and burdens of governorship (Rogers 1976, 176).

Black male clergy, particularly in Baptist and Sanctified (Holiness-Pentecostal) churches, are invested with extraordinary authority and charisma. In most black communities, preachers come closer to royal status than does any other professional group. The installation of a new pastor of a significant congregation has all the drama of a coronation, replete with dignitaries, gifts, music, money, and a feast. Black female clergy in these denominations report that they have not been similarly invested with the community's unqualified loyalty and respect. Rather than relinquish the pulpit and the call to ministry to men, however, black women are struggling against patriarchal structures by pursuing theological education, by affiliating with churches that ordain women, and by gradually subverting sexist practices within the patriarchal churches.

Following the experience summarized in the exodus motif, Israel later became a kingdom in which some of its political leaders were faithful religious persons. Blacks followed with interest the move from viewing the religious leader as liberator (Moses) to viewing the leader as a governor (Saul, David), one who presides over the community and maintains order and public righteousness.

In addition to this paradigmatic affinity, black clergy do indeed possess historically accumulated wisdom regarding the means by which fragmented selves and institutions can be mended and reconstituted by employing religious resources such as prayer, preaching, song, and ecstatic worship. The towering black scholar of the twentieth century, W. E. Burghardt Du Bois noted that during slavery the black church preceded the formation of the "legal" black family. In fact, both institutions developed symbiotically, and female and male preachers were responsible for creating, through words and structures, the conditions under which persons and families could live with dignity.[1]

---

[1]Despite the patriarchalism of black church leadership culture, black women have contributed immeasurable intellectual, institutional, and material treasures to the tradition. Only now are we beginning to recover documentation of this contribution. See Lillian Ashcraft Webb, "Black Women and Religion in the Colonial Period," in *Women and Religion in America*, eds. Rosemary Radford Ruether and Rosemary

In view of these factors, it is not surprising that black preachers would be expected to provide political leadership for a fragmented, pluralistic society in need of wisdom regarding reconciliation, healing, and moral teaching. Preachers understand the possibilities inherent in a community united around common purposes. And they are masters of presenting visions of the moral life and good society in terms that are poetic, persuasive, and polished. Keenly sensitive to the need for compelling visions of the common good, black preachers have critiqued the paucity of such images in contemporary secular political rhetoric. They have felt compelled to run for office, in part, out of a public need to fill the spiritual and imaginative vacuum untouched by bureaucrats and professional politicians. Hence, elective office has become an extension of the pastoral office.

But not all clergy are explicit politicians. There are different ways of being political. A large number of black and white clergy are implicitly political; that is, in the course of performing their ecclesial roles in a certain manner, they evoke and nurture heightened civic awareness, responsibility, and sometimes radical political sensibilities. In this respect, the slave churches left an important legacy that continues into the present. At a time when blacks possessed prepolitical status, slave churches nurtured what black church historian James M. Washington refers to as the "politics of spirituality," the practice of "resisting imaginatively [through song and story] a white power that could not be overturned literally" (Wills 1989, 14).

Historian of religion Charles Long notes that when African slaves and free blacks organized their own churches, it was an act of overcoming their invisibility in American culture. As he puts it: "The very organization of black people meant that they were not invisible to each other; their humanity was affirmed within their communities" (Long 1986, 153). Hence, we could say that all of the activity in which blacks engaged within their churches was in some sense political. And it was the job of the preachers to lead the people every Sunday through rituals of empowerment that enabled them to resist racism, dismantle legal discrimination, and focus their hopes upon creating a nonracist America.

Skinner Keller (San Francisco: Harper & Row, 1983), 2:233–259; and Jualyne E. Dodson and Cheryl Townsend Gilkes, "Something Within: Social Change and Collective Endurance in the Sacred World of Black Christian Women," ibid., 3: 80–130. Also see selected volumes from the significant Schomburg Library of Nineteenth-Century Black Women Writers, Henry Louis Gates, Jr., general editor (New York: Oxford University Press, 1988).

The most significant ways in which the implicitly political preachers have fulfilled their political responsibilities have been through the ministries of education, community organization, and mobilization in behalf of social change and justice. Because the church was the one institution established and controlled by blacks, it was the most significant power institution in the community. Preachers took advantage of the captive audiences they attracted. The pulpit was used to inform people of public concerns, to educate persons, to organize movements for community action, and to instill within people the confidence, hope, and joy necessary for sustained struggle.

Let us consider two examples of this ministry of politicization: the civil rights movement and one of Chicago's more fascinating mayoral elections.

In a very insightful book, *The Origins of the Civil Rights Movement*, sociologist Aldon Morris observes:

> The black church functioned as the institutional center of the modern civil rights movement. Churches provided the movement with an organized mass base; a leadership of clergymen largely economically independent of the larger white society and skilled in the art of managing people and resources; an institutionalized financial base through which protest was financed; and meeting places where the masses planned tactics and strategies and collectively committed themselves to the struggle.
>
> (Morris 1984, 4)

He continues:

> The black church supplied the civil rights movement with a collective enthusiasm generated through a rich culture consisting of songs, testimonies, oratory, and prayers that spoke directly to the needs of an oppressed group. Many black churches preached that oppression is sinful and that God sanctions protest aimed at eradicating social evils. Besides, the church gave the civil rights movement continuity with its antecedents in the long-standing religious traditions of black people. Finally, the black church served as a relatively autonomous force in the movement, being an indigenous institution owned and controlled by blacks.
>
> (Morris 1984, 4)

In Montgomery, Alabama, in 1955, grass-roots leaders such as Rosa Parks and Jo Ann Gibson Robinson set in motion the bus boycott that launched the modern civil rights movement and the career of Martin Luther King Jr.[2] Initially, King was reluctant to assume leadership of the nascent grass-roots effort. He was young, a newcomer to Montgomery, an untested pastor, a newlywed, and a new father. But King was also a child of the black church and understood the tradition of public obligation that black ministers bear precisely because they lead the only autonomous institution in the black community. He had no choice; his presidency of the Montgomery Improvement Association was an extension of his pastoral responsibilities to the people of Dexter Avenue Baptist Church. Also, he had been socialized into the black Christian leadership tradition during his years as a student at the historically black Morehouse College in Atlanta. While at Morehouse, he acknowledged his call to ministry, and his view of black ministers as public theologians and activists found embodiment in the college president, Benjamin E. Mays, a Baptist minister and alumnus of the University of Chicago.

During the course of the Montgomery campaign and subsequent dramas, the black churches ably performed the tasks of educating, organizing, and mobilizing the masses for the purpose of struggling to transform America's political economy and race relations. King believed that the movement that black churches led should be joined and supported by all religious agents. Indeed, many white and Jewish clergy and laypersons marched with and supported the movement in a variety of ways. Still, he was disappointed with the large number of white churches that failed to apprehend the *Zeitgeist* and the theology of human interrelatedness that seemed to be leading the nation and the world away from racial polarization in pursuit of authentic pluralism and interethnic group respect and collaboration.

Exhibiting considerable political savvy, King urged the churches to translate their ministries of politicization into concrete political gains. King observed that political power might well become the most effective new tool of the black's liberation (King 1963, 148–151).

King was also concerned about the quality of political leadership in the nation, and offered the following comments concerning the need for better candidates:

> Until now, comparatively few major Negro leaders of talent and unimpeachable character have involved themselves actively in

---

[2]For an excellent account of the leadership roles played by women during the movement, see Jo Ann Gibson Robinson, *The Montgomery Bus Boycott and the Women Who Started It* (Knoxville: University of Tennessee Press, 1987).

partisan politics. Such men as Judge William Hastie, Ralph Bunche, Benjamin Mays, A. Philip Randolph, to name but a few, have remained aloof from the political scene. In the coming period, they and many others must *move out into political life as candidates and infuse it with their humanity, their honesty and their vision.*

(King 1963, 151. Emphasis mine.)

In this statement, King urges his own ministerial mentor, Benjamin Mays, to offer himself as a political candidate. And in his last book, *Where Do We Go from Here?* King praises and chides the leadership performance of another friend and clergyperson-politician, Congressman Adam Clayton Powell of Harlem's Abyssinian Baptist Church.

By virtue of being the first black preacher of the twentieth century to be elected to Congress (1944–1970), Adam Clayton Powell is the patron saint of all latter-day black clergy politicians and merits some attention here. Moreover, his career in public life provides important lessons for all clergypersons who enter elective office.

Like King, Powell was born into the ranks of the black elite. He attended prominent educational institutions (Colgate University) and was the son of a Baptist pastor of a prestigious church, where he assisted his father before succeeding him as pastor in 1937. At the age of twenty-two, Powell led a successful boycott to protest racial discrimination at Harlem Hospital. Capitalizing on his ability to bring together (especially within his father's 10,000-member Abyssinian Baptist Church) the black middle class, who supported the National Association for the Advancement of Colored People, and the black masses, who had supported Marcus Garvey's Universal Negro Improvement Association, Powell was elected to the New York City Council in 1941 and to Congress in 1944.

Political scientist Martin Kilson observes that Powell, a "man of more than usual vanity," portrayed himself as a savior of oppressed Harlem blacks, and that he "exploited the tendency of the black American lower classes to elevate political leaders, who represent secular authority, to messiahs, who represent sacred authority (a tendency I consider an Africanism)" (Kilson 1982, 267).

Powell's messianism authorized him to confront racist congresspersons and policies with great gusto and pardonable arrogance. When Congressman John Rankin (D-Miss.) stated that the bombastic and flamboyant Powell's election to Congress was a "disgrace" and he would not let Powell sit near him,

Powell replied that the only people "fit for him [Rankin] to sit by are Hitler and Mussolini" (Kilson 1982, 269). Thereafter, whenever Rankin entered the Chamber, Powell says in his autobiography, *Adam by Adam*, "I followed after him, sitting next to him or as close as I could. One day the press reported that he moved five times" (270).

Beyond such mischievous ways of confronting political white supremacy, after becoming chairman of the House of Representatives powerful Education and Labor Committee in 1961, Powell began to attach a "pro-black or pro-civil rights amendment (Powell Amendment) to crucial legislation emanating from his committee" (Kilson 1982, 271). Although this often led to delays and defeat of important legislation, he was faithful to his role as the sacred symbol of black defiance of racism and exclusive power.

Ultimately, Powell's inability to "suppress the egotistical and flamboyant elements in his personality" (Kilson 1982, 273) led to his political demise. He was subjected to press criticism and government scrutiny following his trips to Europe and the Caribbean with black and white female staff members. In 1967 the House stripped him of his chairmanship and denied him his seat in the 90th Congress. Although the U.S. Supreme Court declared that he should be reinstated, by then opposition to him in Harlem was mounting, and he was defeated by Charles Rangel in the 1970 primary. Although turned out by the black establishment, younger, militant blacks bestowed their highest praises upon this uncompromising, defiant preacher-politician.

In light of the quotation by King at the beginning of this chapter, we could say that Powell was indeed a "transformed nonconformist" who displayed "creative maladjustment" in the face of conventional political power structures. He would not cooperate with the system, as did his early black congressional colleagues. However, conservative elements of the black Christian community of the time expressed displeasure with the public moral witness of this highly visible, fun-loving preacher-politician. They expected something he chose not to provide—an upstanding model of middle-class, Christian morality. Perhaps seeking to apologize for the public career of Powell, King observed:

> The circumstances in which Congressman Powell emerged into leadership and the experiences of his career are unique. It would not shed light on the larger picture to attempt to study the very individual factors that apply to him. It is fair to say no other

Negro political leader is similar, either in the strengths he possesses, the power he attained or the errors he has committed.

(King 1967, 175)

As we return to King's analysis, let us bear in mind the
Powell paradigm. Here we find King calling blacks to go
beyond mere registering and voting in fulfilling the obligations
of citizenship.

And so we shall have to do more than register and more than
vote; we shall have to *create leaders who embody virtues* we can
respect, who have moral and ethical principles we can applaud
with an enthusiasm that enables us to rally support for them
based on confidence and trust.

. . . In the future *we must become intensive political activists.*
We must be guided in this direction because we need political
strength more desperately than any other group in American
society.

(King 1967, 175–181. Emphasis mine.)

Thus one of the most respected ministers in America issued
a call to explicit public service, virtuous political leadership,
and relentless political activism. Had he eschewed clergy in
politics, it is doubtful that his own lieutenants would have
pursued public careers following his assassination. Among
those who responded to his call were Atlanta Mayor Andrew
Young, Georgia State Representative Hosea Williams, District
of Columbia Congressman Walter Fauntroy, and the ubiqui-
tous presidential candidate Jesse L. Jackson. But King understood his own role to be prophetic and, therefore, outside the
realm of elective politics, popular sanction, and consent. It is
debatable whether or not he would have modified this posture
and run for office himself. I happen to think that ultimately he
would have yielded to a mass demand for his candidacy.

The civil rights movement was a regional drama that possessed a certain definition and simplicity to it. A single, charismatic leader came to symbolize its goal of dismantling
legalized segregation and infusing blacks into the mainstream
of American society. The post–civil rights movement struggle in the urban context has not enjoyed such clarity and
consensus.

Consider Chicago. During the 1960s, it rejected King's
southern, Christian strategies. Black preachers in the North
were quickened more by the defiant rhetoric and separatist
sensibilities of Malcolm X than by the reconciling suasion of
King, and many northern whites seemed to be unmoved by

King's appeals to good will and conscience. As time passed, younger, militant preachers developed their own strategies for the political resurrection of the black community. It was this generation of clergypersons, led by the African Methodist Episcopal preacher James Cone, who would write the first wave of books in the emerging field of black liberation theology.

Their well-coordinated efforts slowly evolved into a movement that produced dramatic changes in Chicago's 1983 mayoral election. In that year, the "People's Republic of Chicago" elected a true reformer in the person of Mayor Harold Washington. Before that time, this mass energy had been funneled into supporting patronage bosses such as Mayor Richard J. Daley and the famous Chicago machine.

The events that led to the election of Mayor Washington illustrate some of the ethical and practical problems black clergy and other clergy experience relating to Caesar's realm. In that instance, the distinction between accommodationist and prophetic clergy (which I will develop in the typology) was brought into sharp relief.

For most of this century, black professional politicians and a few clergy have entered into mutually beneficial alliances with white political bosses. Harvard political scientist Martin Kilson characterizes this as "clientage politics." In this arrangement, white ethnic power brokers distributed jobs, money, and access to city hall to black leaders or clients in exchange for votes and other favors.

Older, well-established accommodationist clergy found this system to be efficient and rewarding. But, when younger civil rights movement clergy began to accuse their older mentors of selling out and "Uncle Tomism," the cleavage between them widened. The late Mayor Richard Daley's successor, Michael Bilandic, tried to preserve the coherence of the old machine. But the old coalition was growing unstable. Inspired by the spirit of the civil rights movement, many blacks were uncomfortable with the white ethnic hold upon city hall. However, at that point the black community had no single candidate it was ready to support.

In the general election, Bilandic was opposed by Jayne Byrne. Jesse Jackson was the leading voice of local prophetic radicals at that time. Jackson supported the challenger Byrne against the approval of black clerical clients such as Dr. Joseph H. Jackson of Olivet Baptist Church, Bishop Louis H. Ford of the St. Paul Church of God in Christ, and the Reverend Wilbur Daniels of Antioch Baptist Church. After Byrne's victory, the influence of the old black clients was significantly compromised. It appeared that Jesse Jackson might become the new radical client of city hall. But Mayor Byrne's memory seemed to be short. As her administration took shape, blacks were stunned by her refusal to appoint blacks to powerful city posts such as Police Superintendent, Superintendent of Public Schools, and Chair of the Chicago Housing Authority Board. Now it appeared that Jackson and the black electorate were being snubbed and taken for granted.

Black preachers do not accept public embarrassment very well. By the end of 1982, both the old clients and the younger radicals, humbled by defeat and deception, determined to vindicate themselves. As Byrne was courting the old clients in preparation for the next election, Jesse Jackson was challenging Congressman Harold Washington to run for city hall. As it was reported, Washington agreed to run if Jackson's forces could produce 100,000 new registered voters. This challenge evoked a religious and nationalistic crusade. The vigorous voter registration drive that ensued added over 250,000 impatient and aroused voters.

Black preachers learned an important lesson from this episode. A leader's moral authority is linked to his or her political judgment. The old clients discovered the high price of their unqualified "over the pulpit" endorsements of machine candidates. I recognize that this is a highly subjective matter; but on the basis of the public rhetoric of these clergy clients following Byrne's victory, I am persuaded that each of them lost moral credibility in the process. They had gambled and lost. The unsullied reputation of their pulpits was compromised.

The principal lesson that emerged from this experience can be formulated into an ethical guideline for all clergy: in light of the teachings of Jesus regarding the "two kingdoms" that Christians inhabit, and in light of the Constitution's separation of church and state, pastors have a moral obligation to separate their personal political preferences and endorsements from the choices and values of the congregation, denomination, and broader Christian tradition.

The young radicals also learned lessons. They had urged the black community to vote for an alleged reformer, who ignored them after the victory. As we have learned from several sources, rates of voter participation are lowest among the poor and minorities. Mayor Byrne's insensitivity to minorities generated anger and despair among many blacks who were already disaffected with the political process. Once again, their trusted leaders had aroused their expectations only to see them disappointed by the system. This experience did have the effect of convincing certain black clergy not to entrust the fate of the community to professional politicians. Rather, the most trusted and influential leaders in the community should offer themselves for public office. The infusion of clergy into the explicit political arena has generated a lively rivalry between them and secular, professional politicians. This is best illustrated in the recent verbal sparring matches between Virginia Governor Douglas Wilder and the Reverend Jesse Jackson.

The ethical guideline that emerges echoes the psalmist's injunction: "Do not put your trust in princes" (Psalm 146:3). Further, religious leaders have a moral obligation to mistrust secular structures, processes, and leaders who do not acknowledge religious or moral judgments, norms, or claims upon their political behavior. Indeed, Christians have an obligation to apply critical reason to the behavior of all politicians, religious or secular, because we understand all persons to be subject to self-deception, selfishness, and other sin-related distortions of human personality.

Having sketched the historical conditions and prudential reasons for the explicit political activism of black clergy, I turn now to a suggested typology that may assist in organizing its various manifestions. This typology is inspired by H. Richard Niebuhr's classic model *Christ and Culture.* The principal difference in our perspectives is that in the black church community, none of the options is absolutely and uniformly "against" culture or politics. This is evidence of a fundamental difference in the way African peoples tend to perceive the created order and orient themselves to reality. In African ontology, nothing is altogether profane, evil, or irredeemable.

Varieties of Political Activism

The following typology organizes three variables that I consider to be important for analyzing the political behavior of black and other clergy: (1) their moral *ends,* that is, how these leaders conceptualize their religiopolitical goals; (2) their *means* for achieving them; and (3) their *warrants,* or the theological foundations that authorize and guide their choices and action. In the black religious community, the dominant form of theological warrant is not a rational proposition but often a metaphor that seems to express God's concern for human society.

I characterize the first and largest segment of black clergy engaged in political activism as *progressive accommodation-ists.* Since the Reconstruction period, a long line of black clergy engaged in politics have adopted this posture. One of the best examples of this posture would be the Reverend Joseph H. Jackson, pastor of Chicago's Olivet Baptist Church and long-time president of the National Baptist Convention. The moral end that these clergypersons seek is a peaceful *social order* in which they may acquire and enjoy what is thought to be a fair distribution of allocable goods (education, housing, health care, employment).

The principal means employed to achieve social order is *cooperation* and compromise with the status quo. In order to make progress, the utilitarian clergyperson must play the political game as effectively as his or her opponents, insisting that the rules for distributing goods be neutral and fairly applied to all players. Making deals is not only acceptable, but is morally required in order to produce the greatest balance of good over ill consequences for one's parishioners and community.

The most frequently used metaphor for God is that of *creator.* God has provided a bountiful earth with resources adequate to support every living creature. Scarcity is not the moral problem; rather, human will and faulty distributive schemes are responsible for poverty and inequality. God desires that all of God's children have shoes and bread and other basic goods necessary for personal development. This conviction authorizes progressive accommodationist clergy to cooperate with the system in order to wrest from it the maximal amount of welfare provisions for their less fortunate parishioners and constituents. They do not seek to change the basic structure of market capitalism or liberal democracy; rather, they seek reforms that are more inclusive of marginal groups. Personally, these clergy tend to live middle-class lifestyles and are firmly committed to actualizing the American dream.

The second group of politically active clergy can be characterized as *prophetic radicals.* Although there are very few such clergy in elective office (tending to be too radical for the general electorate's taste), this option is attracting large numbers of young clergy who have grown dissatisfied with the progressive accommodationist strategy. It was the strategy employed by numerous slave preachers of the eighteenth and nineteenth centuries, such as Gabriel Prosser and Nat Turner. Although Dr. Martin Luther King Jr. articulated this approach to political activism most fully, it was embodied most compellingly by Congressman Adam Clayton Powell. And, on occasion, it is embraced by the Reverend Jesse Jackson, although he is a particularly complex example, who blends features of the first two types.

Prophetic radicals pursue uncompromisingly the end of *social justice*. In the American context, this entails a radical restructuring of the free market capitalist economy. Their diagnosis of America's social problem focuses on the root causes of economic inequality and seeks to limit private ownership of the means of production. In the quasi-utopian democratic socialist vision that they embrace, dramatic economic disparities are prohibited and full employment is established.

The principal means for pursuing justice is *confrontation* and *negotiation*. Rather than cooperating with the political status quo in order to increase their share of the common pie, prophetic radicals initiate dramatic actions (such as marches or boycotts) in order to create a crisis within the body politic that calls attention to the need for radical change. Reform is not adequate to correct the problems of poverty, unemployment, ignorance, racism, sexism, environmental abuse, and so on. Radical transformation of institutions (and ultimately of human spirits) is warranted and essential. Professor Eleanor Holmes Norton has observed that part of the genius of Dr. King's leadership was his capacity to employ brilliantly both confrontation and negotiation. Recall that his last planned campaign was to return to Washington with thousands of poor people in order to shut down the federal government in pursuit of economic justice. That kind of bold, risky action stands in sharp contrast to the more conciliatory and pragmatic strategies of King's own disciples.

The metaphor of God most commonly pursued by this community is that of God as *liberator* and *judge*. Just as the Hebrew prophets held political authorities to divine accountability, these clergy live in tension with the status quo and seek its radical transformation. Their responsibility is to call the nation to higher, nobler principles and possibilities. King did this in the "I Have a Dream" speech.

The third option for the black clergy is that of the *redemptive nationalist*. Since the beginning of the African presence in the New World, there have been black Christian nationalists such as Martin Delaney and African Methodist Episcopal Bishop Henry McNeal Turner. This option has also been articulated by Albert B. Cleage, Jr., founder of the Shrine of the Black Madonna in Detroit and Atlanta. The most vigorous exponents of this tradition are not Christian but Muslims, the late Malcolm X and Louis Farrakhan.

Redemptive nationalists seek to establish a *separate black nation,* where the dignity and human rights of blacks will be secure. In the 1920s, Marcus Garvey and his ecclesial colleague, the Reverend George Alexander McGuire, urged blacks to return to Africa. Under the influence of Elijah Muhammad, this goal was revised to establishing the black homeland in the Caribbean or within several southern states of the United States. We should note the potency of black nationalist ideas during times when the socioeconomic status of blacks is threatened as it was during the Reagan administration. Although few blacks embrace seriously the notion of a separate black nation, large segments of the black community embrace a thin version of this ideology, insisting that blacks should control the major institutions in their communities. In 1990, this sentiment was expressed dramatically by Catholic priest George Stahling, who established the "Imani Temple" in Washington D.C. for disaffected black Catholics and other spiritual searchers.

Such clergy tend to cultivate an ambiguous relationship to the political status quo, a relationship that at best is characterized as *opportunistic.* That is, they use the system (vote, run for office) in carefully calculated ways to advance their interests while minimizing their future obligations to secular civil authorities. The nationalists would affirm columnist George Will's characterization of the American conservative attitude toward politics: "Politics may be bad but it makes many good things possible."

These clergy tend to employ the metaphor of God as *redeemer* of the lost and fragmented "nation" of the African diaspora. Like the radicals, they call the status quo into judgment and press it to actualize the ideals in the Constitution and Declaration of Independence. But they exhibit no special allegiance to the United States and would prefer to have a separate land and government rather than seek to transform this one. The political orientation of this community has evolved since the civil rights movement in ways roughly parallel to the emergence of the new evangelical religious right. In the 1950s and early 1960s, Malcolm X and others eschewed political involvement as the devil's business. By the 1980s, separatist groups became very savvy about political involvement and began to concentrate their efforts upon electing their own "home grown" candidates. However, they generally do not have a robust vision of, or serious commitment to, the common good as a political or religious matter. Politics is an instrument for imposing their parochial visions of the good community upon the religiously pluralistic landscape of modern America.

The fourth group of black clergy are the *grass-roots revival-ists.* These are the thousands of clergypersons without formal theological education who do their ministries out of storefront buildings and in small rural towns. One of the best-known figures is the Reverend William J. Seymour, father of the black Pentecostal movement.

Grass-roots revivalists seek *personal salvation* of all persons and tend to relate to the political order with *indifference,* apathy, and disdain. Such clergy are primarily interested only in the moral hygiene of their members, and tend not to advo-cate political positions or endorse candidates. They employ the metaphor of God as *savior* of fallen humanity. Sociologists of religion tend to dismiss these groups as escapist and other-worldly cults, but scratching the surface of those descriptions betrays another reality. For instance, there is ample evidence in the public pronouncements of early black Pentecostal de-nominational leaders of a sophisticated political theology. Bishop Charles H. Mason of the Church of God in Christ (1907) proclaimed that God's judgment would visit America because of her mistreatment of poor people, and he urged young pa-rishioners to declare conscientious objector status rather than fight in America's wars. Such positions earned him the atten-tion of the FBI decades before Dr. King was harassed by them. Also, during Jesse Jackson's two campaigns I witnessed the mobilization of grass-roots clergy behind the candidacy of a fellow "man of God." If their level of political involvement increases and if their marginal status evolves into mainline respectable status, I predict that they will follow the path of the progressive accommodationists. But that is arguable. Someone with Dr. King's mass appeal could emerge and help to radicalize these masses. Because I understand this radical style to resemble most closely the "politics of Jesus," I think that such radicalization would be a good thing for all Christian communities, although another less-charged term may need to be adopted.

The final group of black clergy are *positive thought materi-alists.* This is a relatively new school of religious expression in the black community. Hence, there are few significant histori-cal examples, although Depression-era leaders Father Divine and Daddy Grace initiated many of the practices that later groups adopted. The best-known contemporary example of this option is New York radio personality Reverend Ike.

Positive thought materialists seek neither social order, social justice, a separate nation, nor personal salvation. Rather, they seek to maximize their own *health, wealth, and success.* In order to achieve these goods, rigorous personal disciplines are implemented to ensure that persons are thinking positively. They tend to cultivate an *incidental,* indirect relationship to the political status quo. In contrast to the nationalists, who operate from the perspective of moral superiority vis-à-vis the secular political realm and who deploy political activism instrumentally to achieve narrow goals, the materialists become political only if doing so promises to increase their ability to acquire personal material goods. This sort of ethical egoism manifests no concern for the welfare of the wider community and judges the effectiveness of government by the question George Bush repeatedly asked during the 1988 campaign, "Is your life better today than it was eight years ago?"

Materialists tend to employ the metaphor of God as *provider* of all of the goods necessary for personal fulfillment. When they speak of God's "blessings," they refer strictly to the material goods of a capitalist consumerist culture. Because many of their tenets seem to be at odds with traditional Christianity, there is considerable tension between them and the wider black church community. Indeed, if one listens to certain urban black religious radio broadcasts, one may discover that doctrinal and *ad hominem* warfare is being waged via the airwaves.

Despite the roughness of this typology, I hope that it establishes the point that there is no longer any such monolithic entity called "the black church." There are a variety of black clerical voices constantly debating significant theological and political matters. The black church community is now radically pluralistic.

Although I have not tried to do so here, this typology could be applied to Euro-Anglo American religious communities with interesting comparative results. It would not be difficult to categorize persons such as Billy Graham, William Sloane Coffin, Jerry Falwell, Jimmy Swaggart, and Robert Schuller. Comparative analysis would highlight the manner in which certain religious communities perceive and respond to secular realities such as power and force. Also, we might discover that a group's socioeconomic class location might be as significant as its racial identity in shaping positive or negative attitudes toward political activism. The practical payoff would come through discovering sufficient theological common ground to authorize ecumenical Christian political coalitions and interfaith collaborations despite racial-ethnic and ideological boundaries. This was a constant element in Dr. King's vision.

As we have noted, Dr. King mobilized numerous clergy-persons to enter public life. Although he invoked general ethical principles and values to advance his case, he did not offer many practical moral guidelines for how one might be an effective politician and a clergyperson simultaneously. Let us recall that he called persons to "create leaders who embody virtues we can respect, [and] who have moral and ethical principles we can applaud with an enthusiasm that enables us to rally support for them based on confidence and trust" (King 1967, 175–181).

Moral Expectations for Clergy in Politics

In light of the experience of black clergy in politics, I would like to suggest the following moral expectations regarding clergy in politics that may be valid for black and white clergy. Despite our very different historical experiences, whether the descendants of former slaves or impoverished and hopeful immigrants, we are challenged now to live and struggle together for a humane existence.

When I was a political science major at Morehouse College in the early 1970s, I heard a speech by Congressman Mark Hatfield in which he suggested that politics was one means of multiplying the impact of an individual Christian's witness one hundredfold. I think that this sentiment is shared by the black Christian community, for it supports both preachers and moral laypersons in elective office and other forms of political service. Quite aware of the corruption and evil in politics, the black church tradition has produced the sort of leaders whom King called for—leaders who would infuse the public realm with a distinctive moral point of view informed by religious, and more specifically, Christian ethics. Hence, the expectation is that Christian politicians will seek to embody a Christian view of the moral life and strive for a just society in light of Christian values.

From my perspective, clergy ethics is a subfield of Christian ethics and maintains that the life and teachings of Jesus Christ are the decisive norm for Christian existence. As official, full-time representatives of the Christian tradition (some would say, "token Christians"), clergypersons are authorized and expected to be faithful to a somewhat higher standard of consistent, Christlike behavior than is expected from the average believing community. In order to understand this moral double standard fully, the subfield of clergy ethics may benefit from the insights offered by social scientific studies of leadership/followership. A much richer account of the possibilities and limits of contemporary Christian leadership can be purchased by keeping both biblical and theological perspectives in dialogue with theorists such as Weber, Durkheim, Erikson, and Victor Turner.

We should note that King saw Christian faith as a resource for building and broadening public life rather than merely Christianizing it. Unlike the new evangelical right, which supports candidates who seek to impose Christian norms upon all Americans, King believed that authentic Christian love empowers us to acknowledge, respect, tolerate, and be enriched by the differences in human culture and religion. Politicians of this sort are sorely needed to help revitalize our experience and visions of the public good.

In addition to this fundamental commitment to renewing public life, clergy in politics should strive to bear witness to the counterculture values that distinguished Jesus Christ. They include a commitment to caring for and transforming the lives of the poor; a commitment to permitting love to regulate and guide the norms of public justice; freedom from status anxiety and the lust for power; liberation from the fear of failure and, even, death.

Politicians who also wear the mantle of Christian leadership should seek to model healthy and moral relationships to power, money, and sex. Paul Tillich's insightful essay *Love, Power, and Justice* should be required reading for such leaders. In that valuable, brief text he alerts us to the "deep" relationship between these ever-present realities. Because the "power instinct" is a "normal attribute" of politicians, they should seek to keep alive the tension between acts of self-interest and acts of conscience. Although Max Weber thought that it was well-nigh impossible for a person concerned with the salvation of souls to be successful in the political realm of violence, black clergy politicians such as Andrew Young prove that one can "meddle with the infernal powers" and preserve personal integrity. The clergyperson's personal spiritual journey, however, is crucial to his or her Christian faithfulness in secret decision making and in public action. Hence, there is the necessity for what Parker Palmer refers to as rituals of private spiritual renewal (Palmer 1983, 24).

In seeking to be faithful to both callings, clergypersons who hold office and are pastors simultaneously should make it a high priority to enlist a good staff for both offices. Poor performance in either role will engender public contempt for persons who seem to want to be all things to all people. In order to remedy this, Congresspersons Floyd Flake and William Gray have been very deliberate about hiring church assistants who direct the ministry of the church in their absence.

This brings me to some concluding remarks concerning the political mission and performance of black clergy since the premature departure of Dr. King.

In a scathing critique of the political performance of Dr. King's lieutenants, Manning Marable has observed:

> As a group . . . not a single member of King's generation has courageously pursued the logic of his final years. Part of their current dilemma is created by their conscious, class-oriented commitment to infuse the Negro middle class into the present economic order and to perpetuate the inert politics of bourgeois reform.
>
> (Marable 1983, 211)

Notwithstanding his negative tone, he does express some hope that black clergy will overcome their traditional parochialism and preoccupation with gaining a share of the American pie in favor of a more radical Christian agenda: "It is entirely possible that the most decisive ally of the Black working class in its struggle for democratic socialism, at least among the Black elite, will be the Black Church" (213).

Numerous contemporary empirical studies of black church political activism suggest strongly that most black parishioners believe that the church and clergypersons should be actively involved in political activities such as voter registration and education drives, fund raising, distributing campaign literature, candidate debates, and so forth (Brown and Jackson 1988). In a long-awaited national, quantitative study of the black church, C. Eric Lincoln and Lawrence Mamiya have gathered data corroborating what many have observed; namely, that a statistical majority of white parishioners do not expect or seem to appreciate their churches speaking out on daily social and political concerns. It appears that some more liberal white denominations have experienced a "loss in membership and financial support because of their involvement in social and political issues" (Lincoln and Mamiya 1991). Conversely, black Christians expect their churches and religious leaders to be politically active and tend to withdraw support from churches that are not adequately political.

However, in the black community, it remains to be seen whether or not the black masses will follow leadership that pursues a radical "Kingian" agenda for social justice. In order for the black church to maintain its institutional ascendancy in the community, it will have to meet the challenges posed by Marable.

With regard to the white community, we should admit that there are considerable risks facing progressive white clergy and laypersons who refuse to leave well enough alone. But, thanks be to God, there are such leaders around the country who have been agents of Christian creative dissent, especially William Sloane Coffin.

Finally, how can all clergy heighten their various degrees of political (defined as renewing public life) activism? Those who aspire to elective office can learn from the mixed experience of Adam Clayton Powell and from today's exemplary public clergy, William Gray and Andrew Young. But perhaps we can all learn from the exemplary behavior of black churches during the civil rights movement. Through their ministries of lively worship, triumphant singing, prophetic preaching, cathartic shouting, and therapeutic prayer, the churches channeled black rage into the constructive avenues of education, organization, and community mobilization in direct pursuit of justice. At a time when public life needs to be revitalized and our parishioners need to be awakened from a self-indulgent, apolitical slumber, there are things we can do and say while leading worship and while in the community to make more explicit the politics of the gospel of Jesus Christ.

Conclusion

I close with the following summary comments. First, there are a wide variety of black clergy who understand political activism in a variety of ways. Whether explicitly or implicitly political, all of these options should be affirmed. Second, as Dr. King argued, our society stands in special need of prophetic radical leadership. The dilemma is that such leaders have a tough time being elected. The Reverend Jackson seems to illustrate the strategy of accommodating just enough to gain entrance to the system with hope of changing it thereafter. Third, clergy should appreciate the implicit political power inherent in the gospel and available to them as they perform conventional ministries in nonconventional ways. Fourth, clergy must be cautious in aligning themselves and the integrity of the holy office with any particular candidate or policy. To be sure, God has politics or political leanings, but we must be cautious in asserting that we have discerned them more correctly than have others. Fifth, ecclesial and political leaders must embody and proclaim the need for the public virtues of humility and open-minded tolerance without which a democratic, pluralistic society is doomed.

References

Brown, Ronald E., and James S. Jackson. 1988. "Church-Based Determinants of Campaign Participation Among Black Americans." Eastern Michigan University. Unpublished manuscript.

Kilson, Martin. 1982. "Adam Clayton Powell, Jr.: The Militant as Politician." In *Black Leaders of the Twentieth Century,* edited by John Hope Franklin and August Meier. Urbana: University of Illinois Press.

King, Martin Luther, Jr. 1963. *Why We Can't Wait.* New York: Signet Books.

———. 1967. *Where Do We Go from Here? Chaos or Community.* New York: Bantam Books.

Lincoln, C. Eric, and Lawrence Mamiya. 1991. *The Black Church in the African American Experience.* Durham: Duke University Press.

Long, Charles H. 1986. *Significations: Signs, Symbols, and Images in the Interpretation of Religion.* Philadelphia: Fortress Press.

Marable, Manning. 1983. *How Capitalism Underdeveloped Black America.* Boston: South End Press. See esp. the chapter "The Ambiguous Politics of the Black Church."

Morris, Aldon D. 1984. *The Origins of the Civil Rights Movement.* New York: Free Press.

Palmer, Parker. 1983. *The Company of Strangers: Christians and the Renewal of America's Public Life.* New York: Crossroad.

Rogers, Cornish R. 1976. "Black Ministry." In *Creating an Intentional Ministry,* edited by John Biersdorf. Nashville: Abingdon Press.

Tillich, Paul. 1954. *Love, Power, and Justice.* Oxford: Oxford University Press.

Wills, David W. 1989. "Beyond Commonality and Plurality: Persistent Racial Polarity in American Religion and Politics." In *Religion and American Politics* edited by Mark Noll. Oxford: Oxford University Press.

Epilogue

James P. Wind

In 1961 the now-sainted theologian Joseph Sittler surveyed
the situation of his generation of American clergy and
searched for an apt image. Instead of holding up the customary
pulpit orator, social prophet, or neoorthodox theologian, Sittler reached for a violent and grim word to do justice to what
he saw. The American clergy were being "macerated,"
chopped into little pieces. His assessment could be condensed
into one sentence: "The minister's time, focused sense of
vocation, vision of his or her central task, mental life, and
contemplative acreage—these are all under the chopper."[1]
Contending forces from within the parish, the general church
bodies, the minister's own self-image, and from society at large
were tearing coherent images of ministry—and those who
sought to live up to and out of them—apart.

The essays in this book suggest that, if anything, the process
of maceration has intensified since Sittler penned his lines. Our
pluralism has deepened; our traditions have become more eva-
nescent; our exposure to powerful cultural dynamics like individualism, professionalism, feminism, and entrepreneurship
has widened. Once upon a time, James Luther Adams could
speak of clergy as "ethos bearers" and signify by that phrase
a clearly distinctive way of believing and acting that flowed
from a compelling religious tradition. Now, if we ask which
ethos clergy bear, the answer tends toward the "all of the

---

[1]Joseph Sittler, *Grace Notes and Other Fragments* (Philadelphia: Fortress Press, 1981),
57.

above" line following a long multiple choice list of answers. Perhaps the respondent would cite a hefty amount of scriptural tradition, laced with selected historical images, held together by modern psychotherapeutic, sociological, and pragmatic filaments, and tinted with the colors of personal biography and social location. Or maybe another would choose a radicalizing experience of solidarity with oppressed people in third or first worlds, sharpened by a particular seminary community and then molded by a spiritual director. The options multiply; the images clutter our imaginative horizons and jostle each other as ministers move through their workdays.

Are there any signs of hope, or are we doomed to maceration without end? The cover story of the December 1990 issue of *The Atlantic Monthly* seems to promise little relief. In "The Hands That Would Shape Our Souls," Paul Wilkes recounts impressions from a tour of seminary campuses. His portrait of the "deeply troubled world of America's Protestant, Catholic, and Jewish seminaries" indicates that the next generation of ministers is already encountering American maceration, or to shift metaphors, that our would-be ministers are already feeling their way across the new and treacherous terrain we tried to map in these chapters.

Wilkes's portrait is unsparing. Generalizing about the 56,000 students currently enrolled in institutions affiliated with the Association of Theological Schools, he finds them older and of lower quality than earlier generations. They seem lacking in energy, intellectual range, and perhaps even psychological stability. Wilkes wonders about these "charter members" of the "me" generation: "What do they hope to find in religious training—the best way to serve others or a better way to serve themselves?" (p. 66). Their backgrounds are more varied, and their classroom worlds open out into ever more diverse directions. Describing the response of seminaries to the tumult of the 1960s and 1970s, he tells how some "turned to political dialectics, to Marxist critiques, to feminist, gay, and black theologies, as paths through an increasingly complex and threatening world" (p. 72). As their senses of vocation and self fragmented in the face of "piecemeal transmission" (Wilkes retrieves the phrase from H. Richard Niebuhr's 1957 study *The Advancement of Theological Education*) and conflicting ideological signals coming from their professors, seminarians turned to the "swirling" world of spirituality, which increased the repertoire of options at the same time that it promised relief. Meanwhile, back in the classroom, the "disarray" of academic theology seemed to be compensated for primarily by "technological" and "utilitarian" approaches to various tasks of ministry.

When Wilkes completed his survey, he found a common indicator of the shifting ethical ground beneath the feet of future clergy. "Homosexuality is the *timor maximus* within the seminary community, and if openly proclaimed or practiced, is considered by most denominations to be a reason for denying ordination" (p. 79). Charges of homophobia and heterosexism fly back and forth as seminarians struggle to define basic moral and ethical stances. Thus, if Wilkes's vision of our future has any staying power, our next set of ministerial images will be of a troubled, searching, conflict-filled, and beleaguered profession.

Are there any alternatives? One way to look at the preceding chapters is to see them as part of a much larger search for compelling and sustaining images of ministry. The authors reach back into the past for familiar ones: rabbi, prophet, priest, teacher. They probe our present: professional, CEO, entrepreneur, prime minister. Collectively, they reveal the culturewide metaphorical negotiation taking place as American religious communities seek to find their way into a new millennium. To be sure, there are other images contending than those occurring on these pages. One thinks, for example, of Donald E. Messer's recent consideration of the wounded healer, servant leader, political mystic, enslaved liberator, and practical theologian images.[2] So there are signals of creativity and new possibility to qualify the broad-brushed pessimisms that seem to get public attention.

But this book also indicates that the search for new images and for a sense of direction on the postmodern ministerial terrain will be different from earlier ones. We see here a common situation that awaits all American clergy. There is a peculiar American shape to the ethical situation facing our pastors, priests, and rabbis. Distinct traditions of ministry have become fellow travelers across a shared terrain. Few clergy will be untouched by the professionalism of their seminary professors; most will feel the pressure of serving religious consumers; all will seek to fashion a ministerial identity from a dazzling variety of sources; and all will meet unprecedented ethical challenges. Parishioners will bring their medical ethical quandaries that seem to offer only choices between lesser evils. Community members and parishioners will criticize congrega-

---

[2]Donald E. Messer, *Contemporary Images of Ministry* (Nashville: Abingdon Press, 1989).

tions, and those who lead them, for ageism, sexism, classism, racism, and anthropocentrism. People will ask what kind of employers churches and synagogues are, and will challenge the way funds are used and budgets set. Questions will emerge about clergy conflicts of interest, malpractice, and breaches of confidentiality. And congregations will continue to expect more—call it holiness, spirituality, or religious authority—from the people who take on this distinctive role.

For ministers who hope for more than maceration in the years ahead, several strategies seem essential. First, it is time to face our common ethical uncertainty directly and honestly. When publications like the secular *Atlantic Monthly* make the ethical and spiritual confusion of our seminaries into cover stories, it is time to admit that the ecclesiastical cat is out of the bag. The culture knows, our congregational members know, that clergy—like everyone else—are searching to find their way.

The second strategy requires a frank assessment of the many factors that compound the search. The chapters of this book try to bring many of them into view. When considered together, they suggest that new methods for charting a course are needed. Older repristinating strategies that snatch one cherished image out of the past and ignore everything else seem unlikely to take us very far on the slippery slopes and shifting sands of our new topography.

A third strategy is one that seeks to shape collaborative approaches. The burgeoning "clergy support" industry and the lengthening list of ministerial dropouts testify to how costly "go it alone" approaches to ministry can be. Ministers need places where they can search together—where they can share discoveries and come to terms with failure. They need places where they can tell the stories of their ethical and spiritual journeys—where they can consider the right and wrong turns made as they sought to fulfill their callings. They need new places of moral discourse where they can encounter the consequences of their ministry—not just their feelings about them.

In these new places within their professional and ecclesiastical worlds, clergy just might find room to turn in several creative directions. The first is toward cases and practice. Every day of ministry is filled with moments of truth, choice, collision of values. The rich experience of ministry needs to become more than anecdotal material for sermons and shoptalk. It needs to be carefully explored, studied, and pondered.

In addition to mining the daily behavior of clergy and opening it to reorienting reflection—both for clergy themselves and for those who teach them—it is important to identify the enduring practices of ministry (leading worship, preaching, caring for the sick and dying, administering sacraments, pastoral conversation about sin and grace, teaching) and to see if within these practices are hidden sources of wisdom and reorientation. Do practices like forgiving a sinner, feeding a starving person, or rebuking an oppressor provide maps for clergy who are searching?

Perhaps a serious relating of the ancient practices of ministry to the most recent cases of ethical confusion can open a new path or two for tomorrow's clergy. Public discourse about these topics may create room for clergy and those whom they serve to put down some initial landmarks and chart some fresh courses that can move us beyond maceration and fragmentation. But such discourse is costly. It will make demands upon congregations, denominations, seminaries, as well as clergy. It will increase conflict, and it will force each of us to confront our uncertainties—and certainties. But if our future is to include images other than those painted by the Sittlers and Wilkeses and other observers of modern ministry, the path into clergy ethics—onto this terrain; into our traditions, practices, and experiences; and outward into shared public conversation—may be a much more promising path than we originally perceived.

Selected Bibliography

Ahlstrom, Sidney E. 1972. *A Religious History of the American People*. New Haven: Yale University Press.

Barr, Browne. 1990. "Ministry as Midwifery." *The Christian Century* 107, no. 20 (June 27/July 4): 625–626.

Bellah, Robert N., Richard Madsen, William M. Sullivan, Ann Swidler, and Steven M. Tipton. 1985. *Habits of the Heart: Individualism and Commitment in American Life*. Berkeley: University of California Press.

Bledstein, Burton J. 1976. *The Culture of Professionalism: The Middle Class and the Development of Higher Education in America*. New York: W. W. Norton.

Boyajian, Jane A., ed. 1984. *Ethical Issues in the Practice of the Ministry*. Minneapolis: United Seminary of the Twin Cities.

Browning, Don S. 1976. *The Moral Context of Pastoral Care*. Philadelphia: Westminster Press.

——. 1983. *Religious Ethics and Pastoral Care*. Philadelphia: Fortress Press.

Burns, James MacGregor. 1978. *Leadership*. New York: Harper Colophon Books.

Burrows, William R. 1980. *New Ministries: The Global Context*. Maryknoll, N.Y.: Orbis Books.

Camenisch, Paul F. 1983. *Grounding Professional Ethics in a Pluralistic Society*. New York: Haven Publications.

——. 1985. "Are Pastors Professionals?" *The Christian Ministry* 16, no. 4 (July): 12–13.

Campbell, Alastair V. 1984. *Professional Care: Its Meaning and Practice*. Philadelphia: Fortress Press.

Campbell, Dennis M. 1982. *Doctors, Lawyers, Ministers: Christian Ethics in Professional Practice.* Nashville: Abingdon Press.

Capps, Donald. 1984. *Pastoral Care and Hermeneutics.* Philadelphia: Fortress Press.

Chandler, Alfred D., Jr. 1977. *The Visible Hand: The Managerial Revolution in American Business.* Cambridge: Harvard University Press, Belknap Press.

Edelheit, Joseph A. 1989a. "The Rabbi and the Abyss of AIDS." *Tikkun: A Bimonthly Jewish Critique of Politics, Culture, and Society* 4, no. 4 (July/August): 67–69.

————. 1989b. "The Rabbi and the Mandatory Premarital HIV Antibodies Test." *Journal of Reform Judaism* 36, no. 3 (Summer): 1–9.

Epstein, Isidore, ed. and trans. 1935. *The Babylonian Talmud, Tractate* Hagigah. London: The Soncino Press.

Glasse, James D. 1968. *Profession: Minister.* Nashville: Abingdon Press.

Graff, Ann O'Hara. 1986. "Vision and Reality: Discernment and Decision-Making in Contemporary Roman Catholic Ecclesiology." Ph.D. diss., University of Chicago.

Gray, Robert N. 1984. *Managing the Church: Business Administration.* Vol. 1. Austin, Tex.: National Institute on Church Management.

Häring, Bernard. 1978, 1979, 1981. *Free and Faithful in Christ: Moral Theology for Clergy and Laity.* 3 vols. New York: Seabury Press; Crossroad.

Harmon, Nolan B. 1928, 1978. *Ministerial Ethics and Etiquette.* Nashville: Abingdon Press.

Heyward, Carter, ed. 1985. *God's Fierce Whimsy: Christian Feminism and Theological Education.* New York: Pilgrim Press.

Holifield, Brooks E. 1983. *A History of Pastoral Care in America: From Salvation to Self-Realization.* Nashville: Abingdon Press.

Hough, Joseph C., and John B. Cobb, Jr. 1985. *Christian Identity and Theological Education.* Chico, Calif.: Scholars Press.

Hough, Joseph C., and Barbara Wheeler. 1988. *Beyond Clericalism: The Congregation as a Focus for Theological Education.* Atlanta: Scholars Press.

Knobel, Peter. 1982. "The Rabbi, an Interpreter of Religious Experience." In *Rabbinic Authority,* edited by Elliot L. Stevens. New York: Central Conference of American Rabbis.

Larson, Magali Sarfatti. 1977. *The Rise of Professionalism: A Sociological Analysis.* Berkeley: University of California Press.

Lebacqz, Karen. 1985. *Professional Ethics: Power and Paradox.* Nashville: Abingdon Press.

————, and Ronald G. Barton. 1991. *Sex in the Parish.* Louisville: Westminster/John Knox Press.